Arbitration Discourse in Asia

Linguistic Insights

Studies in Language and Communication

Edited by Maurizio Gotti,
University of Bergamo

Volume 208

PETER LANG
Bern · Berlin · Bruxelles · Frankfurt am Main · New York · Oxford · Wien

Vijay K. Bhatia & Maurizio Gotti (eds)

Arbitration Discourse in Asia

PETER LANG
Bern · Berlin · Bruxelles · Frankfurt am Main · New York · Oxford · Wien

Bibliographic information published by die Deutsche Nationalbibliothek
Die Deutsche Nationalbibliothek lists this publication in the Deutsche Nationalbibliografie; detailed bibliographic data is available on the Internet at ‹http://dnb.d-nb.de›.

British Library Cataloguing-in-Publication Data: A catalogue record for this book is available from The British Library, Great Britain

Library of Congress Control Number: 2015949683

Published with the support of Università di Bergamo, programme 'ITALY' (Italian TALented Young ®esearchers)'.

ISSN 1424-8689 pb.
ISBN 978-3-0343-2032-0 pb.

ISSN 2235-6371 eBook
ISBN 978-3-0351-0884-2 eBook

This publication has been peer reviewed.

Hochfeldstrasse 32, CH-3012 Bern, Switzerland
info@peterlang.com, www.peterlang.com

Contents

Vijay K. Bhatia / Maurizio Gotti

Introduction

1. Arbitration discourse in Asia

Arbitration is the most widely used alternative dispute resolution method to resolve commercial disputes between parties. International commercial arbitration is considered a creature of party agreement as it crucially depends on the parties' agreement to resolve disputes through private adjudication by a single arbitrator, or a tribunal of more than one, appointed in accordance with rules of a specific arbitration institution that the parties themselves have agreed to adopt, usually by including an arbitration clause in their contract. The practice of international arbitration has developed in a manner to allow parties from different legal and cultural backgrounds to use any variety of English or other language to resolve their disputes without any interference from the system of courts. Since arbitration in international contexts is equally applicable to all jurisdictions and legal traditions across the world, there has been incessant effort on the part of all jurisdictions to harmonize principles and practices to establish and follow a unified system of arbitration, which is not an easy task. Local laws, arbitrators' background, experience and expertise, language preference, and socio-political as well as economic considerations, in addition to differences in jurisdictional constraints and contestations are often difficult to reconcile, and hence there has been quite a bit of interest and effort invested in the study of some of the key issues and challenges in the field.

This volume reports on one such initiative undertaken by members of an interdisciplinary project on *Asian Arbitration Law*, of which one of the significant components is investigating *Arbitration Discourse in Asia*. The project has been part of the programme 'ITALY' (Italian TALented Young ®esearchers)' financed by the University of Bergamo

(Italy).[1] The main objective of this two-year project is to investigate the norms and arbitral practices in some of the important Asian countries, such as China, India, Singapore, Hong Kong, Malaysia and Japan, not only from a juridical point of view, according to the perspectives of civil trial law and employment law, but also from the point of view of discursive practices prevalent in these jurisdictions.

From the linguistic-textual point of view, the project focuses on the main documents used in arbitration in some of these Asian countries and often compares them with the discursive practices employed in Italy and other countries of the European Union. The investigated documents include not only norms and awards, but also interviews with professionals in the field so as to gain direct insights into the linguistic and textual choices employed in the drafting of these documents. In particular, the investigation attempts to verify the degree of interdependence that discursive practices in Asia show when compared to the ones used in other civil law and common law jurisdictions. Some of the findings from this project were presented at the International Conference on *Asian Arbitration Discourse* held in Bergamo on 18–19 September 2014.

In addition, there is an attempt to analyse the extent to which arbitral practices in Asia are being 'colonized' by those used in litigation, a phenomenon recently observed in alternative dispute resolution proceedings in several Western countries. This issue of the extent to which integrity of arbitration as non-legal practice is maintained in international commercial arbitration was the focus of two earlier international projects in which more than 20 international teams of researchers both from discourse analysis and law as well as arbitration collaborated over a period of more than eight years. These projects were *Generic Integrity in Legislative Discourse in Multilingual and Multicultural Contexts* and *International Commercial Arbitration Practices: A Discourse Analytical Study*.[2]

---

1 The project is co-ordinated by Prof. Mariacarla Giorgetti and Prof. Maurizio Gotti, of the University of Bergamo, in collaboration with Prof. Vijay Bhatia in Hong Kong.

2 For further details of these projects cf. the webpage at <http://www1.english.cityu.edu.hk/arbitration/arbitration/index.html>.

By drawing on discourse-based data (narrative, documentary and interactional), these projects investigated the extent to which the 'integrity' of arbitration principles is maintained in international commercial arbitration practice, and to what extent, if indeed at all, there is an increasing level of influence from litigative processes and procedures over arbitration practice. This was achieved by analyzing *arbitration in action* to investigate the extent to which legal expertise, training, and experience in relation to arbitration processes and procedures are essential and helpful in international commercial arbitration practice.

Some of the major findings were published in a number of edited volumes (Bhatia *et al.* 2003a, 2003b, 2005, 2008a, 2008b, 2010, 2012a and 2012b) as well as special issues of two international journals (Bhatia/Engberg 2004; Bhatia 2011), in addition to several international conferences organized by the project members.

2. Contents of the volume

The present volume is divided into three sections, each investigating a particular issue relevant to the analysis of arbitration discourse in the Asian context and focussing on different types of textualizations: namely, normative texts, discursive practices, and arbitration awards.

2.1 Focus on normative texts

In the opening chapter of the first section, MAURIZIO GOTTI provides an analysis of the Arbitration Law of the People's Republic of China (PRC) in order to highlight a few of its legal and linguistic features that are indicative of some of the characteristics of the arbitration process which are typical of the Chinese system. The comparison of this text with that of the UNCITRAL Model Law shows both similarity in terms of topical content and coverage, but also interesting divergences in terms of clarity of expression and conceptual and terminological precision, which may also depend on the common law tradition reflected in the UN document and the civil law perspective adopted by Chinese legislators. Moreover, the investigation confirms that the drafting of the PRC text has been influenced by the linguistic constraints and legal traditions of the local community to which the provision is addressed, as can be seen in the choice of particular terms to refer to the local socio-cultural system as well as the analysis of the specificity of information included in the two texts taken into consideration, which differ significantly, due to differences in socio-cultural expectations and practices that constrain social behaviour in local contexts.

Girolamo Tessuto investigates the Singapore Arbitration Act from the perspective of language use in order to identify specific aspects of accessibility/readability of this legal discourse. The analysis shows that the drafting practices used in the statute replicate several linguistic resources implemented in the common law tradition, thus revealing generic similarities across Western European and Eastern (Asian) legal cultures and systems. In particular, the linguistic and discursive properties of the statute align the law applicable to domestic arbitration with the provisions of the UNCITRAL Model Law and the 1996 UK Arbitration Act. This alignment betrays the willingness of the drafters of the Singapore statute to adopt a globally harmonized and convergent philosophy of arbitration, which is meant to increase Singapore's attractiveness as a national as well as international arbitration venue.

In the following chapter, Patrizia Anesa and Francesca Locatelli discuss the main features of arbitration in Japan as provided by the local Arbitration Law. The authors also investigate the reasons why arbitration is scarcely used in the Japanese context, mainly tracing them in the non-litigative tradition of the local legal system. Anesa and Locatelli then investigate the role and the characteristics of the Rules of the Japanese Commercial Arbitration Association (JCAA), which is the main arbitral institution there. In particular, the analysis focuses on the comparison between the JCAA Rules and those of the International Chamber of Commerce, highlighting some interesting differences in how a few problematic issues are dealt with in both texts.

Maurizio Gotti, Piera Pellegrinelli and Elena Signorini investigate the texts of both the PRC Arbitration Law and the Law on Mediation and Arbitration of Labour Disputes in order to examine, in particular, the norms concerning the appointment and challenge to appointment of arbitrators. with the aim of detecting relevant legal and cultural aspects. The analysis of the two texts highlights that, from a juridical point of view, the intent of the Chinese legislature was to place arbitration in China in line with international practice, by introducing a few key, internationally recognized principles. However, the procedures for the appointment and challenge of arbitrators do not always prove to be as smooth as Chinese arbitration norms indicate. This study confirms that the issue of impartiality of arbitrators is a very complex matter, which needs to be regulated in a careful way in order to guarantee a smooth and fair resolution of both commercial and labour disputes.

2.2 Focus on discursive practices

The second section focuses on the discursive practices employed in some Asian countries concerning arbitration. In her chapter, TARJA SALMI-TOLONEN examines surveys and dispute indexes, cases, and media coverage representative of Eastern and Western arbitration discourse so as to discover both pragmatic and linguistic markers of similar or diverse attitudes towards the demands of global trading relationships both in partnership and conflict. The purpose of this chapter is also to find a methodology for a more detailed discursive and textual comparative study of arbitration approaches in the Western world and in Asia. Salmi-Tolonen concludes that – because of the multifaceted nature of international commercial arbitration – the approach will inevitably have to be multidisciplinary for the answer to be as accurate as possible. Moreover, to better understand the specific characteristics, attention should be paid to the historical, political, societal and linguistic contexts of the arbitration events and their participants.

JOANNA JEMIELNIAK's chapter examines the legal, cultural and discursive particularities of the hybrid process which combines arbitration with mediation or conciliation, as used in the Chinese legal tradition. By examining historical accounts of the use of hybrid processes in imperial China as well as in the Western legal tradition, the chapter unveils the historical roots and determinants of modern-day approaches to this hybrid process of dispute resolution. The chapter also explores methodological aspects of research on this issue, demonstrating how the presence of 'soft', conciliatory components in hybrid processes makes the results of a legal doctrinal, text-oriented analysis incomplete, as many of the key aspects of arb-med proceedings are oral. Jemielniak also argues that the existing quantitative studies of this subject should be supplemented by qualitative ones, so as to allow for an in-depth, comparative interpretation of the various local types of hybrid processes, of the functions they fulfil and of their legal and social consequences.

Ulisse Belotti and Mariacarla Giorgetti discuss some critical aspects of arbitration practices in Singapore, highlighting the complexity of its sets of regulations, both for domestic and for international arbitration. Their study then analyses the results of interviews with professionals involved in arbitration practice in Singapore, in which the respondents express their considerations about the local arbitration practices and also rate areas of concern which, in their view, are likely to make this process less attractive as an instrument of alternative dispute resolution. The most critical issues identified are: arbitration clauses, confidentiality and privacy in arbitration proceedings, costs and duration of arbitration, and cross-examination. Moreover, the interviewees discuss the common perception that arbitration has recently become similar to litigation.

2.3 Focus on arbitration awards

The third section of the volume deals with the document that expresses the final judgment of the dispute examined, i.e. the arbitration award. The various chapters in this section explore the main linguistic, textual and pragmatic features of this textual realization, also comparing the rhetorical features of the specific documents taken into consideration to the principal characteristics of this genre as described in previous studies.

Giuliana Garzone examines the features of arbitration awards issued in both Eastern and Western countries, in order to verify whether they differ to any extent in terms of structure or textual/discursive traits. In particular, she investigates Internet domain name dispute resolutions, a field which has become quite popular due to the great increase in the misuse of website names, with frequent recourse to cybersquatting, domain name hijacking or domain theft. The corpus investigated in this chapter includes awards issued by Western providers (one based in Geneva and the other in Minneapolis) as well as by Asian providers (Chinese and Indian). Garzone's detailed analysis of their generic structure, discursive organisation and lexical peculiarities highlights an unexpected degree of uniformity in the drafting and organization of texts in macro-structural terms. The reasons for these similarities are found in the coordinating role of the Internet Corporation for Assigned Names and Numbers (a not-for-profit public-benefit corporation based in the U.S.) and in the common background of many arbitrators, most of whom are presumed to have been trained in law schools (mainly in English-speaking countries) adopting a similar approach.

The chapter by MICHELE SALA examines the linguistic, rhetorical and pragmatic features of arbitral awards drafted in English by the Hong Kong International Arbitration Centre (HKIAC), with a specific focus on those resources which are meant to enhance deonticity and authoritativeness, and thus increase the degree of unchallengeability of these pronouncements. Indeed, if arbitrators want their judgments to be recognized as binding, they need to make them sound highly authoritative so that their decisions cannot be considered arbitrary, biased, or partial. Sala's investigation shows that the conventional expressions to which HKIAC arbitrators usually resort when codifying their decisions succeed in harmonizing these rhetorical constraints, possibly even without the drafters being fully aware of their pragmatic potential.

The last two chapters of the volume focus on arbitration awards written in the Indian context. In the first of these, STEFANIA M. MACI analyses the role of evidentiality in these texts. The purpose of the chapter is to investigate the extent to which knowledge is linguistically expressed by the parties involved in the arbitral procedure in terms of evidence, intended as a source of information. Maci's analysis shows that evidentials are mainly concentrated in two particular sections of the award: when the arbitrator establishes the facts of the case and when he highlights the motivations for his decision. These are indeed the most important sections of the arbitral award, where the case is reconstructed and where the objective and juridical reasoning path followed by the arbitral panel is explained. It is in these parts that the arbitrator makes the best use of his argumentative skills as he is aware that the way in which language intersects with the law is of primary relevance here.

In the final chapter, Patrizia Anesa focuses on a corpus of Indian awards in order to observe their general characteristics and their linguistic and discursive peculiarities, with the aim to contribute to the identification of areas of concern and potential improvements to be implemented. Although from a macro-structural perspective the awards analyzed here are in line with the rhetorical structure which characterizes international and domestic awards in other countries, the micro-linguistic analysis shows some significant peculiarities. In spite of the fact that awards in general tend to display a relatively high level of formality and linguistic accuracy, this does not always hold true in the awards analyzed. Anesa explains this finding with the inevitable trade-off that exists between time and cost efficiency on the one hand and linguistic precision on the other, with the former aspect being favored in many cases.

3. Closing remarks

In the chapters of this volume, arbitration discourse has been analyzed in various forms of its textualization: not only focusing on normative texts and final awards, but also on its communicative and discursive practices. Moreover, the investigation has been carried out from different viewpoints: not only from a merely linguistic angle, with a focus on the description of the forms and genres commonly used in arbitration contexts, but also from a legal perspective, with the identification of the juridical intent and tools to be adopted in this process. Another complex standpoint that has been adopted is the vast array of social and cultural contexts in which arbitration is practised in Asia, from China to India, from Japan to Singapore, just to mention some of the countries explored.

The topic is so vast that we do not claim to have been comprehensive and offered a complete, definitive account of the multifarious discursive practices that are commonly employed in arbitration processes in such a wide continent as Asia. Rather, we hope that the chapters in this volume will open up new perspectives, provide subjects for fresh discussion, and stimulate debate among all those scholars and practitioners interested in arbitration discourse and practices, and – more broadly – in the relationship between language and law.

References

Bhatia, Vijay K. (ed.) 2011. *Interdiscursive Colonisation of International Commercial Arbitration Practice.* Special issue of *World Englishes* 30/1.

Bhatia, Vijay K. / Candlin, Christopher N. / Engberg, Jan (eds) 2008a. *Legal Discourse across Cultures and Systems.* Hong Kong: Hong Kong University Press.

Bhatia, Vijay K. / Candlin, Christopher N. / Engberg, Jan / Trosborg, Anna (eds) 2003a. *Multilingual and Multicultural Contexts of Legislation: An International Perspective.* Frankfurt am Main: Peter Lang.

Bhatia, Vijay K. / Candlin, Christopher N. / Evangelisti, Paola (eds) 2008b. *Language and Legal Concepts across Systems and Cultures. Bern: Peter Lang.*

Bhatia, Vijay K. / Candlin, Christopher N. / Gotti, Maurizio (eds) 2003b. *Arbitration in Europe: Legal discourse in a Multilingual and Multicultural Context.* Bern: Peter Lang.

Bhatia Vijay K. / Candlin, Christopher N. / Gotti, Maurizio (eds) 2010. *The Discourses of Dispute Resolution.* Bern: Peter Lang.

Bhatia Vijay K. / Candlin, Christopher N. / Gotti, Maurizio (eds) 2012a. *Discourse and Practice in International Commercial Arbitration.* Farnham: Ashgate.

Bhatia, Vijay K. / Engberg, Jan (eds) 2004. Special issue of *HERMES, Journal of Linguistics* 32.

Bhatia, Vijay K. / Engberg, Jan / Gotti, Maurizio / Heller, Dorothee (eds) 2005. *Vagueness in Normative Texts*. Bern: Peter Lang.

Bhatia, Vijay / Garzone, Giuliana / Degano, Chiara (eds) 2012b. *Arbitration Awards: Generic Features and Textual Realisations*. Newcastle upon Tyne: Cambridge Scholars.

Focus on normative texts

Maurizio Gotti

A Linguistic Insight into China's Arbitration Law

1. Introduction

International business exchanges with China have increased enormously over the last few years and even the recent economic recession has not slowed down this growth, which has made China the biggest Asian market in terms of import-export trade (WTO International Trade Statistics 2014). As a natural consequence, this increase in business deals and contracts has brought about a rise in the number of trade disputes. To resolve these disputes, the three most common ways are either litigation in court or Alternative Dispute Resolution (ADR) proceedings such as arbitration and conciliation (Berger 2006).

Arbitration has become a very popular method of dispute resolution for foreign companies in the People's Republic of China (PRC) for many practical reasons, such as the relative ease of enforcement, economy of costs and time, privacy of proceedings and the finality of the award. Indeed, it is commonly assumed that it is easier to enforce arbitral awards than it is to enforce court judgments; moreover, the time period for litigation has generally been found to be longer; another advantage is that arbitration is generally considered to be a more private forum (Ali/Huang 2012). A further reason for preferring arbitration may be the fact that proceedings brought before the ordinary PRC People's Courts can be risky, as judges may be inclined to follow the instructions of PRC administrative bodies and therefore protect the interests of the local enterprises. Moreover, it is often more advantageous for non-Chinese companies to submit a dispute to arbitration in China, since foreign judgments may not be recognized and may not be enforceable in the PRC due to a lack of reciprocity. Indeed when becoming a contracting state to the New York Convention, in its Declaration of Accession the

PRC made a reciprocity reservation, thus not being bound to automatically recognize and enforce all awards made in the territory of another contracting state of the New York Convention. Although the probability of enforcing a foreign award against a PRC individual or a PRC company has increased significantly in the last few years, there are still cases in which local courts refuse the enforcement of foreign awards in order to protect the local party (Glück/ Lichtenstein 2014). This is due to the fact that the New York Convention is ultimately implemented in China through a unitary court system that has less judicial independence.

The different matters concerning arbitration are dealt with by specific provisions (The People's Republic of China Arbitration Law 1994 – PRCAL, for short). PRCAL was promulgated by the Standing Committee of the National People's Congress of the PRC on 31 August 1994 and came into force on 1 September 1995. This law was a very important step in the development of arbitration in China. Although its main emphasis was on the reorganization of the local arbitration system, it also had a great impact on international arbitration carried out by Chinese companies. Following the entry into force of PRCAL, more than 200 domestic arbitral institutions have been established in the PRC. These domestic arbitral institutions are also entitled to administer foreign-related disputes, if so agreed by the parties. However, the best known foreign-related arbitral institution is the China International Economic and Trade Arbitration Commission (CIETAC), which is headquartered in Beijing.

It is the aim of this chapter to investigate the text of The People's Republic of China Arbitration Law in order to highlight a few of its legal and linguistic features that are indicative of some of the characteristics of the arbitration process which are typical of the Chinese system. When useful, this text will be compared to that of the UNCITRAL Model Law, which has been used as a starting document by many countries all over the world when producing their own individual statutory provisions for commercial arbitration. Although the original text was written in Standard Chinese, also known as Mandarin and Putonghua, here we will be examining its English version.

2. Topical and definitional aspects

As illustrated in the Appendix, the coverage of the Chinese text (PRCAL) and the Model Law (ML) does not always correspond in terms of topical content, also due to juridical differences between the two documents. Indeed, the organisation of content reflects the different context in which they are embedded: most PRCAL provisions also apply to domestic commercial arbitration, with only Chapter VII dealing specifically with international awards. Instead, ML approaches the matter more systematically, with no allowance for domestic cases. ML opens with a definition of legal scope, status and interpretation (Chapter I) and then follows a chronological progression from the drafting of a commercial contract to the eventual recourse against the award (particularly in Chapters III–VI). However, in PRCAL further articles have been inserted, where emphasis is given to other aspects, such as reference to local arbitration commissions or special provisions for arbitration involving foreign elements. The amount of legal mapping clearly depends on the different origin of these two texts as well as their purpose.

Moreover, PRCAL gives hardly any terminological definitions, whereas ML devotes several articles to this purpose: for example, Art. 2 of ML provides the definition of the basic concepts of this field, such as 'arbitration', 'arbitral tribunal' and 'court', while Art. 7 clearly specifies the concept of 'arbitration agreement'. This is in line with the common law drafting tradition, which places a great emphasis on the precise and detailed wording of the text in order to limit any possibility of ambiguity or misunderstanding (Driedger 1982). This more precise way of drafting the text is also visible in the choice of the ML drafter to give a title to every article of the Model Law, which is meant to facilitate the comprehension of each specific provision. Such headings are missing in the Chinese text.

The greater detail in wording the text results in longer formulations of the provisions. Indeed, although the Chinese text has more articles (80 vs 36), the ML document contains more words (7,207 vs 4,659). In terms of word count (summarised in Table 1), this means that each article in ML is longer and more structured, with a higher number of words per article.

	ML	*PRCAL*
Articles	36	80
Average article length (words)	200	58
Total length (words)	7,207	4,659

Table 1. Quantitative data.

An example of the difference in the formulation of similar concepts can be seen in the following two quotations referring to the specification of the concept of international arbitration. The Chinese text does not clearly define this concept but merely implies its meaning in a very vague manner in the first article of Chapter VII which provides special provisions for 'arbitration involving foreign elements':

(1) The provisions of this Chapter shall apply to the arbitration of disputes arising from economic, trade, transportation and maritime activities involving a foreign element. For matters not covered in this Chapter, the other relevant provisions of this Law shall apply. (PRCAL Art. 65)

The Model Law instead provides a very long and detailed explanation of the concept:

(2) (3) An arbitration is international if:

(a) the parties to an arbitration agreement have, at the time of the conclusion of that agreement, their places of business in different States; or

(b) one of the following places is situated outside the State in which the parties have their places of business:

(i) the place of arbitration if determined in, or pursuant to, the arbitration agreement;

(ii) any place where a substantial part of the obligations of the commercial relationship is to be performed or the place with which the subject-matter of the dispute is most closely connected;

or

(c) the parties have expressly agreed that the subject matter of the arbitration agreement relates to more than one country.

(4) For the purposes of paragraph (3) of this article:
  (a) if a party has more than one place of business, the place of business is that which has the closest relationship to the arbitration agreement;
  (b) if a party does not have a place of business, reference is to be made to his habitual residence. (ML Art. 1 (3), (4))

As can be seen, in order to facilitate the comprehension of this long text, the drafter uses numbers and letters providing a well-structured provision thus avoiding the risk of the reader getting lost in the long series of embeddings and subordinating clauses. Another particularly striking example of this drafting technique used in ML is the following:

(3) Grounds for refusing recognition or enforcement
  (1) Recognition or enforcement of an arbitral award, irrespective of the country in which it was made, may be refused only:
    (a) at the request of the party against whom it is invoked, if that party furnishes to the competent court where recognition or enforcement is sought proof that:
      (i) a party to the arbitration agreement referred to in article 7 was under some incapacity; or the said agreement is not valid under the law to which the parties have subjected it or, failing any indication thereon, under the law of the country where the award was made; or
      (ii) the party against whom the award is invoked was not given proper notice of the appointment of an arbitrator or of the arbitral proceedings or was otherwise unable to present his case; or
      (iii) the award deals with a dispute not contemplated by or not falling within the terms of the submission to arbitration, or it contains decisions on matters beyond the scope of the submission to arbitration, provided that, if the decisions on matters submitted to arbitration can be separated from those not so submitted, that part of the award which contains decisions on matters submitted to arbitration may be recognized and enforced; or
      (iv) the composition of the arbitral tribunal or the arbitral procedure was not in accordance with the agreement of the parties or, failing such agreement, was not in accordance with the law of the country where the arbitration took place; or
      (v) the award has not yet become binding on the parties or has been set aside or suspended by a court of the country in which, or under the law of which, that award was made; or

(b) if the court finds that:
  (i) the subject-matter of the dispute is not capable of settlement by arbitration under the law of this State; or
  (ii) the recognition or enforcement of the award would be contrary to the public policy of this State. (ML Art. 36)

By arranging content schematically, the drafter can construct a denser, more cognitively demanding text such as the one cited above. The advantages of good paragraphing is thus pointed out by Driedger:

> [It] provides a visual aid to comprehension by breaking up solid blocks of type; it delivers the sentence in packages, so to speak, making it easier for the mind to grasp the whole. It does visually what the reader would do mentally without it. (Driedger 1982: 78)

This greater effort towards the attainment of a more 'reader-friendly' text is also visible in the higher degree of concern for clarity of expression in the UNCITRAL text, which pays particular attention to conceptual and terminological unambiguity. This feature can be associated with the emphasis normally placed by common law legislation on precision and detail for action in specific circumstances (Campbell 1996). Another reason for this greater need for clarity is the broader scope of the Model Law, which targets the whole international community and as such is potentially more prone to ambiguity or misinterpretation. This explains why ML devotes various parts of its text to very detailed terminological explanations:

(4) 'Arbitration agreement' is an agreement by the parties to submit to arbitration all or certain disputes which have arisen or which may arise between them in respect of a defined legal relationship, whether contractual or not. An arbitration agreement may be in the form of an arbitration clause in a contract or in the form of a separate agreement. (ML Art. 7 (1))

PRCAL, instead, gives hardly any terminological definitions. This is also due to the fact that the monocultural background of PRCAL is in fact less likely to require such specifications. Moreover, the Chinese text displays a high degree of intertextual linking as this new law is embedded in the extant body of legislation, and therefore has to be interpreted in the light of several other texts of greater or equal authority, whereas ML is a stand-alone law.

3. Terms with a specific local meaning

The analysis of the PRCAL text has highlighted the use of some terms which have a specific local meaning. Indeed, the formulation of particular legal norms relies on typical cultural implications involved in dispute resolution in the Chinese legal system. This shows that the cultural environment has greatly influenced the outcome of the drafting process.

3.1 Arbitration commission

Some of the terms contained in PRCAL have given rise to disputes as regards their true interpretation as they seem to have a specific local meaning. One of these terms can be found in art. 10 of PRCAL:

(5) Arbitration commissions may be established in municipalities directly under the Central Government and in cities that are the seats of the people's governments of provinces or autonomous regions. They may also be established in other cities divided into districts, according to need. Arbitration commissions shall not be established at each level of the administrative divisions. (PRCAL Art. 10)

The term *arbitration commission* is not commonly used in documents on international arbitration, where the term *arbitral institution* is usually employed. Although the common interpretation is to consider these two terms as synonymous, in practice they are not, because elsewhere arbitral institutions are independent institutions, while in China they are seen as strictly linked with the complex system of local and national government and cannot therefore be established in an autonomous way. This strict link with local and national government can be pernicious to a fair and independent resolution of the dispute. As Glück and Lichtenstein aptly observe:

> While the legislation requires a strict legal separation between the administrative authorities and these domestic arbitral institutions, it should be noted that, in reality, these legal safeguards are not always effective. Not all domestic arbitral institutions are free from judicial and administrative interference. Local protectionism and political influence are common problems. (Glück/Lichtenstein 2014)

Other scholars have expressed much stronger criticism towards the close links between arbitral tribunals and local government. Here is Moser and Yuen's opinion about the degree of independence of the arbitration tribunal of CIETAC (China International Economic and Trade Arbitration Commission):

> Foreign parties have frequently voiced concerns about the independence and impartiality of CIETAC tribunals. Despite specific provisions in the Arbitration Law and the 2000 Rules aimed at ensuring impartiality, the fact remains that many Chinese members of the CIETAC Panel of Arbitrators are either current or retired government officials and CIETAC itself, while officially independent, enjoys close ties to government departments. (Moser/Yuen 2005: 396)

Further problems concerning the term *arbitration commission* derive from its usage in Article 16 of PRCAL, which reads:

(6) [...] An arbitration agreement shall contain the following particulars:
(1) an expression of intention to apply for arbitration;
(2) matters for arbitration; and
(3) a designated arbitration commission. (PRCAL Art. 16)

The missing designation of a specific arbitration commission in the arbitration agreement has led to the invalidity of the agreement itself and therefore to the impossibility of carrying out such procedure. This has also happened in case of an imprecise formulation of the commission's name or to its vague reference as *local arbitral institution* or a similar expression.

Another question raised by the use of the indeterminate term *arbitration commission* is whether such expression only refers to Chinese arbitration institutions or also encompasses foreign arbitration institutions. Although the *arbitration commission* referred to in Article 16 of PRCAL could also be interpreted in a broad sense so as to cover any arbitration body wherever it is domiciled (Chang 2001), it is commonly assumed that only local arbitration commissions may be indicated in the arbitration agreement. This interpretation also guarantees a safer recognition of the final award. Indeed, as aptly pointed out by Tao and Von Wunschheim:

> [...] even when an arbitration clause expressly refers to the foreign arbitration institution, it is uncertain whether such an arbitration clause would be regarded as valid in China considering the controversy as to the interpretation of the term 'arbitration commission'. This will not prevent a foreign arbitration institution from handling a Chinese arbitration case, but it may endanger the enforceability of the resulting award. (Tao/Von Wunschheim 2007: 324)

This consideration helps to explain the fact that there are no foreign arbitration institutions operating in China and that it is still rare for a foreign arbitration institution to deal with an arbitration proceeding taking place in China. On the other hand, there is a continuous growth in the number of local arbitration institutions being set up.

3.2 Foreign-related arbitration

Another expression which has proved ambiguous in interpretative terms is *foreign-related arbitration*. This term appears in several provisions mainly grouped in Section 7 of PRCAL dealing with "special provisions for arbitration involving foreign elements". The first article in this section defines international arbitration in very vague terms:

(7) The provisions of this Chapter shall apply to the arbitration of disputes arising from economic, trade, transportation and maritime activities involving a foreign element. (PRCAL Art. 65)

The following article deals with the organization of foreign-related arbitration commissions, but does so in an indeterminate way, which is clearly shown by the use of *may* (instead of *shall*) in two of the three sentences of the provision:

(8) Foreign-related arbitration commissions *may* be organized and established by the China Chamber of International Commerce. A foreign-related arbitration commission shall be composed of one chairman, a certain number of vice chairmen and members. The chairman, vice chairmen and members of a foreign-related arbitration commission *may* be appointed by the China Chamber of International Commerce. (PRCAL Art. 66, emphasis added)

The use of *may* is meant to give greater decisional powers to the China Chamber of International Commerce, again an institution strictly linked with the local government. Also the analysis of the use of modal verbs in the PRCAL text carried out by Bhatia and Candlin (2008: 135) has led them to conclude that "[a]lthough not stated explicitly, it is clear [...] that executive bodies are assigned more power than the parties in the arbitration process". The powers of the China Chamber of International Commerce in this matter are also clearly strengthened by a subsequent article of the law, which reads:

(9) Foreign-related arbitration rules may be formulated by the China Chamber of International Commerce in accordance with this Law and the relevant provisions of the Civil Procedure Law. (PRCAL Art. 73)

In this way the law does not explicitly confer exclusive jurisdiction over foreign-related cases to foreign-related arbitration commissions, but rather implies that jurisdiction is meant to be concurrent with local arbitration commissions. Indeed, it has often been pointed out (e.g. Zhou 2006) that the law would have used *shall* instead of *may* if it had intended to reserve jurisdiction on foreign-related cases exclusively to foreign arbitration commissions.

However, the fact that foreign-related cases are dealt with in a specific section of the law seems to imply that international arbitration cases may be seen as separate from the domestic ones. Indeed, it has been noted that international arbitration cases are commonly dealt with somewhat differently: judicial review of international arbitration is mainly focused on procedural issues, while review of domestic arbitration concentrates on more substantive aspects (Yifei 2012).

The choice of *foreign-related* rather than *non-domestic* or *international,* two adjectives commonly found in documents concerning international commercial arbitration, seems to imply the willingness to guarantee complete autonomy to the Chinese adjudicating system, without any necessary application of criteria followed elsewhere. Also the use of the expression *foreign-related arbitration award* found in this law is meant to provide greater autonomy of decision on the part of Chinese institutions as this term is so indeterminate as to be applicable not only to foreign-related arbitration cases carried out in China, but also to those proceedings dealt with in a foreign country and which thus would be ruled by the New York Convention. However, since China did not sign a reciprocity agreement within that convention, the Chinese legislators did not want to run the risk of an automatic recognition of an award issued in a foreign country.

When PRCAL came into force, the expression *foreign-related arbitration award* was used also for awards deriving from arbitration proceedings held in Hong Kong since at that time this area was still a British colony. When the Hong Kong territory was annexed to the People's Republic of China as a Special Administrative Region, an agreement on mutual recognition and enforcement of arbitral awards between Hong Kong and Mainland China was signed and became effective on February 1, 2000. This agreement permits the High Court of Hong Kong to enforce Mainland Chinese awards made pursuant to the Arbitration Law of the People's Republic of China, and the Intermediate People's Court in China to enforce awards made in Hong Kong. Under this agreement, awards from either place are to be considered domestic, and no longer to be examined according to the New York Convention.

3.3 Public interest

Another element which strengthens the autonomy of the Chinese legal system and its great power over the arbitration decision is the concept of 'public interest'. This concept is explicitly mentioned in PRCAL in Article 58:

(10) If the people's court determines that the arbitration award violates the public interest, it shall rule to set aside the award. (PRCAL Art. 58)

Although this concept is not explicitly mentioned in Section 7 of PRCAL as a reason for challenging or invalidating a foreign-related award, this possibility is implicitly evoked in an indirect way. Indeed, Article 71 states:

(11) If the party against whom the enforcement is sought presents evidence which proves that the foreign-related arbitration award involves one of the circumstances set forth in the first paragraph of Article 260 of the Civil Procedure Law, the people's court shall, after examination and verification by a collegial panel formed by the people's court, rule to disallow the enforcement. (PRCAL Art. 71)

If one analyses the circumstances set forth in the first paragraph of Article 260 of the Civil Procedure Law, one finds that this provision states that Chinese courts may deny the recognition and enforcement of foreign-related arbitral awards according to the 'public interest' criterion. This concept, of course, is quite vague and thus enables local courts to act in an autonomous way. The use of this term has aroused intense criticism as this term is found only in the Chinese context and is thus more liable to be employed and interpreted in an idiosyncratic way. In traditional international law, instead, the term commonly used is *public policy*, a term which has amply been discussed and clarified in specialised literature all over the world (e.g. Lew/Mistelis/Kröll 2003). For example, in publications concerning the interpretation of this term as used in the New York Convention, public policy is usually conceived of as narrowly limited to the violation of a state's "international public policy or order public international" (Zhou 2006: 448). The meaning of *public interest*, instead, seems to be wider than that of *public policy* and seems to go beyond notions of morality and justice, and include general financial, cultural, environmental and other interests. As Zhou aptly remarks:

> Technically, any enforcement may have a substantial impact on the financial situation of an interest group, and the public interest defense may therefore be abused as a ground for defending arbitral awards. This wide-open ground offered a convenient channel for local protectionists in China. (Zhou 2006: 448)

4. Vagueness

As we have seen, the text of PRCAL presents several cases of vague and indeterminate formulations. Apart from the reasons pointed out in the specific cases dealt with above, a further explanation may be provided by the fact that the vagueness of the English translation examined here may derive from the typical traits of Chinese legal language. Indeed, Chinese legal language has been found vaguer and more ambiguous than other traditions, such as English legal language (Ross/Ross 2000).

Peerenboom (2002), for example, claims that Chinese legislation is characterised by generality and vagueness, with frequent cases of undefined terms and inconsistent usage. Keller (1994) attributes this greater vagueness and indeterminacy to the particular need for generality and flexibility that is at the basis of legislative drafting in that country. This higher degree of flexibility derives from the need to guarantee the unitary nature of the state while preserving respect for regional diversity. This also favours greater legislative stability, since it allows broader generality of application by means of varying interpretations of the law rather than actual changes to existing legislation. This is also due to the fact that specific meanings attached to many legislative terms shift with their contexts, a trait that has always characterised Chinese legal language based on Confucian tradition (Liao 2012). According to Potter (2001) this traditional indefiniteness of legal terms is also due to the preference of Chinese administrative bodies for broadly drafted laws that may grant them greater freedom in their application in specific contexts. A more general explanation may be found in the fact that China has a civil law tradition, which generally favours broader and more general legal drafting compared to that of common law countries.

To exemplify the indefiniteness of Chinese legal language, Cao (2008) mentions the case of the frequent use of the word *deng* (meaning *etc.*, *such as*, *including*) in Chinese legal texts. She adds:

> The habitual and sometimes over-frequent use of *deng* which allows for open-ended interpretations can cause a great deal of uncertainty and ambiguity. A further problem is that *deng* can indicate both open-endedness when listing things and can also be used to end a listing, a closure, to be all inclusive, depending on actual use and context. (Cao 2008: 112)

Indeed, several cases of open-endedness have been found in the English translation of PRCAL, deriving from the use of *deng* in the original text. Here are a couple of examples (emphasis added):

(12) An arbitrator shall meet one of the conditions set forth below: [...] To have acquired the knowledge of law, engaged in the professional work in the field of economy and trade, *etc.*, possessing a senior professional title or having an equivalent professional level. (PRCAL Art. 13)

(13) A foreign-related arbitration commission may appoint arbitrators from among foreigners with special knowledge in the fields of law, economy and trade, science and technology, *etc.* (PRCAL Art. 67)

Moreover, the text often includes 'weasel words' (Mellinkoff 1963: 21), i.e. words and expressions which have flexible meanings, such as *serious, equitable, justified, reasonable*:

(14) In arbitration, disputes shall be resolved on the basis of facts, in compliance with the law and in an *equitable* and *reasonable* manner. (PRCAL Art. 7)

(15) If an arbitrator is involved in the circumstances described in item (4) of Article 34 of this Law and the circumstances are *serious* or involved in the circumstances described in item (6) of Article 58 of this Law, he shall assume legal liability according to law and the arbitration commission shall remove his name from the register of arbitrators. (PRCAL Art. 38)

(16) The arbitration commission shall notify the parties of the date of the hearing within the time limit specified in the rules of arbitration. A party may, within the time limit specified in the rules of arbitration, request a postponement of the hearing if he has *justified* reasons therefore. The arbitration tribunal shall decide whether or not to postpone the hearing. (PRCAL Art. 41)

Also the issues that can be subjected to arbitration are not specified in a clear way. The matter is dealt with in Article 3:

(17) The following disputes may not be arbitrated:
(1) marital, adoption, guardianship, support and succession disputes;
(2) administrative disputes that shall be handled by administrative organs as prescribed by law. (PRCAL Art. 3)

As can be seen, while the issues concerning civil cases are listed in subclause 1, the ones concerning 'administrative disputes' are stated in a vague way and are even more indeterminately referred to law in general. This indeterminacy has led to the challenging of arbitration awards due to the claim that the matter was not arbitrable. One of these cases was the dispute over product quality defect between a hospital in Zhouzhou City and Mr Ding reviewed in Yifei (2012). The hospital did not accept the arbitration award of the Zhouzhou Arbitration Commission (which was unfavourable to them), and applied to the Zhouzhou Intermediate Court to cancel it, arguing that the Arbitration Commission did not have the right to accept disputes involving product quality defects, as this matter concerned medical malpractice, and was therefore to be considered an administrative dispute.

5. Conclusion

The analysis of the text of PRCAL has highlighted a few of the legal and linguistic features that may be considered indicative of some of the chacteristics of the Chinese arbitration process and, more in general, of the Chinese legal system. Also the comparison with the UNCITRAL Model Law has proved useful, as it has provided interesting insights into the differentiations between the provisions of the PRC and those of many other countries based on the UN document. This comparison has shown that in spite of the fact that the two texts are similar in terms of topical content and coverage, they suggest interesting divergences in terms of clarity of expression and conceptual and terminological precision, which may also depend on the common law tradition reflected in the UN document and the civil law perspective adopted by Chinese legislators. Whereas the former favours precision and detailed guidelines for action in specific circumstances, the latter takes a more systematic approach, with arbitration firmly embedded within the country's highly codified domestic legislation.

Moreover, the analysis carried out in this chapter has also confirmed that the phenomenon of legal drafting is greatly influenced by the linguistic constraints and legal traditions of the local community to which the provision is addressed. As language is inseparable from set cultural implications and is deeply involved in social norms, linguistic and cultural factors are bound to arise in the complex process of formulation of legal norms. This can be seen, in particular, in the choice of particular terms to refer to the local socio-cultural system as well as the analysis of the specificity of information included in the two texts taken into consideration here, which differ significantly, due to differences in socio-cultural expectations and practices that constrain social behaviour in local contexts.

Our analysis has also shown that the legislation on arbitration in the People's Republic of China is not always precise and unambiguous, which has given rise to the fear that the system does not always guarantee equal opportunities and fair treatment to non-Chinese parties. However, in spite of these criticisms, the recourse to arbitration in solving both internal and international disputes in the PRC has increased significantly in the last few years. Indeed, also due to the difficulty in recognizing and enforcing foreign judgments from ordinary courts of law in China, arbitration has proved to be the preferred option for the settlement of international commercial disputes with counterparties located there. As a consequence, with China's increasing role in world trade, international arbitration in that country is expected to grow as a preferred method of resolving commercial disputes.

References

Ali, Shahla / Huang, Hui 2012. Financial Dispute Resolution in China: Arbitration or Court Litigation?. *Arbitration International* 28/1, 77–100.

Berger, Klaus P. 2006. *Private Dispute Resolution in International Business: Negotiation, Mediation, Arbitration*. The Hague: Kluwer Law International.

Bhatia, Vijay K. / Candlin, Christopher 2008. Interpretation across Legal Systems and Cultures: A Critical Perspective. In Bhatia/ Candlin/ Engberg (eds), 127–144.

Bhatia, Vijay K. / Candlin, Christopher / Engberg, Jan (eds) 2008. *Legal Discourse across Cultures and Systems*. Hong Kong: Hong Kong University Press.

Campbell, Lisbeth 1996. Drafting Styles: Fuzzy or Fussy? *ELaw. Murdoch University Electronic Journal of Law* 3/2. <http://www.murdoch.edu.au/elaw/issues/v3n2/ campbell.html>.

Cao, Deborah 2008. Is the Chinese Legal Language More Ambiguous and Vaguer?. In Wagner, Anne / Cacciaguidi-Fahi, Sophie (eds)

Obscurity and Clarity in the Law: Prospects and Challenges. Aldershot: Ashgate, 109–125.

Chang, Wang Sheng 2001. Formation of the Arbitral Tribunal. *Arbitration International* 17/1, 401–410.

Driedger, Elmer A. 1982. Legislative Drafting Style: Civil Law *versus* Common Law. In Jean-Claude Gémar (ed.) *Langage du droit et traduction / The Language of the Law and Translation*. Montreal: Linguatech / Conseil de la Langue Française, 63- 81.

Glück, Ulrike / Lichtenstein, Falk 2014. *Arbitration in the People's Republic of China*. CMS Guide to Arbitration, Vol I. at <http://eguides.cmslegal.com/pdf/arbitration_volume_I/CMS%20GtA_Vol%20I_CHINA.pdf>.

Keller, Perry 1994. Sources of Order in Chinese Law. *The American Journal of Comparative Law* 42/4, 711–759.

Lew, Julian / Mistelis, Loukas / Kröll, Stefan 2003. *Comparative International Commercial Arbitration*. The Hague: Kluwer Law International.

Liao, Meizhen 2012. Courtroom Discourse in China. In Tiersma, Peter / Solan, Lawrence (eds) *The Oxford Handbook of Language and Law*. Oxford: Oxford University Press, 395–407.

Mellinkoff, David 1963. *The Language of the Law*. Boston: Little, Brown & Co.

Moser, Michael / Yuen, Peter 2005. The New CIETAC Arbitration Rules. *Arbitration International* 21/3, 391–403.

Peerenboom, Randall 2002. *China's Long March toward Rule of Law*. Cambridge: Cambridge University Press.

Potter, Pitman B. 2001. *The Chinese Legal System: Globalisation and Local Legal Culture*. London: Routledge.

PRCAL = The People's Republic of China Arbitration Law (1994). <http://www.wipo.int/wipolex/en/text.jsp?file_id=182634>.

Ross, Claudia / Ross, Lester 2000. Language and Law: Sources of Systemic Vagueness and Ambiguous Authority in Chinese Statutory Language. In Turner, Karen G. / Feinerman, James V. / Guy, R. Kent (eds) *The Limits of the Rule of Law in China*. Washington: The University of Washington Press, 221–270.

Tao, Jingzhou / Von Wunschheim, Clarisse 2007. Articles 16 and 18 of the PRC Arbitration Law: The Great Wall of China for Foreign Arbitration Institutions. *Arbitration International* 23/2, 309–325.

UNCITRAL Model Law on International Commercial Arbitration 1985 (With amendments as adopted in 2006) <http://www.uncitral.org/pdf/english/texts/arbitration/ml-arb/07-86998_Ebook.pdf>.

Yifei, Lin 2012. Judicial Review of Arbitration Agreements in China. *Arbitration International* 28/2, 243–293.

Zhou, Jian 2006. Judicial Intervention in International Arbitration: A Comparative Study of the Scope of the New York Convention in U.S. and Chinese Courts. *Pacific Rim Law & Policy Journal* 15/2, 403–455.

Appendix

Comparison of contents of UNCITRAL and PRCAL statutory provisions

ML	*PRCAL*
CHAPTER I. GENERAL PROVISIONS Article 1 – Scope of application Article 2 – Definitions and rules of interpretation Article 2A – International origin and general principles Article 3 – Receipt of written communications Article 4 – Waiver of right to object Article 5 – Extent of court intervention Article 6 – Court or other authority for certain functions of arbitration assistance and supervision	CHAPTER I. GENERAL PROVISIONS Article 1 – Legislative intent Article 2 – Nature of arbitral disputes Article 3 – Subjects excluded from arbitral disputes Article 4 – Reaching of arbitration agreement Article 5 – Arbitration vs Litigation Article 6 – Selection of arbitration commission Article 7 – Basis for dispute resolution Article 8 – Extent of court intervention Article 9 – Setting aside of award CHAPTER II. ARBITRATION COMMISSIONS AND THE ARBITRATION ASSOCIATION Article 10 – Establishment of arbitration commissions

ML	*PRCAL*
CHAPTER II. ARBITRATION AGREEMENT Article 7 – Option 1: Definition and form of arbitration agreement Article 7 – Option 2: Definition of arbitration agreement Article 8 – Arbitration agreement and substantive claim before court Article 9 – Arbitration agreement and interim measures by court CHAPTER III. COMPOSITION OF ARBITRAL TRIBUNAL Article 10 – Number of arbitrators Article 11 – Appointment of arbitrators Article 12 – Grounds for challenge Article 13 – Challenge procedure Article 14 – Failure or impossibility to act Article 15 – Appointment of substitute arbitrator CHAPTER IV. JURISDICTION OF ARBITRAL TRIBUNAL Article 16 – Competence of arbitral tribunal to rule on its jurisdiction CHAPTER IV A. INTERIM MEASURES AND PRELIMINARY ORDERS Section 1. Interim measures Article 17. Power of arbitral tribunal to order interim measures Article 17 A. Conditions for granting interim measures	Article 11 – Conditions for an arbitration commission Article 12 – Composition of arbitration commissions Article 13 – Selection of arbitration commissions Article 14 – Independence of arbitration commissions Article 15 – China Arbitration Association CHAPTER III. ARBITRATION AGREEMENT Article 16 – Forms and contents of arbitration agreement Article 17 – Validity of arbitration agreement Article 18 – Reaching of arbitration agreement Article 19 – Independence of arbitration agreement Article 20 – Challenge of the validity of the arbitration agreement CHAPTER IV- ARBITRATION PROCEEDINGS Section 1. Application and Acceptance Article 21 – Application for arbitration Article 22 – How to apply for arbitration Article 23 – Specifications to be inserted in a written application for arbitration Article 24 – Duties of an arbitration commission Article 25 – Notification of an application for arbitration Article 26 – Ignorance of an arbitration agreement Article 27 – Renouncing or amending an arbitration claim. Article 28 – Property preservation Article 29 – Appointing a lawyer or other agent to carry out arbitration activities Section 2. Formation of Arbitration Tribunal

ML	*PRCAL*
Section 2. Preliminary orders Article 17 B. Applications for preliminary orders and conditions for granting preliminary orders Article 17 C. Specific regime for preliminary orders Section 3. Provisions applicable to interim measures and preliminary orders Article 17 D. Modification, suspension, termination Article 17 E. Provision of security Article 17 F. Disclosure Article 17 G. Costs and damages Section 4. Recognition and enforcement of interim measures Article 17 H. Recognition and enforcement Article 17 I. Grounds for refusing recognition or enforcement Section 5. Court-ordered interim measures Article 17 J. Court-ordered interim measures CHAPTER V. CONDUCT OF ARBITRAL PROCEEDINGS Article 18 – Equal treatment of parties Article 19 – Determination of rules of procedure Article 20 – Place of arbitration Article 21 – Commencement of arbitral proceedings Article 22 – Language Article 23 – Statements of claim and defence Article 24 – Hearings and written proceedings Article 25 – Default of a party	Article 30 – Number of arbitrators Article 31 – Appointment of arbitrators Article 32 – Failure in appointing arbitrators Article 33 – Formation of arbitration tribunal Article 34 – Grounds for challenge Article 35 – Challenge procedures Article 36 – Withdrawal decision Article 37 – Appointment of substitute arbitrator Article 38 – Removal of arbitrator from the register Section 3. Hearing and Award Article 39 – Oral hearings Article 40 – Private proceedings Article 41 – Notification of arbitration hearing Article 42 – Failure to appear before the arbitration tribunal Article 43 – Providing evidence Article 44 – Appraisal requirements Article 45 – Presentation of evidence Article 46 – Preservation of the evidence Article 47 – Right to carry on debate Article 48 – Records of the hearings Article 49 – Private settlement Article 50 – Repudiation of the settlement agreement Article 51 – Conciliation prior to giving an arbitration award Article 52 – Conciliation statement Article 53 – Arbitration award Article 54 – Specifications of an arbitration award Article 55 – Partial award Article 56 – Errors in the arbitration award Article 57 – Legal effectiveness of the arbitration award

ML	*PRCAL*
Article 26 – Expert appointed by arbitral tribunal Article 27 – Court assistance in taking evidence CHAPTER VI. MAKING OF AWARD AND TERMINATION OF PROCEEDINGS Article 28 – Rules applicable to substance of dispute Article 29 – Decision making by panel of arbitrators Article 30 – Settlement Article 31 – Form and contents of award Article 32 – Termination of proceedings Article 33 – Correction and interpretation of award; additional award CHAPTER VII. RECOURSE AGAINST AWARD Article 34 – Application for setting aside as exclusive recourse against arbitral award CHAPTER VIII. RECOGNITION AND ENFORCEMENT OF AWARDS Article 35 – Recognition and enforcement Article 36 – Grounds for refusing recognition or enforcement	CHAPTER V. APPLICATION FOR SETTING ASIDE ARBITRATION AWARD Article 58 – Applying for setting aside an arbitration award Article 59 – Deadline for applying for setting aside an arbitration award Article 60 – Ruling on setting aside an arbitration award Article 61 – Ruling to stay the setting-aside procedur CHAPTER VI. ENFORCEMENT Article 62 – Performing the arbitration award Article 63 – Disallowing the award Article 64 – Suspending the procedure of enforcement CHAPTER VII. SPECIAL PROVISIONS FOR ARBITRATION INVOLVING FOREIGN ELEMENTS Article 65 – Scope of the provisions of this Chapter Article 66 – Establishment of foreign-related arbitration commissions Article 67 – Appointment of a foreign-related arbitration commission Article 68 – Applying for preservation of the evidence Article 69 – Records of the hearings Article 70 – Evidence of the circumstances set forth in the first paragraph of Article 260 of the Civil Procedure Law Article 71 – Disallowing the enforcement Article 72 – Enforcement of a legally effective arbitration award Article 73 – Foreign-related arbitration rules

ML	*ML*
	CHAPTER VIII. SUPPLEMENTARY PROVISIONS Article 74 – Prescription for supplementary provisions Article 75 – Provisional rules of arbitration Article 76 – Payment of arbitration fees Article 77 – Regulations concerning arbitration of labor disputes and agricultural contractor's contract disputes Article 78 – Conflict between provisions Article 79 – Reorganization of arbitration institutions Article 80 – Effectiveness of this law

Girolamo Tessuto

Legislating on Arbitration in Singapore: Linguistic Insights

1. Introduction

Arbitration is one of the ADR methods used for resolving commercial disputes, and increasingly is a popular, cost-effective and expeditious alternative to the more formal and public litigation. Arbitration takes place within complex and important national and international legal frameworks where legislation, rules, and conventions provide specialized regimes for arbitration practices. Coinciding with a strong interest taken by (applied) linguists since the early 2000s, the relevance of arbitration has led to a burgeoning of scholarly studies appearing in edited collections of papers (Bhatia/ Candlin/Gotti 2003, 2010, 2012; Bhatia/Candlin/ Engberg/Trosborg 2003; Bhatia/Candlin 2004; Bhatia/ Candlin/Engberg 2008; Bhatia/Candlin/Evangelisti 2008; Salmi-Tolonen/Tukiainen/ Foley 2011; Bhatia/Garzone/Degano 2012) as well as individual papers (Evangelisti 2008; Garzone 2008; Gotti 2008; Bhatia 2011). While these insightful works reveal the important context of the institutional and professional practices of arbitration from which different texts and genres originate, they also show the dynamism of arbitration language and discourse in a variety of situational genres, enhancing knowledge of arbitration practice and its integrity across languages, cultures, and legal systems. The reviewed studies therefore provide evidence of the commitments made by the academic strand of linguists to respond to an agenda that arbitration continuously sets in an increasingly globalised world.

In keeping with this important agenda, a vital linguistic research opportunity is now offered by the legislative practice of arbitration in the Asia Pacific region. In this part of the globe, the increased economic interaction between the East (Asia) and the West as well as within

Asia demonstrates that Asia is a very important region to the global economy. The region's increasing participation in global commerce is coupled with the arbitration procedures available in the many Asian countries, such as China, India, Singapore, Taiwan, or Vietnam, which rely on Civil Law and Common Law jurisdictions to resolve national and international disputes. In this framework, Singapore (a Common Law jurisdiction) has recently been attempting to boost its image as a world-class arbitration centre across the Asian region, and various measures have been taken to foster this image under the auspices of the Singapore International Arbitration Centre (SIAC). In addition to the SIAC arbitration rules and other provisions promoting arbitration as a viable alternative to litigation, legislative steps have also been taken to amend the dual-track regime of international and domestic arbitration for private commercial disputes in Singapore, namely the International Arbitration Act 2002 and the domestic Arbitration Act 2001 (AA). While these amended acts derive from previous changes to the legislative framework of (international and domestic) arbitration, their names suggest that they differ from each other in terms of the conduct required for the arbitral process in Singapore. Broadly speaking, the international regime concerns arbitrations that are conducted under international arbitration agreements where the parties to the arbitration are of different nationalities. The domestic regime, on the other hand, concerns arbitrations that are conducted under domestic arbitration agreements, and the AA thus operates whenever the subject matter of the dispute involves Singapore, in which the parties are nationals.

It is against this background that this chapter seeks to examine the new Singapore Arbitration (Amendment) Act 2001 from the perspective of language use by contributing to our linguistic knowledge of arbitration practice manifested in the Eastern (Asian) context. The chapter thus analyzes quantitatively and qualitatively the linguistic and discursive features of arbitration laws written in the institutional and professional context of the Asian (Singapore) genre, and identifies specific aspects of accessibility/readability of legal discourse within the genre itself. The chapter draws conclusions from contextualized material and data, and highlights the hypothesis for generic integrity (Bhatia 2004) when the Asian legal discourse of arbitration is set against the Western European style of legislating on a similar topic.

2. Material and Method

2.1 The data

The Singapore Arbitration (Amendment) Act 2001 (Chapter 10 – Revised Edition 31 July 2002)[1] was retrieved from the Attorney-General's Chambers (A-GC) Singapore institutional website[2] where other online Singapore Statutes are found as part of the Chambers' Legislation Editing and Authentic Publishing System. The data source for this study is a 12,910-word corpus of electronically published laws, but excludes the 'Legislative History' and 'Comparative Table' short sections at the back of the Act as they are irrelevant for the purpose of this study. Expectedly, the text sample in this corpus is a well-defined piece of 'legislative' or 'statutory writing' (Bhatia 1983a: 2; Bhatia/ Candlin/Engberg 2008: 13) serving a 'prescriptive function' (Šarčević 2000: 9), and provides the internal operating prescriptions of the arbitration regime and practice in this country. Like any other enacted legislation across the world, the statute is a generic form of institutional communication that involves various participants as 'real writers' (draftsmen, legislators, government departments) and 'real readers' (ordinary citizens, lawyers, judges, members of the executive arms of the government), who "do not share the same level of legal and background knowledge in the discipline" (Bhatia 2004: 126).

---

1 This Act became law on 1 March 2002 and replaces entirely the previous (1985) Arbitration Act (Cap 10). The text is available at <http://statutes.agc. gov.sg/aol/ home.w3p>.

2 <http://statutes.agc.gov.sg/aol/home.w3p> as of 10 March 2014.

2.2 Analytic procedure

The analysis in this study primarily relies on the functional organization of the lexico-grammatical units that describe written legal language and discourse in English (Bhatia 1993, 1994a/b, 2004, 2005a/b, 2010), combined with other functionally descriptive units of English language and discourse, whether or not in the field of law (e.g. Coates 1983; Quirk et al. 1985, Tiersma 1999; Garzone 2001, 2013; Gotti 2003, 2012; Hiltunen 2001, 2012; Palmer 2001; Williams 2005). Descriptive findings of the current study therefore involve a great deal of textual analysis linked with discourse properties of the text from the chosen genre. Given that much linguistic work has already been published on the subject of investigation, the aim of this study is also therefore to draw on comparable data from Western-styled English-language arbitration texts appearing in edited volumes (e.g. Bhatia/ Candlin/Gotti 2003, 2010), as well as other individual investigations dealing with (Western) non-arbitration legislative texts (Williams 2011; Garzone 2013). Qualitative and quantitative data results of ongoing study design and procedure were obtained via computer scanning and manually analysed for specific linguistic items and frequencies.

3. Results and Discussion

3.1 Macro-structural organization: a unity of communicative purpose

To begin with, the general layout and format of the Singapore Arbitration Act have much in common with traditional standards of legislative drafting as found in the English Arbitration Act 1996 (Tessuto 2003: 339), and include ten Parts as descriptive components of the statute, in addition to metadata ('Legislative History' and 'Comparative Table'). In keeping with these Parts, Table 1 clearly shows that the statute is laid out in sequential order, starting with the arbitration agreement, through to jurisdiction, proceedings and finally to the award and the role of the court.

Singapore Arbitration Act 2001 – Chapter 10 – Contents	*Number of sections*
Part I – PRELIMINARY	3
Part II – ARBITRATION AGREEMENT	2
Part III – STAY OF LEGAL PROCEEDINGS	3
Part IV – COMMENCEMENT OF ARBITRAL PROCEEDINGS	3
Part V – ARBITRAL TRIBUNAL	9
Part VI – JURISDICTION OF ARBITRAL TRIBUNAL	2
Part VII – ARBITRAL PROCEEDINGS	10
Part VIII – AWARD	13
Part IX – POWERS OF COURT IN RELATION TO AWARD	8
Part X – MISCELLANEOUS	14
Legislative History	–
Comparative Table	–
Total number of sections	67

Table 1. Singapore Arbitration Act 2001: overall textual organization.

In addition to these conventional Parts grouping provisions of a similar kind, other legislative standards of the kind found in the 1996 English Act are based on the division of text into sections and subsections grouped together with numbering and lettering systems. The use of short, clear headings to Parts and individual sections/ subsections therefore provides the essential contents of the enactment, serving a unity of communicative purpose. This can be seen in Part headings and section headings, where words that indicate the main topic are used as specifically as possible and substantive law matters (Part I – PRELIMINARY; Part II – ARBITRATION AGREEMENT) come before procedural law matters (Part III – STAY OF LEGAL PROCEEDINGS and subsequent Parts). As Table 1 shows, the resulting structure is a totality of 67 sections included in the statute where they govern Singapore's arbitration regime in both substantive and procedural law rules. Predictably, the topics of the arbitration regime covered in this structure are also determined by a different number of sections, as shown by a greater emphasis given to issues for rule on Arbitral Tribunal, Arbitral Proceedings, Award and Miscellaneous (Table 1), and this is presumably determined by the legislative intentions that the Singapore Parliament had in mind in amending and passing the statute. Within this macro-structure, then, the 'enacting formula' (Kurzon 1986) is placed at the very front of the statute to introduce the main provisions of Singapore arbitration law enacted by the legislature. As such, the formula can be said to characterize the legislative machinery and institutional practice of the genre since it declares the source from which the relevant law claims to derive its authority:

(1) An Act to provide for the conduct of arbitration. [**Long title**]
Be it enacted by the President with the advice and consent of the Parliament of Singapore, as follows: [**Enacting formula**]

As a result of this authority, the conventional formula is one which also conveys the binding force of the statute for the people at large, or similarly the "perpetual, speaking command from the sovereign power to its subjects" (Maley 1994: 20), as realized by the *be it enacted* 'passive imperative' (Kurzon 1986: 10), or 'old jussive subjunctive' (Maley 1994: 20). Compared to the English Arbitration Act (1996), where the enacting formula still contains antiquated, formulaic expressions derived from the historical tradition (*BE IT ENACTED by the Queen's most Excellent Majesty, by and with the advice and consent of the Lords Spiritual and Temporal, and Common, in the present Parliament assembled, and by the authority of the same, as follows*), the formula in the Singaporean statute is no more than a stylistic variant version of the English statute, though closer to being plain in language.

3.2 Syntactic features: text length

The macro-structural features resulting from the legislative machinery and institutional practice of the genre have their effect on the total length of the text noted above (12,910). Table 2 illustrates that the total number of sentences separated by a full stop (248) and the average sentence length (52.06) naturally reflect the textual development across the variously headed rules.

Singapore Arbitration Act 2001	
Word length (tokens)	12,910
Number of sentences	248
Average sentence length	52.06
Words per sentence: min/max	Minimum: 6 / Maximum: 304

Table 2. Text length per total number of words, total sentences and sentence length.

Viewed comparably, the average sentence length in the table above shows a greater degree of variability with the average sentence length found in previous studies on a different set of arbitration rules in legislative and non-legislative texts from the Western-European law tradition (Belotti 2003: 33; Garzone 2003: 186; Salmi-Tolonen 2003: 319; Tessuto 2010: 241), as well as the average sentence length found in other types of legal language (Gustafsson 1975: 10; Kurzon 1997: 131) and British statutes (Hiltunen 2001: 56, 2012: 41). In addition to this average trend, sentence length in the current data can also be appreciated by the massive range between minimum (6) and maximum number of words (304) used in a sentence as is necessary for the drafters to present the complete substance of the rule.

3.2.1 Syntactic arrangement: sentence type

The need for the presentation of substance in a provision means that sentence length is reflected in the structure and meaning of a legislative sentence. In keeping with these contents, Table 3 shows that less than one sentence out of five in the corpus is either a simple or compound sentence type, while almost half of the sentences there are complex in type. Indeed, four out of five sentences are complex or complex-compound.

Sentence type	*no.*	*%*
Simple	15	6.0
Compound	31	12.5
Complex	110	44.3
Complex-compound	92	37.1

Table 3. Distribution of sentence types: occurrences and percentages.

The proportionally higher incidence of complex and complex-compound sentences in the corpus therefore provides evidence of very intricate patterns of sentence structure in the genre, and is at some variance with the previously investigated (Western) European/non-European arbitration/mediation texts of the non-legislative genre (Belotti 2003: 34; Tessuto 2010: 242), where complex sentences alone are found to occur in greater use. Clearly, it is a mistake to think that legislation 'can' be drafted in simple and compound sentences alone, since the requirement for precision and non-ambiguity discussed in the sections below allows the other pair of sentences to necessarily take precedence in the corpus. Generalizing, therefore, 'complexity' (including length) and 'organization' (coordination, subordination) of sentence structure corroborate other studies on English legal language and discourse outside Asian contexts (Hiltunen 1990: 70; Bhatia 1993: 105–106; Tiersma 1999: 56; Gotti 2003: 85–90, 2012: 53–54; Salmi-Tolonen 2008: 119). In an attempt to visualize these four types of sentences, reference is made to the basic building blocks of English sentence structure rules identified in Quirk et al.'s (1985: 987–991) traditional Grammar of English, since they appear to accommodate the legal sentence structure of the genre we are dealing with. With these rules in mind, simple sentences are therefore used in the text with only one predicate about the subject, and correspondingly hold simplicity of expression only when the content of the rule so requires:

(2) This Act shall bind the Government.

(3) The date of the award and place of arbitration shall be stated in the award.

Since too many simple sentences would naturally sound choppy and undeveloped in the ongoing text, as noted before, compound sentences make their appearance with two or more coordinate main clauses:

(4) The arbitral tribunal shall act fairly and impartially and shall give each party a reasonable opportunity of presenting his case.

Complex sentences overflow into the text with one main clause and one or more subordinate clauses, as in the following examples of rule structure:

(5) If all parties to any arbitral proceedings consent in writing and for so long as no party has withdrawn his consent in writing, an arbitrator may act as a mediator.

(6) Where any provision in this Act refers to a claim, it shall also apply to a cross-claim or counter-claim, and where such provision refers to a defence, it shall also apply to a defence to such cross-claim or counter-claim.

Indeed, expressing the interrelationships among the ideas conveyed by the words and phrases becomes more intricate when complex-compound sentences slide into the text with two or more coordinate clauses and one or more subordinate clauses. This can be seen in the following lengthy provision constructed in 142 words:

(7) – 1 Notwithstanding subsection (3), where a court gives grounds of decision for a judgment in respect of proceedings to which this section applies and considers that judgment to be of major legal interest, the court shall direct that reports of the judgment may be published in law reports and professional publications but, if any party to the proceedings reasonably wishes to conceal any matter, including the fact that he was such a party, the court shall –
(a) give directions as to the action that shall be taken to conceal that matter in those reports; and
(b) if it considers that a report published in accordance with directions given under paragraph (*a*) would be likely to reveal that matter, direct that no report shall be published until after the end of such period, not exceeding 10 years, as it considers appropriate.

This example clearly shows that drafters are able to knit a range of different pieces of information into a single sentence and to order them in relationship to each other. Despite this intellectual effort by the drafters, the example is not saved from the difficulty posed by the syntactic and semantic complexity of the sentence consisting of three main clauses, each modified by as many subordinate and conjoined clauses as necessary to help understand the nature and content of the provision.

3.3 Lexico-grammatical and discoursal resources of Singapore arbitration provisions

As already seen from some of the examples quoted, writing complex and complex-compound sentences also requires the use of a variety of lexico-grammatical resources that account for the consistency of discourse patterning in the genre in terms of its conventionalized communicative purpose. Naturally, reliance on those resources within a sentence also brings into play the question of readability for a specific group of readers for whom the domestic arbitration regime should be 'successful' and 'party friendly', as discussed below. With this in mind, the following sections provide descriptive findings of such resources that characterize the clausal structure of those sentences.

3.3.1 Qualifications and syntactic discontinuities

Writing long and intricate provisions in the statute conventionally relies on the three types of 'qualifications' that provide different types of information about those provisions – namely, 'preparatory qualifications', 'operational qualifications', and 'referential qualifications' (Bhatia 1993: 115). Adherence to "qualificational insertions within [the] syntactic boundaries" (Bhatia 1993: 111) of the provisions often leads to syntactic discontinuities in the structure of legislative sentences (Gustafsson 1975: 19–22; Bhatia 1993: 111–113, 1994a: 147). In the present material, such discontinuities and their varying frequencies are commonly traced within:

- the main verbal phrase (22%);
- the restrictive/non-restrictive clause (16%) and adverbial clause (38%); and
- the binomial or multinominal (*and*, *or*) parallel structures (24%).

The examples below illustrate the use of diverse qualificational devices (italics) conflating in variable positions of the statutory provisions and interacting with the main clause of the provision (bold):

(8) Where any party to an arbitration agreement institutes any proceedings in any court against any other party to the agreement in respect of any matter_*which is the subject of the agreement*, **any party to the agreement may**, *at any time*

after appearance and before delivering any pleading or taking any other step in the proceedings, **apply to that court to stay the proceedings so far as the proceedings relate to that matter**.

(9) Where the parties fail to agree on a procedure for appointing the arbitrator or arbitrators –
(a) in an arbitration with 3 arbitrators, **each party shall appoint one arbitrator, and the parties shall** *by agreement* **appoint the third arbitrator**; *or*
(b) in an arbitration with a sole arbitrator, *if the parties are unable to agree on the arbitrator*, **the arbitrator shall be appointed**, *upon the request of a party*, **by the appointing authority**.

(10) Where the terms of an arbitration agreement to refer future disputes to arbitration provide that a claim *to which the arbitration agreement applies* shall be barred *unless* –
(a) *some step has been taken to begin other dispute resolution procedures which must be exhausted before arbitral proceedings can be begun*;
(b) *notice to appoint an arbitrator is given*;
(c) *an arbitrator is appointed*; *or*
(d) *some other step is taken to commence arbitral proceedings*,
within a time fixed by the agreement and a dispute to which the agreement applies has arisen, **the Court may**, *if it is of the opinion that in the circumstances of the case undue hardship would otherwise be caused*, **extend the time for such period and on such terms as the Court thinks fit**.

As we can see, the resulting sentence structures are tightly woven, dense and clausally complex, and the elements that are semantically and structurally related end up being separated from each other by various qualifications constructed at different word length, thus creating syntactic discontinuities. Not only do these qualificational insertions provide additional information about the execution of the rule (operational qualifications), but they also interact with preparatory qualifications that are realized mostly by *where*-adverbial clauses throughout the corpus. Such initial, pre-main clauses describe a set of circumstances (cases/conditions) in which the substantive or procedural law provision applies in domestic arbitration, or function as initial focus of the whole sentence in grammatical terms (Quirk et al. 1985: 491).

No wonder that syntactic complexity and discontinuity resulting from qualificational insertions are closely connected with the drafting standards of legislation used in the Common Law jurisdictions, which favour an expansive and detailed approach to law by legislating for any and every imaginable scenario, as found in other Western-styled arbitration texts (e.g. Bhatia 2005a: 338–343; Bhatia/Candlin 2008: 136; Gotti 2012: 58–59; Tessuto 2003: 343–347, 2010: 242–249). Consequently, the frequent use of qualifications in the Asian, Common Law text as well has a rightful place, since it makes the textualization of the genre "precise, clear, unambiguous and all-inclusive" (Bhatia 1993: 117) by "creat[ing] conditions of homogeneity between the insiders [through] shared genre knowledge" (Bhatia 2004: 192), and similarly retaining "the generic integrity of legislative discourse" (Bhatia 2004: 194). Clearly, this form of textualization is not destitute of other purposes outside the statute because it allows Singapore judges and lawyers alike to restrict expansive rules to the specific facts they are intended to cover in the particular case as it does for other Common Law judges and lawyers.

Quite apart from these purposes, however, this textualizing form enables to appreciate the far-reaching significance of parliamentary law by emphasizing the dynamics of "power and control in [the] legislative context" (Bhatia 2004: 193–194), where the role of the Asian draftsman is to give effect to the unicameral intention of Singapore Parliament in amending the current statute. There obviously comes a point when this all-inclusive principle of arbitration laws in the genre unveils to a certain extent the law-making processes within such a Parliament, and "gives a relatively high degree of transparency to legislative intentions" (Bhatia 2004: 194; 2010: 8) in line with the institutional goals of the legal community as a whole (draftsmen, legislators, government departments).

3.3.2 *Paragraphing: effecting a compromise between comprehensibility and precision*

Yet, exploring every imaginable scenario by qualifications within the criterion of complexity of sentence length and structure is likely to backfire. This undesirable result can be seen in the linguistic examples quoted above (7, 9, 10), where the close nexus between semantic and structural elements may become less obvious to ordinary readers, who are affected by the content of arbitration laws but are mostly unused to those conventional elements. This is unfortunate indeed if the goal of writing laws on arbitration is also "to facilitate comprehension of the unfolding text for ordinary readership" (Bhatia 1993: 103), or even to make the arbitration process more transparent and accessible for the training of new arbitrators (Bhatia/Candlin/Sharma 2009).

One step towards this goal is achieved by the typological device of paragraphing used in one fifth of complex and complex-compound sentences across the statute. Such a device may have the effect of simplifying the text at those points where linguistic resources alone fail, and therefore makes for easy access to integrity of the rule by those readers. Thus, in the same examples above (7, 9, 10), paragraphing helps to reveal at a glance the logical structure of a lengthy and intricate sentence by showing which grammatical units are parallel to each other through cumulative (*and*) or alternative items (*or*) in paragraphs, and to indicate how different parts of a sentence are linked to each other by avoiding ambiguity about the objects of modifiers, such as adverbial clauses, relative clauses and preposition phrases.

As a "visual aid to comprehension" (Driedger 1982: 78) as well as a Plain Language technique advocated in diverse legal drafting manuals across the world, paragraphing the statute thus provides one of the functional *easification* devices (Bhatia 1983b; 2010: 10–13) conventionally used to give readers the key structural elements of each legislative sentence as early as possible. Which practice to follow (paragraphed or unparagraphed sentence) will naturally be determined by the rule content in line with the scope and function of the statute, as much as by a conscious decision on the part of the drafters to abide by the legislative intentions themselves. However, a sentence in a paragraphed form seems to always ensure completeness of rule content in terms of its communicative purpose, and to similarly encourage ordinary readers to move forward in the text, thus providing an added bonus in terms of readability.

3.3.3 Binomial and multinomial structures

Just as informational density and complexity of sentence structure effects a compromise, as it were, between accuracy and comprehensiveness, so it is for binomials and multinomials flowing into the genre to make legislative provisions precise and all-inclusive (Gustafsson 1984:

132; Bhatia 1993: 108, 1994a: 143–144; Bhatia/Candlin/Engberg 2008: 23–24), as found in other arbitration/mediation texts (Garzone 2003: 202–203; Giannoni 2003: 231–234; Tessuto 2010: 249–250).

In the present material, the all-inclusive effect of bi- and multinomials is identified by lexical strings in various parts of speech, such as adjectives and verbs in addition to nouns, and placed in semantic relations of (near) synonymy, antonymy, or complementarity by *and/or* conjunctions. This effect is equally achieved by the syntactic parallel units based on coordination (*and*) and alternative coordination (*or*), as noted before about syntactic discontinuity, which are indented from the opening clauses and numbered in the same series. In both cases, therefore, semantic parallelism is as important as the syntactic to explain the relations that exist in the word or clause strings.

Connecting strings of words and placing them in stereotyped semantic relations can be traced in the notable proportion of bi- and multinomial structures below used in almost every provision of the statute:

(11) role *and* function
ready *and* willing
null *and* void
fairly *and* impartially
admissibility, relevance, materiality *and* weight of <u>any</u> evidence
proper *and* expeditious conduct
inordinate *and* inexcusable delay
jointly *and* severally liable
fees *and* expenses

(12) institution *or* organization
a panel of arbitrators *or* an arbitral institution
instituted *or* heard
any arbitral *or* other institution *or* person authorised by the parties
agreement *or* contract
arbitral *or* legal proceedings
information generated, sent, received *or* stored by electronic, magnetic optical *or* similar means
any written law *or* rule of law
interim *or* supplementary orders
claiming through *or* under such party
which the Court orders to be set aside *or* declares to be of no effect

Although these resources contribute to the peculiar conventionality and formality of legislative provisions in the Asian statute, as they do indeed in Common Law texts, they also cleverly help remove ambiguities lurking within long, intricate sentences. Yet, as the set of linguistic examples above illustrates, the all-inclusive effect of bi- and multinomials can also be seen by the grammatical feature of *any* ('whichever of a specified class'), used abundantly in the statute (210 times) to make the whole sentence as comprehensive as possible, and extends to all-inclusive sentences constructed outside bi- and multinomial structures. Thus, we read:

(13) Where *any* provision in this Act allows the parties to determine *any* issue, the parties may authorize [....].

3.3.4 Lexical repetition, anaphora and gender neutrality

The need to avoid latent ambiguity within syntactic structures of the statute can also be seen by the tendency towards repetition of lexical items. In the example below, the nouns *party* and *procedure* (accompanied by *such* as a determiner) are reiterated five times each in the provision to ensure clarity and precision:

(14) If, under an appointment *procedure* agreed upon by the *parties* –
(a) a *party* fails to act as required under such *procedure*;
(b) the *parties* are unable to reach an agreement expected of them under *such procedure*; or
(c) a third *party*, including an arbitral institution, fails to perform any function entrusted to it under such *procedure*,
any *party* may apply to the appointing authority to take the necessary measure unless the agreement on the appointment *procedure* provides other means for securing the appointment.

While the example above illustrates that lexical repetition is an overriding principle of precise reference chains in the generic writing, other examples from the corpus show that lexical repetition is circumvented by the use of pronoun reference and anaphora (*he*, *his*, *him*, *they*, *their*, *them*). This can be seen in the provision below, where a substitute word (*he*) refers back to a lexical item that would otherwise have been reiterated, and contributes to the internal cohesion of the rule:

(15) The authority of an arbitrator shall not be revoked by the death of any party by whom *he* was appointed.

At the same time, the provision above illustrates the gender-neutral language achieved in the statute by the use of the masculine pronoun *he* to refer to antecedents (*arbitrator* or *party*) of indeterminate gender, whether masculine or feminine, although neutrality of language here is also ensured by the neutral word or phrase (*person* or *no person*) used almost throughout the statute. Clearly, gender neutrality through pronouns is traditional of Common Law legislative writing and emanates from the 'Interpretation' statutes of many law-making institutions in the West. But where the choice for gender-neutral pronouns is meant to legislate for both sexes in arbitration matters, then it will not only ensure the equality of gender in the statute but will also in some way bring us round to the overriding principle of all-inclusiveness by precisely encompassing both gender categories in those matters.

3.3.5 Nominalization

Drafters make rather extensive use of nominalization (78 times) realized in the form of verbs that are changed into nouns (Tiersma 1999: 77–79; Jackson 1995: 120–122), as in:

(16) A court […] shall *give directions* as to whether […]. ('direct')

(17) the court may, on its own motion, *make an order* discontinuing the proceedings […] ('order').

It is easy to see that these nominalized forms (*give directions/make an order*) are preferred over the strong, more effective verbs (*direct, order*) to express the same meaning, suggesting that drafters are unaware of the warnings made against the overuse of nominalizations in legal discourse that "[o]verall, it is best to use straightforward, active verbs rather than nominalizations" (Tiersma 1999: 207), or that "[i]f you use nominalizations instead of base verbs, surplus words begin to swarm like gnats" (Wydick 2005: 23). By avoiding the reference to the results of actions their base verbs would do in the same circumstances, the nominalized forms above can thus be said to strip the legal action of its immediacy by introducing a degree of abstractness in arbitration rule-making.

Apart from nominalization in the form of longer nouns created by verbs, the corpus shows that nominalization is often employed for the purpose of inserting as many details as possible into a single sentence, thus conveying "a greater degree of precision and all-inclusiveness" (Bhatia 1994a: 142) in the construction of arbitration laws:

(18) An *application* for the leave of the Court to appeal or an *application* referred to in section 21(10)21A(1), 36(6) or 49(3)(*b*) or (7) shall be made in such manner as may be prescribed in the *Rules* of *Court*.

(19) If all parties to any *arbitral* proceedings consent in *writing* and for so long as no party has withdrawn his consent in *writing*, an *arbitrator* may act as a *mediator*.

Of these and other nominal examples that enable informational density in almost every provision across the statute, nominalization takes the most typical *-al* (*arbitral*), *-ance* (*accordance, substance*), *-ence* (*reference*), *-ion* (*arbitration, institution, satisfaction*), *-ment* (*agreement*), *-ity* (*authority*), and *-or* (*arbitrator*) suffixes, as identified in the categories of derivational noun endings (Biber 1988; Biber et al. 1999; Biber et al. 2002), and occurs in the form of noun phrase modifiers, including attributive adjectives (*<u>arbitral</u> proceedings*, *<u>arbitral</u> tribunals*), nouns as pre-modifiers of a head noun (*<u>party</u> representative*), and prepositional phrases as post-modifiers of a head noun (*a single agreement <u>in settlement of a dispute</u>*). By squeezing more information into a sentence, these nominal elements thus provide a further grammatical phenomenon that is communicatively and discursively necessary in the expression of arbitration laws.

3.3.6 Modality, mood and active/passive construction

The statute provides the legally binding framework in which duties/ obligations, permissions, powers, and liabilities are defined, or rights conferred upon the subjects involved in arbitration. In this framework, the modals used in the grammar of active and passive sentence structures and the mood grammatical categories (imperative, subjunctive and indicative forms) play a significant role in the generic discourse where they are pragmatic vehicles of communication. In this section, the analytical perspective on the discourse functions of modals and semi-modals is drawn from established empirical studies of modality categories in English, whether in legal or non-legal contexts (e.g. Coates 1983; Quirk et al. 1985; Leech 1987; Trosborg 1997; Garzone 2001, 2013; Palmer 2001; Huddleston/Pullum 2002; Williams 2005), while the mood grammatical categories are drawn from traditional English grammar books (Quirk et al. 1985: 149; Huddleston/Pullum 2002: 172).

3.3.6.1 Central modal and semi-modal verbs

Table 4 shows the distribution of central modal verbs across the statute, where the highest incidence is held by *shall* accounting for just over a half, followed by *may* being just over one third of all modals used. Except for *might*, missing across the current sample, the frequency list in Table 4 therefore leaves all other modal auxiliaries far behind in the sample, as is the case of *should* and *would* forms used collectively in less than one in twenty cases, and includes the *be to* semi-modal form used only on five occasions.

Central modal verbs	*no.*	*%*
Can	2	0.5
Could	3	0.8
May	137	38
Might	0	0
Must	2	0.5
Shall	198	55
Should	7	1.9
Will	2	0.5
Would	10	2.8
Total	*361*	*100*
Semi-modals	*no.*	*%*
Be to	5	100

Table 4. Distribution of central modal and semi-modal auxiliaries: occurrences and percentages.

Comparatively, the higher incidence of *shall* in the current data is congruent with other findings of the modal in larger corpus-based data sets from UNCITRAL texts (Gotti 2008: 238), as well as from contracts (Bondi/Diani 2010), or legislative texts (Hiltunen 1990: 75; Garzone

2001: 156). Where the aggregate sum of *shall* and *may* modals in the reference data is also taken into account, the proportionally higher incidence of these modal aggregates is consistent with previously investigated (Western European) arbitration/mediation texts (Belotti 2003: 26; Dossena 2003: 104; Tessuto 2003: 347, 2010: 252).

Despite the relatively small-sized corpus here, the heavy incidence of legislative *shall* in the recorded data takes on greater significance if compared to other Western, diachronic (large corpus-based) data sets from (UK) Common Law legislative texts, where the tendency has been towards *shall* being substantially dropped from those texts since the 2000s. On this point, Williams (2011: 143) reports on the "frequency of *shall* dwindling to 0.2 occurrences per 1000 words" and, rather similarly, Garzone (2013: 71) reports on the *shall* "residual number of occurrences [becoming] negligible, approximating 0" after 2005. While, as these authors argue, this tendency to oust *shall* from the Western legislative drafting practices is largely contingent upon the varying pace of progress made by the Plain Language modernizing movement in Common Law countries and EU institutions, the tendency to keep *shall* in the Asian statute suggests that the effects of this movement have not filtered down to Singapore yet. In discussing Plain English in Asia, in fact, Bhatia (2005b: 45, 'Abstract') notes that this movement "has apparently not gained a strong presence in many Asian countries, including India, China, Singapore and Hong Kong", where "public and bureaucratic writing shows a distinct lack of awareness of plain English".

In keeping with these data and arguments, therefore, it is fair to say that the preference for *shall*-bound provisions instead of clearer drafting alternatives in the current sample depends purely on a conservative legal-making bias of Singaporean drafters, who are accustomed to this modal as the most conventional – however less modernizing – verb form to convey the essential features of deontic or non-deontic meaning in the genre, as discussed below. In addition to the discretion given to drafters, however, the preference for *shall*-bound provisions is not without the power and control of other community members (legislators, government departments) committed to legislating arbitration laws in this particular manner.

3.3.6.2 Active/passive sentence structure

It is also interesting to see how Singapore drafters prefer the active sentence structure over the passive sentence structure when drafting in the most popular *shall* as well as *may* provisions. Table 5 shows the patterns and frequency of these modal items in active/passive sentence structures, where the modal auxiliary *shall* (*shall/shall not* + main verb) is almost always in the active verb form (94.5%) with a third-person (singular/plural) subject of the main clause, and hardly ever in the passive form (5.5%) of the same clause (*shall/shall not be* + *past participle*). No use is made of *shall* in subordinate clause types. The second most common modal auxiliary *may* shows a similar preference for the active verb form (68.5%) with a third-subject (singular/plural) of the main clause, although this preference is less marked than the *shall* construction, while the passive form (*may* + *be* + *past participle*) is used in almost one in three cases (31.5%). Again, no use of *may* is made in subordinate clauses.

Top-two modal verbs	*active voice (no. / %)*		*passive voice (no. / %)*	
Shall	187	94.5	11	5.5
May	94	68.5	43	31.5

Table 5. *Shall/May* active and passive verb constructions: occurrences and percentages.

The preference for an active sentence structure in the reference data is therefore a clear sign of the Asian drafters sticking fast to many Plain Language legal drafting manuals (e.g. Asprey 2003: 102–103), where the active voice is recommended. The propensity for an active-voice sentence in the statute openly suggests that the subject-verb relationship and the sentence structure in an active form are more direct, and consequently easier to process than those in the passive voice sentence. In the latter (passive) construction, the agent is often realised as a prepositional phrase, most typically with *by* (Carter/ McCarthy 2006) across the statute, typifying what has been referred to as 'central passives' (Quirk et al. 1985: 167, on a tripartite division into 'central passives', 'semi-passives' and 'pseudo-passives'). Although passive verb constructions tend to avoid 'actual' work in the statute, they are employed for three main reasons. Firstly, to describe the short title by referring to the statute itself (*This Act may be cited as the Arbitration Act*), and therefore to provide a mandatory principle for writing in the genre. Secondly, and as Hiltunen (1990: 81) points out, to enable the drafters to arrange the material so that 'old' information appears in the subject position and 'new' information appears in the final position, which receives end stress by enhancing the semantic link. Thirdly, to enable the drafters to confer an impersonal and objective tone to the provisions. Allied to the tendency to slip easily into the active mode is the preference for the positive to the negative forms of *shall* and *may* provisions, suggesting that only a few actions need to be expressly prohibited (and therefore stated negatively) on account of the rule content.

However, the emphasis on active/passive *shall* and *may* provisions is no less useful to specify the incidence of the types of third-person subjects, who are concerned with the legal effect of those provisions purposively established by the legislature. In these modalized provisions, animate subjects (48%) in active sentences are almost as frequent as inanimate subjects in such sentences (52%), and animate or inanimate subjects are also generally specified in passive sentences (object position).

3.3.6.3 Shall

Predictably, *shall* modal flows into the text with a deontic (prescriptive), agent-oriented meaning (e.g. Coates 1983: 190–194; Trosborg 1997: 45–46; Gotti 2001: 93; Williams 2005: 114–120; Garzone 2001: 165, 2013: 72), by laying down obligations or duties on animate subjects (individuals) who are required to perform in the specified manner:

(20) Where the parties fail to agree on a procedure for appointing the arbitrator or arbitrators –
(a) in an arbitration with 3 arbitrators, <u>each party</u> *shall* appoint one arbitrator, and <u>the parties</u> *shall* by agreement appoint the third arbitrator; or
(b) in an arbitration with a sole arbitrator, if the parties are unable to agree on the arbitrator, <u>the arbitrator</u> *shall* be appointed, upon the request of a party, by the appointing authority.

This (strong) obligation/duty meaning is no more than an alternative, however much unconsciously made by the drafters, to the isolated instances (2) of *must* modal in the data:

(21) Provision may be made by Rules of Court amending the provisions of this Act –
(a) with respect to the time within which any application or appeal to the Court *must* be made;
(b) […].

More often than not, positive *shall* extends to include other instances where negation or prohibition of obligative *shall* is encoded by a negative particle (*shall not*) in the content of the 'action rules' (Gunnarsson 1984: 84). However, the complex meaning of *shall* provisions in the corpus also lends itself to other possible readings. Following Garzone (2001: 157–158; 2013: 73–74), who argues for the performative/constitutive (adeontic/thetic) value of *shall*, this value is readily apparent in the active (positive/negative) *shall* provisions appearing with inanimate subjects in 'stipulation rules' (Gunnarsson 1984: 84):

(22) This Act *shall* apply to any arbitration where the place of arbitration is Singapore and where Part II of the International Arbitration Act (Cap. 143A) does not apply to that arbitration.

(23) An appeal from the decision of the High Court made under section 21 *shall* lie to the Court of Appeal only with the leave of the High Court.

Although, as a matter of wisdom, no obligation/duty can be imposed on an *Act* or an *appeal* as inanimate subjects of the rule content, the *shall* provisions above containing those subjects and stative verbs (*apply*, *lie to*) can be said to be performative/constitutive in function – they express the immediate fulfillment of the legal state of affairs prompted by the utterances themselves outside obligations. By stating that *This Act shall apply to any arbitration* (thesis), the wording of the provision thus becomes constitutive (thetic) of what it rules under the authority of the Act, and is therefore performative in character. As such, the wording of the provision is accountable for in terms of the entire authority of the Singapore Parliament (the 'source') intending to legislate and amend arbitration in this manner.

On other occasions, however, difficulty of interpretation arises from *shall* provisions that equally involve inanimate subjects, as in the following rule setting out the 'Effect of Award':

(24) An award made by the arbitral tribunal pursuant to an arbitration agreement *shall* be final and binding on the parties and on any person claiming through or under them and may be relied upon by any of the parties by way of defence, set-off or otherwise in any proceedings in any court of competent jurisdiction.

Where the expression of meaning in statutory rule-making is context-dependent, the *shall* verb form above may serve an imperative (deontic) function – by setting the finality and binding requirement of the award for the recipients of the rule – or a performative/constitutive function – by framing the technical elements (state of affairs) that bring out the 'constitution' of the rule. In this and other cases, therefore, we are faced with the essential indeterminacy opened up by the *shall* modal, in terms of ambiguity and merger (e.g. Coates 1983: 11–17). This fuzzy phenomenon of *shall* modal can also be observed in isolated instances shown below, using *There* as a 'dummy' subject with part of the verb *be* followed by a noun phrase:

(25) Where in any arbitral or legal proceedings, [...] *there shall be deemed* to be an effective arbitration agreement as between the parties to the proceedings.

(26) *There shall be no appeal against* a refusal for grant of leave of the High Court.

(27) Failing such determination, *there shall be* a single arbitrator.

On the face of it, each of the provisions allows yet for two possible interpretations: to deliver obligation or requirement, or to constitute and perform by themselves the state of affairs they deal with in the treatment of the arbitration matters. Whatever the reading, the prescriptive/performative (pragmatic) framework of *shall* in the quoted provisions will always be rooted in the authority of the Act which gives effect to those provisions, as part of the discourse-external source of the legislature. In this framework, negating a duty/obligation falling upon subjects by *shall not* active (19 times) or passive negative forms (11 times) adds to similar cases where variations are sometimes used to express such negations or prohibitions (e.g. *No person shall be compelled under any such subpoena to produce any document ... / No appeal shall lie against ... / No appointment by the appointing authority shall be challenged ...*), and are determined by conventional choices for writing in the genre.

3.3.6.4 May

As part of the deontic modality related to permission that is characteristic of any prescriptive legal genre, *may* modal proceeds steadily across the text to confer or deny (*may not*) a power, privilege, or right to animate subjects. The deontic notion of discretion embraced by the modal is evident in the provisions below (action rules) conferring discretionary powers to those subjects:

(28) The Chief Justice *may*, if he thinks fit, by notification published in the *Gazette*, appoint any other person to exercise the powers of the Chairman of the Singapore Mediation Centre under subsection (1).

(29) The parties *may* agree on the powers which *may* be exercised by the arbitral tribunal in the case of a party's failure to take any necessary action for the proper and expeditious conduct of the proceedings.

However, it is not unusual for discretionary *may* to also deontically affect inanimate subjects of the provision in rather few instances. This can be seen in the examples below, where discretionary (deontic) *may* also combines with the prescriptive-performative value of *shall* modal in the same provision, thus influencing the realization of actions or situations with different modal meanings and functions in legislative discourse:

(30) An application for the leave of the Court to appeal or an application referred to in section 21(10)21A(1), 36(6) or 49(3)(*b*) or (7) shall be made in such manner as *may* be prescribed in the Rules of Court.

(31) A notice or other document *may* be served on a person by any effective means.

(32) An arbitration agreement *may* be in the form of an arbitration clause in a contract or in the form of a separate agreement.

In addition to deontic *may* appearing in active and passive constructions as above, there are marginal instances in which the modal seems to express an epistemic (possibility) meaning:

(33) In this Act, 'arbitration agreement' means an agreement by the parties to submit to arbitration all or certain disputes which have arisen or which *may* arise between them in respect of a defined legal relationship, whether contractual or not.

(34) An order made by the Court under this section shall cease to have effect in whole or in part (as the case *may* be) if the arbitral tribunal, or any such arbitral or other institution or person having power to act in relation to the subject-matter of the order, makes an order which expressly relates to the whole or part of that order of the Court.

Although, as seen, *may* deontic modality predominates to a large extent, the data are still important to emphasize the degree of fuzziness (e.g. Coates 1983: 11–17) between the (deontic/epistemic) boundaries of the modal form in question.

3.3.6.5 Be to

The semi-modal auxiliary *be to* form occurs only marginally in the sample (Table 4), where it is used exclusively in the '*be* + passive infinitive' construction to equally emphasize the legal effect of the arbitration rules and procedures:

(35) For the purposes of this section, arbitration proceedings *are to be taken* as having commenced on the date of the receipt by the respondent of a request for the dispute to be referred to arbitration, or, where the parties have agreed in writing that any other date *is to be taken* as the date of commencement of the arbitration proceedings, then on that date.

As we can see, the legal effect conveyed by *is/are* semi-modal forms in the provision is one which may serve "a performative or deontic value" (Garzone 2013: 77), and is therefore entrenched in the nature and scope of the statute via ad-hoc predictable elements of the rule purposively established by the legislature. When read deontically, the forms do seem to replace the most traditional, legalistic form of *shall* (Williams 2005: 135; Garzone 2013: 77) that is massively employed in the sample, as noted.

3.3.6.6 Mood

Apart from these modal meanings and functions, the legislative discourse in the genre also attracts the pattern of occurrence of mood in its own right. The frequency list in Table 6 shows that the indicative form of the present simple occurs in over three quarters of non-modal verb categories, followed by one out of five cases of subjunctive and only one single case of imperative.

Mood categories	*no.*	*%*
Present simple	31	77.5
Subjunctive	8	20
Imperative	1	2.5
Total	*40*	*100*

Table 6. Distribution of mood (verb) categories: occurrences and percentages.

3.3.6.7 Present simple

Where provisions do not go with the flow of *shall* and *may* modals in the main clauses, the major strand of verbal structures is provided by the simple present indicative, regarded in English as the 'unmarked' mood (Quirk et al. 1985: 149) or 'unmodalised' (Huddleston/Pullum 2002: 174), in contrast to the subjunctive and imperative moods. Found in 31 instances across such clauses, the simple present tense invariably appears in definition rules and stipulation rules, where it often occurs in the active construction using *be*, *mean*, *have* and *include* verb forms alone, as in:

(36) 'award' *means* a decision of the arbitral tribunal on the substance of the dispute and *includes* any interim, interlocutory or partial award but *excludes* any order or direction made under section 28;

(37) The parties *are* free to determine the number of arbitrators.

Clearly, these cases add to others where the present simple also appears in (restricted/non-restricted) *that*-clauses and *if* or *where* clauses to treat the relevant meaning of the provision, as in:

(38) Where an arbitrator *ceases* to hold office, the parties are free to agree [...].

(39) A decision by the arbitral tribunal that the contract *is* null and void shall not entail ipso jure [...].

Using the present simple not only implies that the drafter naturally 'thinks' in terms of the future (because whatever is set out there will always affect events in the future), but also provides a default option for the more traditional use of *shall* for authoritatively (deontically) setting a requirement in the form of 'normative indicative' (Williams 2005:

154), or to realize the "same typically constitutive value" as *shall* (Garzone 2013: 75) in the relevant pragmatic contexts of the provisions.

3.3.6.8 Subjunctive

Next in the non-modal frequency data are the relatively few occurrences of the subjunctive (8 times), or 'mandative subjunctive' (Quirk et al. 1985: 156), used as a formal feature of the text we are dealing with. In the current data, the subjunctive mood only consists of the verb *be* retaining its present subjunctive form, and figures in main *that*-clauses alone to express a requirement of the action:

(40) Where a court stays proceedings under section 6, the court may, if in those proceedings property has been arrested or bail or other security has been given to prevent or obtain release from arrest, order that –
(a) the property arrested *be* retained as security for the satisfaction of any award made on the arbitration; or
(b) the stay *be* conditional on the provision of equivalent security for the satisfaction of any such award.

3.3.6.9 Imperative

Finally, there is the solitary case of the 'passive imperative' (Kurzon 1986: 10), or 'old jussive subjunctive' (Maley 1994: 20) in the *Be it enacted* form, already discussed above with regard to the macro-structural organization of the statute. Indeed, we are dealing with a statute that is a textual amendment or repeal of previous arbitration laws in Singapore, so we should reasonably expect other imperative forms as well to be deployed in the text by clause 'amending verbs' ('deleting' or 'inserting' verbs), as found in other analyses of imperatives in European/non-European legislative texts (Williams 2005: 145–147; Garzone 2013: 78). Surprisingly, though, current data reveal that no other such companions are used to 'imperatively' amend or replace provisions under the statute.

3.3.7 Semantically indeterminate expressions

On a lexical level, semantically indeterminate expressions that naturally lead to ambiguity and vagueness (Cortese 2005: 267–280; Gotti 2005: 234–237; Bhatia/Engberg/Gotti/Heller 2005: 9–15; Tessuto 2005: 297–301; Schane 2006: 15) make their appearance only when so required by the content of the rule, and occur in adjectival, adverbial, or phrasal forms:

(41) *sufficient* reason
things *necessary* to the *proper* conduct of the arbitration
for the *satisfaction* of any such award
such considerations as are *likely* to secure the appointment
where there are *justifiable* doubts
as the court *thinks fit*

Like those found in texts dealing with the subject matter of arbitration/mediation in the Western European legal tradition (Tessuto 2003: 368–369, 2010: 259), these vague, general standards are inescapable attributes of the Asian legal discourse in the genre as well. This is because, by regulating arbitration practice and procedure through 'all-inclusive' rules (Bhatia 1993), those standards support more than one interpretation when placed in concrete, factual situations that involve a more rational process of specification by Singapore judges and lawyers, as noted before. When put in those situations, vague, general standards therefore evolve in the content of arbitration, and make the legal effect of semantically indeterminate expressions more precise than the statutory effect.

3.3.8 Ordinary versus specialized words and phrases

Aside from the unavoidable phenomenon of semantic indeterminacy, the text alternates between ordinary language choices and technical terms. In the latter case, the statute conventionally helps to determine the specialized, monoreferential meaning of seven terms by 'interpretation' clauses, namely *appointing authority*, *arbitral tribunal*, *arbitration agreement*, *award*, *court*, *party*, *place of arbitration*, as in:

(42) (1) In this Act, unless the context otherwise requires –

'appointing authority' means the appointing authority designated under section 13(8) or (9);

'arbitral tribunal' means a sole arbitrator or a panel of arbitrators or an arbitral institution, and includes an emergency arbitrator appointed pursuant to the rules of arbitration agreed to or adopted by the parties including the rules of arbitration of an institution or organisation;

'arbitration agreement' means an arbitration agreement referred to in section 4;

> 'award' means a decision of the arbitral tribunal on the substance of the dispute and includes any interim, interlocutory or partial award but excludes any order or direction made under section 28;
>
> 'Court' means the High Court in Singapore;

As part of the nature and purpose of the text, these terms are expressly subject to the cautionary exception clause of the statute (*unless the context otherwise requires*), which thus gives the terms a wider interpretation. Implicit in the legislative purpose of defining a word or phrase is the normative indicative of the verb *mean* in the examples above, where it is used to close off the relevant meaning and to exclude other meanings, thus putting a rigid (normative) fence around what the word or phrase means according to the communicative context of the genre. This case is part of two general types of definitions used in the statute, those that stipulate what the word/phrase 'means' and those that stipulate what the word/phrase 'includes', as in:

(43) 'award' *means* a decision of the arbitral tribunal on the substance of the dispute and *includes* any interim, interlocutory or partial award but excludes [...].

Although hybrid in wording, the scope of *includes* in the second clause aims to clarify the scope of *means* in the first clause. Apart from the two general, conventional types of definitions, technically defined terms illustrated above are naturally part of the meanings established within the context of the subject matter. However, they are ancillary in nature and are not therefore regarded as an operative component of the statutory provision. In other words, the Singapore legislature does not regulate arbitration practice and procedure by means of 'interpretation' clauses.

3.3.9 Complex prepositional phrases

The text is relatively imbued with complex prepositional phrases, which have endured through time in traditional English legal language. As Table 7 shows, different types of complex prepositional phrases are used to somewhat influence the drafting of the statute in a totality of 53 occurrences, although the items *in accordance with* and *in respect of* are proportionally higher in such occurrences.

Complex prepositional phrases	*no.*
During/in the course of	4
For the purpose of	8
In accordance with	22
In respect of	10
In the event of	2
In pursuance of	2
On the basis of	2
Upon the request of	3
Total	*53*
Simple preposition	*no.*
Under	83

Table 7. Complex prepositional phrases and simple preposition: types and occurrences.

Although these items may still represent wordy nominalizations and often occur in positions where qualifications are used, they mostly function to indicate 'textual authority' and facilitate 'textual mapping' (Bhatia 1998: 2–3), as is the case of specific devices (*for the purpose of*, *in accordance with*, *in respect of*, and *in pursuance of*), or to avoid ambiguity in the text (Bhatia 1994b: 107), as in other instances (*during/in the course of*, *in the event of*, *on the basis of*, *upon the request of*). In both cases, they serve to maintain the completeness of rule-making in the genre. However, the table above also shows that a serious attempt is made by the draftsman to replace the complex prepositions in textual-authority/mapping function with the simple preposition *under*, which spreads throughout the statute in a proportionally higher incidence than the complex ones.

The greater emphasis given to the simple preposition in the data is also useful in deploying the web-styled version of the statute, where the reference to the content of other sections in the same statute (*any order or direction made under* *section ...*) is available at a mouse click, and consequently allows the reader to identify other sets of provisions by internally-coherent textual relations.

3.4 Latin words and phrases

Unlike traditional legal English texts of the last few decades, the tendency in the statute is to dispense with conservative lexis as much as possible. This is shown by the marginally occurring instances of the Latin noun *subpoena* (6 times), the adjective *interim* (6 times) qualifying different nouns (*award*, *custody*, *injunction*, *sale*, *order*) in bi- and multinomial expressions, and the adverb *ipso jure* (1 time) interjecting other English text in brackets to clarify the Latin meaning:

(44) A decision by the arbitral tribunal that the contract is null and void shall not entail *ipso jure* (as a matter of law) the invalidity of the arbitration clause.

3.4.1 Archaisms

As with Latin expressions, antiquated words of legalist style are still marginally used throughout, although their usage may also be jargon in the guise of specialized terms as Latinity-derived expressions.

Archaisms	*no.*
Therein	2
Thereof	4
Thereto	1
Notwithstanding	7
Total	*14*

Table 8. Archaisms: types and occurrences.

In addition to the formal pronominal adverbs (*therein*, *thereof*, *thereto*) used to refer deictically to specific times and places within the statute, the prepositional use of the formal, legalistic word *notwithstanding* also carries weight and falls on its own from *There*-words. The rhetorical purpose of this word is to express a conflicting rule in the statute in the same way as a simple preposition *in spite of* or *despite* in a 'concession' functioning clause, and is exclusively achieved in the initial qualifying (adverbial) clause of a long and intricate sentence structure. Where this word appears, it serves to introduce the current provision into a conflicting provision, and to similarly indicate that the scope of the provision at hand is restricted, or otherwise conceded by the content of another provision (operational qualification):

(45) – 1 *Notwithstanding subsection (3)*, where a court gives grounds of decision for a judgment in respect of proceedings to which this section applies and considers that judgment to be of major legal interest, the court shall direct [...].

Yet, it seems that an alternative to a *notwithstanding* clause is a qualifying *subject to* clause used nine times in the statute, signalling again that the current provision is restricted in scope by another provision (*Subject to subsection (3), any provision...*). Overall, privilege for complex prepositional phrases, Latinisms and archaisms does not depend on the rationale of rule content but on the need to give pleasing resonances towards traditional English (Common Law) legislative writing. Despite this, ordinary readers are still likely to misunderstand the intended effect of those conventional items. Once again, the statute reflects the lexical strategies used in other Western European arbitration texts (Tessuto 2003: 341, 2010: 262–263).

4. Conclusion

The detailed analysis carried out in this chapter has shown that the drafting practices constructed and used in the statute replicate a good number of linguistic (textual, lexico-grammatical and discoursal) resources implemented in the legislative genre from the influential Western European Common Law tradition, and consequently provide a reasonable stability to the macro- and micro-level resources of the statute. The effect is that a fair degree of generic integrity (Bhatia 2004) is maintained in the legislative discourse examined, thus revealing a satisfactory number of generic similarities across Western European and Eastern (Asian) legal cultures and systems. Such generic integrity becomes apparent from the macro-textual organization of the statute that is a relatively standardized structure of the genre used in the English arbitration legislation (1996). As such, then, the Singapore statute reflects a recognizable structure that is shared by the members of the institutional/professional legal community from the English Common Law jurisdiction.

A sufficient degree of generic integrity also becomes apparent from a complex range of micro-level resources brought about by the statute: qualifications, easified devices, lexical repetition, anaphora and gender neutrality, bi- and multinomials, nominalization, semantically indeterminate expressions, complex prepositional phrases, Latin and archaic terms. Not only do these syntactic resources flesh out arbitration laws as discursive statements about the principles and procedures for conducting arbitration in Singapore, but most importantly they closely reflect the archetypal and conservative style features of contemporary Common Law legislative and non-legislative language on arbitration or other topics. Evidence of these features is also provided by the use of the most traditional (Common Law) legal style form of (prescriptive/performative) *shall* in the genre, where it allows for one of the substantive levels of normative force in addition to (deontic) *may*.

The analysis also reveals that the genre does at times respond to traditional (Common Law) legislative sentence length and syntactic complexity with *easifying* devices (paragraphing), and consequently makes sentence complexity of the provisions less than a matter for Plain Language concern. Clearly, the genre is more responsive to the Plain Language syntax of the more vigorous and concise active-voice structure of *shall* and *may* provisions, unless drafters consciously decide that the passive-voice structure is the most appropriate for writing those provisions. Strangely enough, drafters make no attempt to find a valid substitute for traditional *shall*-bound provisions in their statute, and are consequently in the dark when it comes to influential Plain Language calls to remove the outmoded and imprecise *shall* word from their statute.

As an aside, it should be noted that the linguistic and discursive properties of the statute align the law applicable to domestic arbitration with the provisions of the Model Law and the International Arbitration Act, as well as the provisions of the 1996 UK Arbitration Act. This alignment, to form the subject of a separate 'interdiscursive' analysis of the text, means that the drafting of laws in the Singapore statute not only becomes part of a Western philosophy of arbitration law and practice, but also of a broader globally harmonized and convergent philosophy of arbitration. This, then, allows the key linguistic and discursive features of the existing domestic arbitration regime in the statute to respond to continuing efforts by Singapore to develop its attractiveness as a national as well as international arbitration venue.

References

Asprey, Michèle 2003. *Plain Language for Lawyers*. Annandale, NSW: The Federation Press.

Belotti, Ulisse 2003. Generic Integrity in Italian Arbitration Rules. In Bhatia/Candlin/Gotti (eds), 19–40.

Bhatia, Vijay K. 1983a. *An Applied Discourse Analysis of English Legislative Writing*. PhD thesis (unpublished) Birmingham: University of Aston.

Bhatia, Vijay K. 1983b. Simplification v. Easification – The Case of Legal Texts. *Applied Linguistics* 4/1, 42–54.

Bhatia Vijay K. 1993. *Analysing Genre. Language Use in Professional Settings*. London: Longman.

Bhatia, Vijay K. 1994a, Cognitive Structuring in Legislative Provisions. In Gibbons (ed.), 136–155.

Bhatia, Vijay K, 1994b. Syntactic Discontinuities in Legislative Writing and its Implications for Academic Legal Purposes. In Pugh, A. K / Ulijn, J. M (eds) *Readings for Professional Purposes: Studies and Practices in Native and Foreign Languages.* London: Heinemann, 90–96.

Bhatia, Vijay K. 1998. Intertexuality in Legal Discourse. *The Language Teacher* 22/11, 13–39.

Bhatia, Vijay K. 2004. *Worlds of Written Discourse: A Genre-based View*. London: Continuum.

Bhatia, Vijay K. 2005a. Specificity and Generality in Legislative Expression: Two Sides of the Coin. In Bhatia/Engberg/Gotti/Heller (eds), 337–356.

Bhatia, Vijay K. 2005b. Plain English in Asia. *Clarity* 53, 45–47.

Bhatia, Vijay K. 2010. Drafting Legislative Provisions: Challenges and Opportunities. *THE LOOPHOLE. Journal of the Commonwealth Association of Legislative Counsel* 3, 5–15.

Bhatia, Vijay K. 2011. Interdiscursive Colonization of Arbitration Practice. *World Englishes* 30/1, 76–80.

Bhatia, Vijay K. / Candlin, Christopher N. 2004. Analysing Arbitration Laws across Legal Systems. *Hermes* 32, 13–43.

Bhatia, Vijay K. / Candlin, Christopher N. 2008. Interpretation across Legal Systems and Cultures. A Critical Perspective. In Bhatia/Candlin/Engberg (eds), 127–143.

Bhatia, Vijay K. / Candlin, Christopher N. / Sharma, Rajesh 2009. Confidentiality and Integrity in International Commercial Arbitration Practice. *Arbitration* 75, 2–13.

Bhatia, Vijay K. / Candlin, Christopher N. / Engberg, Jan (eds) 2008. *Legal Discourse across Cultures and Systems*. Hong Kong: Hong Kong University Press.

Bhatia, Vijay K. / Engberg, Jan / Gotti, Maurizio / Heller, Dorothee 2005. Introduction. In Bhatia/Engberg/Gotti/Heller (eds), 9–23.

Bhatia, Vijay K. / Candlin, Christopher N. / Engberg, Jan / Trosborg, Anna (eds) 2003. *Multilingual and Multicultural Contexts of Legislation: An International Perspective*. Bern: Peter Lang.

Bhatia, Vijay K. / Candlin, Christopher N. / Evangelisti Allori, Paola (eds) 2008. *Language, Culture and the Law*. Bern: Peter Lang.

Bhatia, Vijay K. / Candlin, Christopher N. / Gotti, Maurizio (eds) 2003. *Legal Discourse in Multilingual and Multicultural Contexts: Arbitration Texts in Europe*. Bern: Peter Lang.

Bhatia, Vijay K. / Candlin, Christopher N. / Gotti, Maurizio (eds) 2010. *The Discourses of Dispute Resolution*. Bern: Peter Lang.

Bhatia, Vijay K. / Candlin, Christopher N. / Gotti, Maurizio (eds) 2012. *Discourse and Practice in International Commercial Arbitration: Issues, Challenges and Prospects*. Farnham, Surrey: Ashgate.

Bhatia, Vijay K. / Engberg, Jan / Gotti, Maurizio / Heller, Dorothee (eds) 2005. *Vagueness in Normative Texts*. Bern: Peter Lang.

Bhatia, Vijay K. / Garzone, Giuliana / Degano, Chiara (eds) 2012. *Arbitration Awards. Generic Features and Textual Realisations*. Newcastle upon Tyne; Cambridge Scholars.

Biber, Douglas 1988. *Variation across Speech and Writing*. Cambridge: Cambridge University Press.

Biber, Douglas / Conrad, Susan / Leech, Geoffrey 2002. *Longman Student Grammar of Spoken and Written English*. Essex: Longman.

Biber, Douglas / Johansson, Stig / Leech, Geoffrey / Conrad, Susan / Finegan, Edward 1999. *The Longman Grammar of Spoken and Written English*. Essex: Longman.

Bondi, Marina / Diani, Giuliana 2010. Conveying Deontic Values in English and Italian Contracts: A Cross-cultural Analysis. *ESP across Cultures* 7, 7–24.

Carter, Ronald / McCarthy, Michael 2006. *Cambridge Grammar of English. A Comprehensive Guide. Spoken and Written English Grammar and Usage*. Cambridge: Cambridge University Press.

Coates, Jennifer 1983. *The Semantics of Modal Auxiliaries*. London: Croom Helm.

Cortese, Giuseppina 2005. Indeterminacy in 'Rainbow' Legislation: The Convention on the Rights of the Child. In Bhatia/Engberg/Gotti/Heller (eds), 255–285.

Dossena, Marina 2003. Arbitration in Scotland: Local Specificity and International Homegeneity. In Bhatia/Candlin/Gotti (eds), 87–109.

Driedger, Elmer A. 1982. Legislative Drafting Style: Civil Law versus Common Law. In J-C. Gémar (éd.) *Langage du Droit et Traduction / The Language of the Law and Translation*. Montreal: Linguatech / Conseil de la Langue Française, 63- 81.

Evangelisti Allori, Paola 2008. The Linguistic Formulation of Power: Modality and Power Relations in Two Sets of Sports-Related Arbitration Rules. In Bhatia/Candlin/Evangelisti Allori (eds), 75–97.

Garzone, Giuliana 2001. Deontic Modality and Performativity in English Legal Texts. In Gotti/Dossena (eds),153–170.

Garzone, Giuliana 2003. Arbitration Rules across Legal Cultures: An Intercultural Approach. In Bhatia/Candlin/Gotti (eds), 177–220.

Garzone, Giuliana 2008. International Commercial Arbitration Rules as Translated/Re-written Texts: An intercultural Perspective. In Bhatia/Candlin/Evangelisti Allori (eds), 47–73.

Garzone, Giuliana 2013. Variation in the Use of Modality in Legislative Texts: Focus on *Shall*. *Journal of Pragmatics* 57, 68–81.

Giannoni, Davide S. 2003. The UNCITRAL Model and Italian Statute Law: A Linguistic and Topical Description. In Bhatia/Candlin / Gotti (eds), 221–246.

Gibbons, John (ed) 1994. *Language and the Law*. New York: Longman.

Gotti, Maurizio 2001. Semantic and Pragmatic Values of *Shall* and *Will* in Early Modern English Statutes. In Gotti/Dossena (eds), 89–112.

Gotti, Maurizio 2003. *Specialized Discourse. Linguistic Features and Changing Conventions*. Bern: Peter Lang.

Gotti, Maurizio 2005. Vagueness in the Model Law on International Commercial Arbitration. In Bhatia/Engberg/Gotti/Heller (eds), 227–253.

Gotti, Maurizio 2008. The Formulation of Legal Concepts in Arbitration Normative Texts in a Multilingual, Multicultural Contexts. In Bhatia/Candlin/Evangelisti Allori (eds), 23–45.

Gotti, Maurizio 2012. Text and Genre. In Tiersma/Solan (eds), 52–66.

Gotti, Maurizio / Dossena, Marina (eds) 2001. *Modality in Specialized Texts*. Bern: Peter Lang.

Gunnarsson, Britt Louise 1984. Functional Comprehensibility of Legislative Texts: Experiments with a Swedish Act of Parliament. *Text* 4/1–3, 71–105.

Gustafsson, Marita 1975. Some Syntactic Properties of English Law Language. *Publications of the Department of English* 4. Turku: University of Turku.

Gustafsson, Marita, 1984. The Syntactic Features of Binomial Expressions in Legal English. *Text* 4/1–3, 123–141.

Hiltunen, Risto 1990. *Chapters on Legal English: Aspects Past and Present of the Language of Law*. Helsinki: Suomalainen Tiedeakatemia.

Hiltunen, Risto 2001. Some Syntactic Properties of English Law Language. In Hiltunen, Risto / Battarbee, Keith / Peikola, Matti / Tanskanen, Sanna-Kaisa (eds) *English in Zigs and Zags: A Festscrift for Maita Gustafsson*. Anglicana Turkuensia, 23 Turku: University of Turku, 53–66.

Hiltunen, Risto 2012. The Grammar and Structure of Legal Texts. In Tiersma/Solan, 39–51.

Huddleston, Rodney / Geoffrey, Pullum K. 2002. *The Cambridge Grammar of the English Language*. Cambridge: Cambridge University Press.

Kurzon, Dennis 1986. *It is Hereby Performed: Explorations in Legal Speech Acts*. Philadelphia, PA: John Benjamins.

Kurzon, Dennis 1997. Legal Language: Varieties, Genres, Registers, Discourses. *International Journal of Applied Linguistics* 7, 119–139.

Jackson, Bernard S. 1995. *Making Sense in Law*. Liverpool: Deborah Charles Publications.

Leech, Geoffrey 1987. *Meaning and the English Verb*. London: Longman.

Maley, Yon 1994. The Language of the Law. In Gibbons (ed), 11–50.

Palmer, Frank R. 2001. *Mood and Modality*. Cambridge: Cambridge University Press.

Quirk, Randolph / Greenbaum, Sidney / Leech Geoffrey / Svartvik, Jan 1985. *A Comprehensive Grammar of the English Language*. London: Longman.

Salmi-Tolonen, Tarja 2003. Arbitration Law as Action: An Analysis of the Finnish Arbitration Act. In Bhatia/Candlin/Gotti, 313–336.

Salmi-Tolonen, Tarja. 2008. *Language and the Functions of Law. A Legal Linguistic Study*, Akta Universitatis Lapponiensis.

Salmi-Tolonen, Tarja / Tukiainen, Iris / Foley, Richard (eds) 2011. *Law and Language in Partneship and Conflict*. Special issue of *Lapland Law Review* 1/1.

Šarčević, Susan 2000. *New Approach to Legal Translation*. The Hague: Kluwer Law International.

Schane, Sanford. 2006. *Language and the Law*. London: Continuum.

Tessuto, Girolamo 2003. Legislative Discourse in Arbitration Language: The English 1996 Arbitration Act and the UNCITRAL Model Law. In Bhatia/Candlin/Gotti (eds), 335–379.

Tessuto, Girolamo 2005. Ambiguity and Vagueness in Human Rights Discourse. In Bhatia/Engberg/Gotti/Heller (eds), 288–311.

Tessuto, Girolamo 2010. US Commercial Arbitration Rules and Mediation Procedures: Linguistic and Discoursal Features of a Genre in Action. In Bhatia/Candlin/Gotti (eds), 231–270.

Tiersma, Peter 1999. *Legal Language*. Chicago: University of Chicago Press.

Tiersma, Peter M. / Solan, Laurence M. (eds) 2012. *The Oxford Handbook of Language and Law*, Oxford: Oxford University Press.

Trosborg, Anna, 1997. *Rhetorical Strategies in Legal Language. Discourse Analysis of Statutes and Contracts*. Tübingen: Gunter Narr.

Williams, Christopher 2005. *Tradition and Change in Legal English*. Bern: Peter Lang.

Williams, Christopher 2011. Legal English and Plain Language: An Update. *ESP across Cultures* 8, 139–151.

Wydick, Richard C. 2005. *Plain English for Lawyers*. Durham, NC: Carolina Academic Press.

Patrizia Anesa / Francesca Locatelli[1]

Arbitration in Japan: Insights into the Arbitration Law and the JCAA Rules

1. Introduction

Arbitration worldwide has received considerable scholarly attention and in the last few decades its use as a dispute resolution method has increased considerably in most countries. However, in Japan the use of arbitration is still relatively limited. Japan is a signatory to the New York Convention on the Recognition and Enforcement of Foreign Awards of 20 June 1961, which came into force on 18 September 1961. Japan applies the Convention with the adoption of the reciprocity reservation, i.e., only for the recognition and the enforcement of those awards rendered in another Convention state. Besides this general international convention, Japan has also signed several bilateral agreements on arbitration.

The main source of law on arbitration is represented by the Arbitration Law, namely Law no. 138 of 2003, which came into effect on 1 March 2004. This normative text regulates both domestic and international arbitration and its scope of application is limited to proceedings that take place in Japan. The Arbitration Law applies to both commercial proceedings and arbitration in general and is essentially based on the UNCITRAL Model Law. Indeed, many of the regulatory provisions of the Japanese Arbitration Law reproduce the text of the Model Law, but there are some notable differences: for example, Art. 13(4) allows the use of electronic means to make the arbitration agreement, for

1 Although the authors have collaborated at every stage in the production of this chapter, Patrizia Anesa is responsible for Sections 4 and 5 and Francesca Locatelli is responsible for Sections 2 and 3. Section 1 was jointly written by the two authors.

instance via email. The choice to refer constantly to the basic scheme of the Model Law is clearly determined by the intention of the Japanese government to make arbitration in Japan appealing, not only as regards domestic arbitration, but also in relation to international proceedings. In this regard, it is clear that the purpose is to attract foreign business partners to Japan, with the promise of a speedy resolution of disputes through an instrument which is easy to handle even by foreign parties.

Besides the Arbitration Law, which applies to *ad hoc* arbitration, another important text to be taken into account is represented by the JCAA Rules, which govern the arbitration administered at the main arbitral institution in Japan, namely the Japanese Commercial Arbitration Association (JCAA), based at Osaka. The JCAA was originally set up as an institution devoted primarily to the conduct of international arbitration and, indeed, it was initially named International Commercial Arbitration Association. It changed its name in January 2003, with the intent to expand its activity to domestic arbitration as well. In Japan there are other smaller arbitral chambers founded by Japanese Bar Associations, which seek to boost arbitration as a dispute resolution tool.

In what follows, we will discuss the main features of arbitration as provided by the Arbitration Law, with particular reference to the main differences between this regulatory standard and the JCAA Rules. The normative references listed in this section, therefore, are to be understood as related to the Arbitration Law, unless otherwise specified. The next section of this study describes the main features of arbitration in Japan and particular attention is devoted to the description of the Japanese Arbitration Law. The third one investigates the reasons why arbitration is scarcely used. Section 4 describes the role and the characteristics of the main arbitral institution operating in the country, the JCAA. In particular, the analysis focuses on the JCAA Rules, which were amended in 2014, and a comparison with the International Chamber of Commerce (ICC) Rules is offered. The concluding part summarizes the main findings, highlights problematic areas and discusses possible intervention strategies.

2. Arbitration in Japan: main features

From a strictly procedural perspective, the Arbitration Law contains a number of procedural measures that are mandatory, including Art. 5 (outlining the jurisdiction of the courts), Art. 13(2), which requires that the arbitration agreement be in writing, and Art. 25, which prescribes the principle of equal treatment of the parties. As to the applicable substantive law, the parties are free to choose it. Whenever the parties refer to the law of a particular state as the applicable law, any designation is intended as a direct reference to the substantive law of the state and not to its rules concerning the conflict of laws (Art. 36(1)). However, there is a rule of closure which applies when the parties do not indicate which law is applicable. In this case, the arbitral tribunal will apply the law of the state with which the dispute is most closely connected (Art. 36(2)). In this respect, the Japanese arbitration law deviates from the provisions of the Model Law, which, in such situations, provides instead for the application of the substantive law determined by the conflict of laws that are considered applicable.

Not all disputes are resolvable through arbitration, but only those whose "subject matter is a civil dispute that may be resolved by settlement between the parties" (Art. 13(1)), with manifest exclusions concerning family law, namely separation and divorce and personal status. Limitations are also provided in cases of arbitration agreements concluded between consumers and businesses (see Supplementary Provisions, Art. 3) or concerning individual labor-related disputes (see Supplementary Provisions, Art. 4). The reason for these prohibitions is evident and can be traced back to the desire to maintain control over the resolution of disputes involving interests which are not only of an individual nature. This typically happens in the case of personal status (which relates to the role that the individual plays in society) or situations where there is a weak subject to be protected, such as the consumer or the worker.

The arbitral tribunal may consist of a sole arbitrator or a panel; an arbitrator is expected to be an impartial and independent third party and comply with all the requirements expressed by the parties in the arbitration agreement. In the case of a sole arbitrator, as well as if a third arbitrator must be appointed by the panel, he/she may also be of nationality different from that of the parties, but only after the appropriateness of such a choice has been assessed (Art. 17(6)(iii)). There are some residual provisions related to the appointment of the arbitral tribunal. If the parties have not reached an agreement about the number of arbitrators in accordance with Art. 16(2), it is expected that the panel operate with three members. If it is a multiparty arbitration, "the court shall determine the number of arbitrators upon request of a party" (Art. 16(3)). Also in the case of arbitration with only two parties, when they cannot agree on the panel of arbitrators, each appoints one arbitrator, and these, in turn, appoint a third arbitrator (Art. 17(2)). If a sole arbitrator is needed and the parties do not reach an agreement, it is possible for the parties to resort to the state court to obtain the appointment (Art. 17(4)). There are two supplementary remedies in order to overcome this stalemate: either the law itself provides for what should be done or it is necessary to resort to the state judicial authority, which intervenes with a supporting role so that the arbitration may take place.

The Arbitration Law includes two hypotheses for the challenge of arbitrators. The former case occurs when the arbitrator does not have the qualifications required; the latter deals with cases in which the arbitrator may not be totally impartial or there is a situation which generates doubts about his independence (Art. 18). If the arbitrator is chosen by one of the parties, they "may challenge that arbitrator only for reasons of which it becomes aware after the appointment has been made" (Art. 18(2)). The party who intends to challenge an arbitrator must send a written request to the arbitral tribunal (Art. 19(3)) within 15 days, starting from the constitution of the tribunal or the day they became aware of the reasons why the arbitrator cannot be entirely impartial or independent. The reasons for the challenge must be made explicit in writing and if the parties do not agree with the decision made by the arbitral tribunal in this regard, they may apply to the state court for a review of the decision (Art. 19(4)). This procedure pending before the state court does not prevent the arbitral tribunal from proceeding until the award is rendered (Art. 19(5)). The removal of the arbitrator may also be requested if "the arbitrator becomes *de jure* or *de facto* unable to perform its functions" (Art. 20). The arbitrator, in general, ceases the mandate due to death, resignation for replacement or objection (Art. 21).

The remuneration to the arbitrators, unless otherwise agreed by the parties, is directly determined by the arbitral tribunal (Art. 47). Arbitrators are not allowed to accept gifts or other benefits from the parties, as that may lead to criminal sanctions. There are no forms of liability for arbitrators; only Art. 13 of the JCAA Rules provides that arbitrators are not "liable for any act or omission in connection with the arbitral proceedings", except in case of willful misconduct or gross negligence.

The arbitral tribunal is competent to decide on "assertions made in respect of the existence or validity of an arbitration agreement or its own jurisdiction" (Art. 23(1)), according to the known and firmly established principle of autonomy of the arbitration clause. The related exceptions must however be raised promptly, i.e. "before the time at which the first written statement on the substance of the dispute is submitted to the arbitral tribunal" (Art. 23(2)). The decision of the arbitral tribunal may be challenged before the court of the State within the period of thirty days (Art. 23(2) and (5)).

With reference to the language of the arbitration, if there is no specific agreement between the parties, the decision lies in the hands of the arbitral tribunal; the same principle applies to the determination of the place of arbitration (Art. 28 and Art. 30 respectively).

The arbitration begins on the day a party gives the other one "notice to refer the dispute to the arbitral proceedings" (Art. 29). Subsequently, within the period of time allowed by the arbitral tribunal, the claimant must complete its request for arbitration indicating the subject, the relief or remedy, the facts, and the points at issue. The claimant must also enclose all the relevant documentary evidence or refer to evidence which will be submitted (Art. 31). Similar rules, of course, also apply to the defendant (Art. 32). In this respect the JCAA Rules are partly different as they provide that the party intending to commence the arbitration at the JCAA should also indicate, in addition to the typical content of the request for arbitration just mentioned and prescribed by the Arbitration Law, a clear reference to the arbitration agreement on which the proceeding is based. The JCAA Rules also provide that the request for arbitration must contain all the contact details of the claimant. Interestingly, it is not required to sign this document, which must be drawn up in as many copies as the number of parties and arbitrators (JCAA Rules, Art. 14 and Art. 21).

As traditionally happens in arbitration, in Japan as well there exists the possibility of an *emendatio libelli* or a *mutatio libelli*: the amendment of a statement and even the proposition of new statements is possible throughout the proceedings. However, "the arbitral tribunal may refuse to allow such amendment or supplementation if made in delay": in this case, the arbitral tribunal may declare the new or amended statements inadmissible (Art. 31(3)).

The arbitration proceeding is divided into several oral hearings, in which the parties can present their arguments and discuss or take on the evidence; obviously the right to defense and the principle called *audi alteram partem* must be respected, making sure that the counterparty knows in advance the object of what will be discussed at the hearing, and that must be fixed by the arbitral tribunal and notified in advance to all the parties (Art. 32). Witness evidence taken directly at the hearing is also admitted, but in the Japanese arbitration system written testimonial evidence has long been used (on the basis of affidavits).

Finally, as for the defense, it should be noted that normally in Japan lawyers representing the parties must be officially qualified according to specific rules. However, there is an important exception in the case of international arbitration taking place in Japan, i.e., if one or all parties have "domicile *(jusho)* or principal place of business in a foreign country". Foreign lawyers, in this case, can legally represent such clients in arbitrations celebrated in Japan (JCAA, 2006).

3. The reasons behind its limited use

It was only in 2004 that Japan adopted a specific law on the subject of arbitration in order to revitalize an institution that had been rarely used. Indeed, when the Civil Procedure Law was revised in 1997, the norms on arbitration were excluded and placed in a separate special law, called Public Peremptory Notice and Arbitration Procedure Law.

Previously, arbitration was regulated by the former Civil Procedure Law (no. 29/1980), which was essentially based on the German Code of Civil Procedure of 1877 (Nomura 1986; Taniguchi 1989; Tezuka/Ichiba 2006), but it had very little application.

Towards the end of the seventies, thanks to a study that was done on the subject of arbitration, a real interest in this institution started to grow. The research group in question is known as *Chusai Kenyukyhai* (Ogawa 1990). The project was essentially a comparative study of the rules of arbitration in the main countries, and in 1989 it produced a preliminary draft of what could potentially become the Arbitration Law (*Chusaiho Shian*). The draft, however, was never adopted and, thus, in 2001 it was followed by a second one (*Chusaiho 2001 Shian*), never adopted either (Sawada 2005).

At the beginning of the twenty-first century thanks to the impulse of the government, which wanted to expand the ADR systems in Japan, another study was specifically requested by the Office for Promotion of Justice System Reform, which used the UNCITRAL Model Law as a basis for the new Arbitration Law of 2003, which was enforced in 2004 (McAlinn 2004; Nakamura 2004; Sawada 2005).

Despite a population of over one hundred and thirty million inhabitants and an economy among the most prosperous in the world, in Japan very few arbitration proceedings are held. As regards international arbitration, the situation is not different, although the JCAA has regulations based on the UNCITRAL Model Law: from the date of its establishment (1953) to today there have been only an average of ten arbitrations a year held at the JCAA (Colombo 2011). The JCAA too rewrote its rules completely when the Arbitration Law came into existence in 2003 with the aim to further clarify some issues that had remained obscure. In order to further revitalize arbitration, the JCAA has recently updated its rules, which came into effect on 1 February 2014. The objective is to encourage the choice of arbitration at the JCAA, but the results still need to be evaluated.

The reasons behind its limited use is that, traditionally, arbitration has never been welcomed very favorably in Japan because the use of negotiation to resolve disputes out of court has always been predominant, even in relation to litigation, given that for a Japanese resorting to the court is considered unseemly according to the principles of Confucianism (Haley 1978; Kim/Lawson 1979; Cole 2007; Colombo 2012). Indeed, it is important to note that in Japan, even when one goes to court, the judge strongly recommends a negotiated solution through ADR tools, among which arbitration is not present, which may appear surprising for Westerners. The acronym tends, indeed, to be translated as *amicable dispute resolution.* Consequently, forms of private justice of an adversarial nature such as arbitration are not common (Ortolani 2007; Colombo 2011).

Beside cultural reasons, the failure of arbitration in Japan is also due to the fact that, although the Arbitration Law of 2003 is largely modeled on the UNCITRAL system, it presents certain variants that aim to fit the social and legal Japanese culture and that, in practice, end up making arbitration less desirable (Goodrich/Greer 2010; McAlinn/ Nottage 2010). These include, in particular, the fact that the state court traditionally invites the parties to resolve the dispute amicably, when appropriate, by expressly appointing an arbitrator, who however presents characteristics that are more similar to those of a mediator. Although in theory the legislation seeks to maintain a distinction between the two figures, following an international trend, Art. 38(4) of the Arbitration Law provides for the possibility to operate the aforementioned blend; the only limit is the need to obtain the prior consent of the parties. In the few cases of arbitration proceedings held in Japan, there have been many attempts on the part of the arbitrators to resolve the dispute in a conciliatory manner. This behavior is understandable for Japanese partners because of their cultural background but it has been a source of great discontent among parties of different nationalities and their lawyers, especially in cases in which they were certain of a favorable outcome according to the law (Oghigian/Ohara/Suzuki 2011).

A major limitation to the expansion of arbitration in Japan is that until 1996, when the Lawyers Act was amended, it was forbidden for foreign lawyers practising in Japan to represent the parties in arbitration as this rule was considered a way to defend the Japanese nationality. This approach, however, proved to be an obstacle to the spread of this ADR tool, given that the arbitration procedure is normally desirable especially for those foreign companies based in Japan which have to deal with a dispute and, generally, would rather be represented by lawyers of their country of origin (Nottage 2004). Another obstacle to the diffusion of arbitration is undoubtedly represented by the costs, which are indeed perceived as very high and are not counterbalanced by a high and proven specialization of arbitrators, because of the limited use of this type of procedure.

Even the reform projects examined in recent years have not significantly succeeded in changing this situation and addressing problematic issues. This is considerably different from what happened in other countries, which were also inspired by the Model Law and have introduced different regulations for domestic and international arbitration. In this way, the principles that are particularly important in a specific country are protected and at the same time the tool is more attractive even as regards international disputes involving parties with different legal and cultural backgrounds. The Japanese arbitration law, however, still includes many elements aiming to safeguard the Japanese identity (Nottage 2004).

From a purely technical perspective, undoubtedly one of the limitations of the arbitration law in Japan is the fact that the arbitral tribunal must often refer to the court of the state, for example in relation to the possibility that precautionary measures be granted. While many other countries have now embraced the idea that the arbitral tribunal may order interim and urgent measures, Japan continues to show skepticism towards such a possibility even though it is contemplated by the Arbitration Law (Art. 24(2); see also Oghigian/Ohara/Suzuki 2011). Indeed, there exist serious doubts about the possibility to apply precautionary measures as issued by the arbitrators. This is the classic procedure, adopted for example by Italian legislators, according to which arbitrators, as private judges, are deprived of the power of *imperium* and consequently of coercion.

Japanese arbitral tribunals commonly ask for the assistance of the ordinary court for gathering evidence. It is evident that the continuous need to move stages of the arbitration proceedings to the state court is a huge disincentive to the use of arbitration in Japan. This undermines speed and confidentiality, two features that generally make arbitration an appealing tool (Oghigian/Ohara/Suzuki 2011).

Moreover, in terms of speed, a peculiarity of the way in which arbitrations are conducted in Japan is that they have an excessive duration, because the arbitrators tend not to limit the number of exchanges of documents and briefs and because of the tendency to have several hearings. The latter problem may be solved through the introduction of a single hearing in which most of the activities should be conducted, as often happens in several arbitral institutions (Nottage 2004).

4. The JCAA

As mentioned above, the JCAA is the main arbitral institution in Japan. It was formally created in 1953 as a development of the International Commercial Arbitration Committee, which was established in 1950 within the Japan Chamber of Commerce and Industry. The JCAA is now an independent body. The number of cases dealt with by the JCAA is increasing, but has always been very small as shown in Table 1.

Year	*International*	*Domestic*	*Year*	*International*	*Domestic*
2006	11	0	2009	17	1
2007	12	3	2010	21	6
2008	12	0			

Table 1. Number of JCAA arbitration cases (Goodrich 2012: 1).

Table 2 shows the nationality of law firms representing the parties in JCAA arbitration. Clearly, the majority of them are Japanese and only a very small proportion of foreign law firms are involved in JCAA arbitration.

Year	*Nationality of the law firms representing the parties in JCAA arbitration*
2006	Japan 14, USA 4, Korea 1
2007	Japan 19, USA 3, UK 2, China 1

Year	*Nationality of the law firms representing the parties in JCAA arbitration*
2008	Japan 17, USA 5, Taiwan 1
2009	Japan 22, USA 3, France 2, UK 1, China 1, Korea 1
2010	Japan 38, USA 6, UK 1, France 1, Singapore 1, Mongolia 1

Table 2. The nationality of the law firms in JCAA arbitration (Goodrich 2012: 1).

4.1 The JCAA Rules and the ICC Rules compared: General aspects

The JCAA Rules were considerably modified in 2003 and then in 2014 with the aim to harmonize them in relation to the Japanese Arbitration Law as well as international practices. In particular, these rules present significant similarities with those of the ICC and this section will offer a contrastive analysis of the two documents. The most recent ICC Rules became effective on 1 January 2012. Compared to the 1998 rules, the new ones address some existent issues and deal with some new areas. Key changes regard multiple parties and multiple contracts, the arbitrator's availability, the concept of impartiality, confidentiality, and the role of an emergency arbitrator.

The JCAA published its amended Commercial Arbitration Rules (also referred to as the New Rules) in February 2014. This represents the most significant change since 2004, when the new Japanese Arbitration Law was enacted and the Arbitral Rules of the JCAA were amended accordingly. Some of the main amendments mirror those introduced by the ICC Rules in 2012 as well as the 2010 amendments to the UNICTRAL Rules. Indeed the changes aim to harmonize the JCAA rules in the light of those of other institutions such as the ICC or other Asian bodies, e.g. the Hong Kong International Arbitration Centre (HKIAC) and the Singapore International Arbitration Centre (SIAC).

The JCAA text consists of three main parts: a. Commercial Arbitration Rules; b. Administrative Fee Regulations; c. Regulations for Arbitrator's Remuneration. The Commercial Arbitration Rules of the JCAA as amended and effective on 1 February 2014 are the primary focus of this analysis. The JCAA rules are macrostructually organized in a way that mirrors that of other arbitral institutions, such as the ICC. In particular the ICC Rules present the following elements:

- Introductory Provisions
- Time Limits
- Commencing the Arbitration
- Multiple Parties, Multiple Contracts and Consolidation
- The Arbitral Tribunal
- The Arbitral Proceedings
- Awards
- Costs
- Miscellaneous

These are followed by appendices concerning:

I – Statutes of the International Court of Arbitration;
II – Internal Rules of the International Court of Arbitration;
III – Arbitration Costs and Fees;
IV – Case Management Techniques;
V – Emergency Arbitrator Rules.

The JCAA uses different terms to define specific sections of the text. Every macro-section is called 'Chapter', whereas the ICC Rules simply present the title of the section without using a metatextual reference. As regards the JCAA Commercial Arbitration Rules, the different subsections included in every chapter are clearly defined as 'Rules', whereas in the case of Administrative Fee Regulations and Regulations for Arbitrator's Remuneration we are dealing with 'Articles'. The ICC instead uses the term 'Article' throughout the text and that is employed as an umbrella term that includes both the notion of article and rule.

Before analyzing the different rules, it should be noted that a section devoted to the use of a specific arbitration clause is offered by both institutions. In the case of the JCAA, the standard clause is presented as a preamble even before the list of contents. This suggests an emphasis on the need to apply a standardized clause, which specifically indicates that the Commercial Arbitration Rules of the Japan Commercial Arbitration Association are to be followed. Its standardized nature is made manifest in the heading itself:

(1) STANDARD ARBITRATION CLAUSE
All disputes, controversies or differences which may arise between the parties hereto, out of or in relation to or in connection with this Agreement shall be

> finally settled by arbitration in (name of city) in accordance with the Commercial Arbitration Rules of the Japan Commercial Arbitration Association.

The ICC also presents a similar clause but at the end of the text, after all the articles have been presented:

(2) Standard ICC Arbitration Clause
All disputes arising out of or in connection with the present contract shall be finally settled under the Rules of Arbitration of the International Chamber of Commerce by one or more arbitrators appointed in accordance with the said Rules.

A greater degree of flexibility seems to emerge from the ICC Rules, in that parties are reminded that they "are free to adapt the clause to their particular circumstances" (Standard ICC Arbitration Clause). The text also emphasizes that the parties have a free choice in deciding what elements have to be included, but offers a linguistic warning: "When adapting the clause, care must be taken to avoid any risk of ambiguity. Unclear wording in the clause will cause uncertainty and delay and can hinder or even compromise the dispute resolution process" (Standard ICC Arbitration Clause). Linguistic ambiguity is in fact an oft-quoted problematic issue in legal language (Charnock 2006) in that it needs disambiguation processes, although it should be noted that linguistic vagueness may also be even more intricate to deal with (see Endicott 2000, 2005; Solan 2005; Anesa 2014). This form of linguistic caveat is not present in the JCAA text, where the arbitration clause seems to assume a purely prescriptive function.

Moving to the actual rules, vast uniformity exists between the Rules and Regulations of the JCAA, especially after the 2014 amendments, and the ICC Rules. This uniformity concerns issues such as multi-party arbitration and emergency arbitrators. However, certain differences exist, for example as regards expedited procedures (described in Chapter VI of the JCAA Rules). The following analysis will describe some of the main similarities and differences.

4.2 Insights into the JJCA Rules

4.2.1 Proceedings

As regards the way proceedings are conducted, several similarities are found. In the JCAA the tribunal directs and controls the proceedings (Rule 37.1, JCAA). Similarly, under the ICC Rules the tribunal has discretion as to how to conduct proceedings (Art. 19). The principle of equality in the treatment of parties emerges in both texts as the tribunal is expected to treat the parties equally and give each party sufficient opportunity to state and defend its case (Rule 37.2 JCAA). The ICC Rules also state that "in all cases, the arbitral tribunal shall act fairly and impartially and ensure that each party has a reasonable opportunity to present its case" (Art. 22 ICC). Under the JCAA Rules the tribunal is required to "use reasonable efforts to resolve the dispute expeditiously" (Rule 37.3 JCAA). The ICC similarly states the importance of an expeditious conduct of the proceeding and also emphasizes the importance of cost effectiveness: "the arbitral tribunal and the parties shall make every effort to conduct the arbitration in an expeditious and cost-effective manner, having regard to the complexity and value of the dispute" (Art. 22 ICC).

4.2.2 The arbitrators

The definition of the number of arbitrators is also subject to similar rules. The agreement of the parties remains the first criteria in the establishment of the number of arbitrators. Otherwise, the number of arbitrators is generally one. The JCAA Rules state that, "If the Parties fail to notify the JCAA in writing of their agreement about the number of arbitrators within four weeks from the respondent's receipt of the notice of the Request for Arbitration, such number shall be one" (Rule 26.1). Within this period of time parties may request to have a panel of three arbitrators (Rule 26.2). Under the ICC Rules, "where the parties have not agreed upon the number of arbitrators, the Court shall appoint a sole arbitrator, save where it appears to the Court that the dispute is such as to warrant the appointment of three arbitrators" (Art. 12.2).

Both texts specify that arbitrators must be independent and impartial (Rule 24.1 JCAA and Art. 11.1 ICC). The JCAA presents no specific restrictions on the nationality of arbitrators. However, it is stated that if "a Party requests that the arbitrator be a person of a different nationality from that of any of the Parties, the JCAA shall respect such request" (Rules 27.4). Instead, the ICC Rules specifically establish that, unless provided under specific circumstances, "the sole arbitrator or the president of the arbitral tribunal shall be of a nationality other than those of the parties" (Art. 13.5 ICC). This difference presumably derives from the fact that the JCAA may draw on a more limited number of arbitrators and therefore may be inclined to impose fewer restrictions on the appointment of arbitrators.

As regards the appointment of arbitrators both the JCAA Rules and the ICC Rules stress the importance of the agreement of the parties (Rule 25.2 JCAA and Art. 12 ICC) and describe the procedure to be followed when a sole arbitrator is appointed or in the case of a tribunal of three arbitrators. Both documents have specific sections with separate headings for the two cases:

(3) Article 12 Constitution of the Arbitral Tribunal Number of Arbitrators
Sole Arbitrator
Three arbitrators (Article 12 ICC)

(4) Rule 27. Appointment of Arbitrator – Sole Arbitrator
Rule 28. Appointment of Arbitrators – Three Arbitrators
Rule 29. Appointment of Arbitrators – Three Arbitrators in Multi-Party Arbitration (Rules 27–28-29 JCAA)

4.2.3 Multi-party arbitration

Interestingly, both texts describe the procedure to be followed in the case of multiparty arbitration. Under the JCAA rules such scenario is presented as a separate section, and the rules specify that if the claimant(s) or the respondent(s) do not notify the JCAA of the appointment of an arbitrator, three arbitrators will be appointed by the Association (Rule 29.7). The ICC text does not use the expression 'multi-party arbitration', but contemplates the existence of multiple claimants or multiple respondents:

(5) Where there are multiple claimants or multiple respondents, and where the dispute is to be referred to three arbitrators, the multiple claimants, jointly, and

the multiple respondents, jointly, shall nominate an arbitrator for confirmation pursuant to Article 13 (ICC 12.6).

(6) If there is no joint nomination, the ICC court may then designate the arbitrators (ICC 12.8).

Multi-party arbitration is one of the key points of the New JCAA Rules. The previous rules did not provide for the joinder of third parties, whereas this is now possible (Rule 52). The new rules also provide for the consolidation of separate proceedings, which was possible also under the previous rules but only with the written consent of the parties. The new rules (Rule 53) are less strict in this respect. Indeed, consolidation of an existing proceeding may take place if:

(7) (1) all Parties (including the parties to the other claim(s)) have agreed in writing;
(2) the pending claim(s) and the claim(s) to be consolidated arise under the same Arbitration Agreement; provided, however, the written consent to such consolidation by the party to the other claim(s) is necessary when the party has not been a Party to the pending claim(s); or
(3) both the pending claim(s) and the other claim(s) to be consolidated arise between the same Parties, and
(a) the same or a similar question of fact or law arises from the claims;
(b) the dispute is referred by the Arbitration Agreement to arbitration under the Rules or at the JCAA; and
(c) the arbitral proceedings are capable of being conducted in a single proceeding with regard to the place of arbitration, the number of arbitrators, language(s), and other issues governed by the Arbitration Agreements under which the claims arise. (Rule 53)

Thus, these rules appear to be more in line with the ICC Rules (see Articles 7–8-9–10).

4.2.4 Confidentiality

The way confidentiality is dealt with shows some differences in the two texts. The ICC does not include a specific confidentiality obligation rule, but the tribunal may take measures to protect any confidential information (Art. 22.3). The JCAA Rules specify that proceedings must be held in private, and all records are closed to the public (Rule 38.1). Disclosure of information is prohibited, except where required by law, court proceedings or other justifiable grounds (Rule 38.2). Interestingly, under the Japanese law there is no specific requirement for arbitration to be conducted confidentially. However, it is generally accepted that, unless otherwise agreed, confidentiality must be preserved. The JCAA Rules instead impose confidentially obligations on all the parties involved in the proceedings (Tezuka/Kawabata 2012).

4.2.5 Emergency Arbitrator provisions

Under the JCAA Rules, parties are allowed to apply for emergency measures: (1) before the constitution of the tribunal; or (2) when any arbitrator has ceased to perform his duties (Rule 70.1). The New Rules introduce provisions for the appointment of emergency arbitrators and the granting of emergency relief. These provisions mirror the recent amendments introduced by the HKIAC, the SIAC and the ICC Rules. The JCAA rules set out that "The JCAA shall use reasonable efforts to appoint an emergency arbitrator within two business days from its receipt of the application for Emergency Measures" (Rule 71.4) and a decision must be provided within two weeks from the appointment. Like under the ICC Rules, a party is allowed to apply for the appointment of an emergency arbitrator before the filing of a request, provided that the request is filed within ten days. This is not contemplated in other texts such as the HKIAC and the SIAC Rules.

4.2.6 Expedited procedures

One evident difference between the two texts regards expedited procedures. The JCAA text includes specific rules on the use of expedited procedures. Parties may agree to settle any dispute according to such procedures (Rule 75). The section dealing with expedited rules was already included in the previous text but was amended with the 2014 reform. Previously it was only applicable to claims of ¥ 20m (c. US$ 200,000) or less. With the amendments, the parties may agree to expedited procedures irrespective of the amount claimed. The time limit for delivering the award under these procedures remains three months.

In contrast, the ICC does not explicitly mention the use of expedited procedures. Nevertheless, the parties are allowed to reduce the time limits described in the Rules under Article 38, which deals with Modified Time Limits:

(8) The parties may agree to shorten the various time limits set out in the Rules. Any such agreement entered into subsequent to the constitution of an arbitral tribunal shall become effective only upon the approval of the arbitral tribunal. (ICC, Art. 38)

However, specific sections about expedited procedures are quite common, and also the SIAC and the HKIAC Rules specifically deal with them.

5. Conclusions

The limited use of arbitration in Japan, both as regards domestic and international arbitration, is determined by several factors. From a cultural perspective, Japanese people may tend to avoid an adversarial system of dispute resolution in that it goes against the idea of harmony. Moreover, traditionally for arbitrations taking place in Japan any associated proceedings are conducted in Japanese and this may discourage foreign parties to choose Japan as an arbitration seat in that translation costs may be too high. Furthermore, the Japanese system is widely based on German law and may thus be unfamiliar with those parties used to a Common Law system.

Japan is trying to promote the use of arbitration through a series of reforms aiming at harmonizing Japanese arbitral law and procedures with the international standards. In 2004 a reform of the arbitral law was introduced but did not lead to substantial changes as regards the number of arbitrations filed (Goodrich/Greer 2010). The amendments of the JCAA Rules will inevitably take some years to show their value and significance. In the meantime it should be reminded that these changes have been viewed positively by most scholars and practitioners in that they move towards harmonization and standardization in relation to the rules of other arbitral institutions such as the ICC.

The new rules have also modified the way mediation-arbitration is conducted. The previous rules had been criticized in that the arbitrator's impartiality could be affected by unsuccessful mediation. Under the new rules the ability of the mediator-arbitrator to consult separately with parties has been restricted, which is also seen as a guarantee of a higher level of impartiality.

However, the way to make the JCAA an attractive arbitration seat especially for foreign parties is still complex. In order to improve the actual number of yearly cases, it is necessary to take further steps towards the internationalization of its rules and practices, such as using "English as the first drafting language" and introducing "an advisory board composed of leading international experts" (Markert 2014: 5).

References

Anesa, Patrizia 2014. Defining Legal Vagueness: A Contradiction in Terms? *Pólemos* 8/1, 193–209.

Bhatia, Vijay / Engberg, Jan / Gotti, Maurizio / Heller, Dorothee (eds) 2005. *Vagueness in Normative Texts*. Bern: Peter Lang.

Charnock, Ross 2006. Clear Ambiguity. In Cacciaguidi-Fahy, Sophie / Wagner, Anne (eds) *Legal Language and the Search for Clarity*. Bern: Peter Lang, 65–103.

Cole, Tony 2007. Commercial Arbitration in Japan: Contributions to the Debate on 'Japanese Non-litigiousness'. *New York University Journal of International Law and Politics* 40/1, 29–86.

Colombo, Giorgio 2011. *Oltre il paradigma della società senza liti: la risoluzione extra-giudiziale delle controversie in Giappone*. Padova: CEDAM.

Colombo, Giorgio 2012. La promozione dell'ADR nel Giappone contemporaneo. Riflessioni critico-quantitative sulla litigiosità in Giappone, *Annuario di diritto comparato e studi legislativi* 3, 397–410.

Endicott, Timothy 2000. *Vagueness in Law*. Oxford: Oxford University Press.

Endicott, Timothy 2005. The Value of Vagueness. In Bhatia *et al.* (eds), 27–49.

Goodrich, Mark 2012. Japanese Arbitration – Much Work Done; Much still to Do. <http://www.whitecase.com/files/Publication/1dfe9f46-eed3-45cb-b025-e2503b779d55/Presentation/PublicationAttachment/a627f056-ebe5-4f8a-98b9-e44a779b827e/article-Japanese-Arbitration-Goodrich-022012.pdf>.

Goodrich, Mark / Greer, Joel 2010. The Modernization of Japan's International Arbitration Infrastructure. *International Arbitration Report* 25/12, 31–42.

Haley, John 1978. The Myth of the Reluctant Litigant, *Journal of Japanese Studies* 4, 359–390.

JCAA, 2006. *A Guide to International Commercial Arbitration in Japan.* <http://www.jcaa.or.jp/e/arbitration/docs/brochure.pdf>.

Kim, Chin / Lawson, Craig M. 1979. The Law of the Subtle Mind: The Traditional Japanese Conception of Law. *International and Comparative Law Quarterly* 28, 491–510.

Markert, Lars 2014. The JCAA Arbitration Rules 2014 – One Step Forward In the Modernization of Japanese Arbitration. *JCAA Newsletter* 32, 1–5.

McAlinn, Gerald 2004. New Rules for International Commercial Arbitration in Effect from March 1, 2004. *JCAA Newsletter* 17, 6–10.

McAlinn, Gerald / Nottage, Luke 2004. Changing the (JCAA) Rules: Improving International Commercial Arbitration in Japan. *Journal of Japanese Law* 18, 23–36.

Nakamura, Tatsuya 2004. Salient Features of the New Japanese Arbitration Law Based Upon the UNCITRAL Model Law on International Commercial Arbitration. *JCAA Newsletter* 17, 1–6.

Nomura, Yoshiaki 1986. Some Aspects of the Use of Commercial Arbitration by Japanese Corporations, *Osaka University Law Review* 33, 47–49.

Nottage, Luke 2004. Japan's New Arbitration Law: Domestication Reinforcing Internationalisation. *International Arbitration Law Review* 2, 54–60.

Ogawa, Frank H. 1990. Proposed Draft of Japanese New Arbitration Law. *Journal of International Arbitration* 7/2, 33–41.

Oghigian, Haig / Ohara, Mami / Suzuki, Junra 2011. Japan. In *The Baker & Mckenzie International Arbitration Yearbook: 2010-2011*. Huntington (NY): JurisNet, 63–82.

Ortolani, Andrea 2007. La lingua del diritto in Giappone. In Ajani, Gianmaria / Serafino, Andrea / Timoteo, Marina (eds) *Diritto dell'Asia orientale*. Torino: UTET, 24–43.

Solan, Lawrence M. 2005. Vagueness and Ambiguity in Legal Interpretation. In Bhatia *et al.* (eds), 73–96.

Taniguchi, Yasuhei 1989. Commercial Arbitration in Japan. In Sanders, Peter (ed.) *Arbitration in Settlement of International Commercial Disputes Involving the Far East and Arbitration in Combined Transportation*. London: Kluwer Law International, 29, 37–41.

Tezuka, Hiroyuki / Ichiba, Kazuyuki 2006. Japan, International Arbitration. *The International Comparative Legal Guide*. London: Global legal Group, 250–257.

Tezuka, Hiroyuki / Kawabata, Yutaro 2012. *Japan. Arbitration Guide IBA Arbitration Committee*. <http://www.ibanet.org/Document/Default.aspx?DocumentUid=DBCF3CAB-E985-4A9B-BBA1-D8D9D191EF5E>.

Sawada, Toshio 2005. The 2004 Japanese Arbitration Law in relation to the UNICTRAL Model Law and the Japanese ADR and Attorney Law. In Aksen, Gerlad *et al.* (eds) *Global Reflections on International Law, Commerce and Dispute Resolution: Liber Amicorum in Honor of Robert Briner*. Paris: IIC Publishing, 725–741.

Maurizio Gotti / Piera Pellegrinelli / Elena Signorini[1]

Norms Concerning the Appointment and Challenge of Arbitrators in the Legislation of the People's Republic of China

1. Introduction

In the last few years there has been a large increase in the number of arbitration proceedings carried out in the People's Republic of China (PRC). This is due to the considerable growth of both internal and international trade conducted by Chinese companies, and – as a consequence – of the number of disputes related to it. In many cases these disputes have been settled by means of arbitration. According to Horrigan, Hess and Lin Mok (2011), more than 60,000 arbitration cases are filed in China every year. In 2010 CIETAC, the most important Chinese arbitration institution, filed a total of 1,352 arbitration cases (934 domestic and 418 foreign-related), making CIETAC the most active arbitral institution worldwide by number of published cases.

Also as regards labour disputes, arbitration has become a widespread means of conflict resolution. China has a huge workforce, reaching a total of over 800 million (Brown 2010). In the last few years this workforce has been in a state of flux because of new labour laws, which have brought about greater liberalization and stronger competitiveness in the workers' world. Moreover, the greater emphasis on a market economy and the growth of the private sector have promoted wider workplace protections and the implementation of better safety and social security programs (Lu 2008). These developments – and the recent

1 Although the authors have collaborated at every stage in the production of this chapter, Sections 1 and 2 were written by Maurizio Gotti, Section 3 was written by Piera Pellegrinelli and Section 4 by Elena Signorini. Section 5 was jointly written by the three authors.

economic crisis – have also caused an increase in labour disputes, with the number of arbitration cases in China rising from 10,326 in 1989 to about 350,000 in 2007 (Brown 2010). The number of cases almost doubled the following year with the approval of the Law on Mediation and Arbitration of Labour Disputes (<www. clb.org.hk>).

The different matters concerning commercial and labour arbitration are dealt with by specific provisions, such as The People's Republic of China Arbitration Law and The Law on Mediation and Arbitration of Labour Disputes. The PRC Arbitration Law was promulgated by the Standing Committee of the National People's Congress of the PRC on 31 August 1994 and came into force on 1 September 1995. The Law on Mediation and Arbitration of Labour Disputes was approved by the Standing Committee of the National People's Congress of the PRC on 29 December 2007 and came into force on 1 January 2008. The main aims of these new laws were to simplify the settlement of trade and labour disputes and resolve them fairly and in a timely manner.

It is the aim of this chapter to investigate the texts of both the PRC Arbitration Law and the Law on Mediation and Arbitration of Labour Disputes in order to examine, in particular, the norms concerning the appointment and challenge to appointment of arbitrators. These texts will be compared to those of the UNCITRAL Model Law on International Commercial Arbitration (ML)[2] and of other arbitration norms so as to detect relevant legal and cultural differentiations.

2. An oveview of some Western texts

The analysis of the provisions regarding the selection of arbitrators may reveal some interesting local cultural aspects. This issue is of great importance in the arbitration process, as arbitrators play a very active

2 The UNCITRAL Model Law on International Commercial Arbitration was issued by the United Nations in 1985 (and amended in 2006) for harmonizing purposes and was later used as a starting document by many countries all over the world when producing their own individual statutory provisions.

role and enjoy a great degree of autonomy, due to the fact that no jury is involved in the proceedings and that the majority of the disputes are of a technical and complicated nature. Moreover, arbitrators often make proposals for an amicable settlement of the dispute if they see any feasible solutions. It is important, therefore, that the decision-making process should be totally transparent and that the arbitrator should be impartial and independent. This need is particularly felt in the Chinese context, where arbitration has often been regarded as too sensitive to the local parties' interests and pressures. Here is the opinion of Professor Jerome Cohen from New York University, as quoted by Jane Moir in an article in the *South China Morning Post* (5 October 2001):

> The longer my experience as either an advocate or an arbitrator in disputes presented to CIETAC, the graver my doubts have become about its independence and impartiality. [...] At a minimum, I would surely no longer advise clients to accept CIETAC jurisdiction unless the contract's arbitration clause required the appointment of a third country national as presiding arbitrator. (Cited in Bhatia/Candlin/Wei 2001: 8)

Things do not seem to have improved in the last few years and the general international opinion about Chinese local arbitration institutions seems to be very skeptical. Here, for example, are a couple of remarks about the behaviour of the Hangzhou Arbitration Commission in the procedings over the dispute between the Chinese Wahaha Group and the French Groupe Danone:

> Why the hell would you agree to arbitration in Hangzhou, the home base of your very strong JV [joint venture] partner? Come on, did you have absolutely no leverage in the negotiation process or did someone screw this one up? (Abrams 2007, quoted in Corona 2011: 137)

> Zong filed for arbitration, too, with the Hangzhou Arbitration Commission, the kangaroo court in his hometown. [...] Expecting an independent hearing from the Hangzhou Arbitration Commission is like expecting an honest report about Tiananmen Square from the *People's Daily* newspaper. It just isn't going to happen. (Levant 2007, quoted in Corona 2011: 137)

These considerations provide an explanation for the specific norms that the Chinese arbitration law has laid down to regulate the challenge to appointed arbitrators. In particular, these norms contain specific reference to such important issues as the arbitrator's competence, impartiality and independence. In the UNCITRAL text,[3] instead, this issue is considered in very general terms:

(1) The court or other authority, in appointing an arbitrator, shall have due regard to any qualifications required of the arbitrator by the agreement of the parties and to such considerations as are likely to secure the appointment of an independent and impartial arbitrator and, in the case of a sole or third arbitrator, shall take into account as well the advisability of appointing an arbitrator of a nationality other than those of the parties. (ML 11.5)

It is evident that the choice of an arbitrator is of immense importance: (s)he must be a figure of sufficient professional standing to satisfy the parties of his/her competence in resolving the issue(s) and add personal credibility to the legal validity of the procedure. However, within the text of the Model Law the provisions tend to be quite vague, as can be seen by the use of the adjective *likely* in the following provision dealing with the impartiality and independence of arbitrators:

(2) When a person is approached in connection with his possible appointment as an arbitrator, he shall disclose any circumstances *likely* to give rise to justifiable doubts as to his impartiality or independence. (ML 12.1)

The use of this adjective reinforces the tone of vagueness which particularly characterises the section of the Model Law dealing with the criteria for the choice of an arbitrator. In other normative texts, instead, the requirement of impartiality and independence of arbitrators is more clearly stated as a strong obligation, with the use of deontic modal auxiliaries such as *shall* or *must* and the explicit mention of situations that may impair such impartiality:

(3) All arbitrators conducting an arbitration under these Rules *shall be and remain at all times impartial and independent* of the parties; and *none shall act in the arbitration as advocates for any party*. *No arbitrator*, whether before or after appointment, *shall advise any party* on the merits or outcome of the dispute. (Rules of the London Court of International Arbitration 5.2)

3 The Model Law (with its 2006 amendments) is available at <http://www.uncitral.org/pdf/english/texts/arbitration/ml-arb/07-86998_Ebook.pdf>.

(4) Every arbitrator *must be and remain independent* of the parties involved in the arbitration. (Rules of the International Chamber of Commerce Court of Arbitration 7.1)

(5) An arbitrator *must be impartial and independent.* (Rules of the Stockholm Chamber of Commerce 17)

Some of the provisions drafted in other contexts to regulate the conduct of appointed arbitrators are even more specific and prescriptive. For example, the regulations laid down by a few Italian arbitration chambers contain specific codes of conduct concerning such important issues as the arbitrator's competence, impartiality and independence, which are largely modelled on the Criteria of Arbitral Ethics *(Criteri di Deontologia Arbitrale)* enacted by the Italian Arbitration Association in 1999 (cf. Bartolini/Delconte 2001). For example, the codes of conduct included in the rules of the Milan Arbitration Chamber (MAC)[4] and the Bergamo Arbitration Chamber (BAC)[5] consist of 15 articles, regulating the conduct of arbitrators in a very detailed way, from the moment they accept the appointment and throughout the entire arbitration procedure. Also the rules of the Venice Court of National and International Arbitration (VENCA)[6] have a specific article (Art. 13) stating explicitly that the appointed arbitrator is expected to send a written statement expressing his independence and impartiality and declaring he has no connections with the parties involved in the arbitration process. Moreover, BAC also includes the need for a Roster of Arbitrators (Section 6) and outlines in detail the characteristics of a potential arbitrator and of the application procedures. The specification of a Roster of Arbitrators stresses the wish of this arbitration chamber to exercise strict control over the competence and reliability of prospective arbitrators. Also as regards the procedure for challenging an arbitrator, the UNCITRAL Arbitration Rules (AR)[7] indicate the grounds for challenge in general terms, only mentioning "justifiable doubts as to his impartiality or independence" (Art.10). BAC (Section 8.1), instead, makes a clear reference to

4 Available at <http://www.mi.camcom.it/eng/arbitration-chamber/reging.htm>.
5 Available at <http://www.bg.camcom.it/camera_arbitrale>.
6 Available at <http://www.venca.it/rules.htm>.
7 Available at <http://www.uncitral.org/english/ texts/arbitration/arbitrul.htm>.

the reasons for challenging an arbitrator and refers to a precise external source of jurisdiction for their specification:

(6) The party may reject the arbitrator *in the cases specified in Section 51 of the Italian Code of Civil Practice.* (BAC 8.1.2)

Italian law does not require specific qualifications to become an arbitrator, except for the requirement of impartiality and independence (Section 812 of the Code of Civil Procedure, the statute that sets out the rules for procedures of arbitration). Arbitrators are usually selected according to their particular area of specialisation and expertise. Professional experience is considered particularly important, and most Chambers of Commerce require prospective Presidents of the Board of Arbitrators to have been registered in the relevant professional register for a considerable period (for example, ten years). A significant level of experience is also required of most arbitrators in an attempt to ensure their professional competence (and credibility) within the field of the dispute. In addition, a Chamber of Commerce typically evaluates an individual's previous arbitrary experience when making appointments. Obviously the nature of the dispute(s) and the parties involved are also taken into consideration.

While it is obviously in the interests of a Chamber of Commerce to appoint credible representation, further protection is provided by Section 815 of the Italian Code of Civil Procedure, which states that the appointment of an arbitrator can be challenged if (s)he does not have the qualifications agreed upon by the parties:

(7) Un arbitro può essere ricusato se non ha le qualifiche espressamente convenute dalle parti. (D.L. 40/2006, 815 ter)
[An arbitrator can be challenged if (s)he does not have the necessary qualifications agreed on by the parties.]

One of the fundamental principles upon which arbitration is based is that arbitrators can be appointed on the basis of their expertise in the subject that has given rise to the dispute. This is particularly important in cases where the nature of the disagreement calls for very specific technical or specialised competence. As Italian law does not specify what kinds of professionals may be appointed as arbitrators, the role could potentially be assumed by any professional, but, in more practical terms, arbitrators belong to a limited number of categories: for example, lawyers, accountants, university professors and researchers, architects, chemists and engineers. Allowing the arbitrator to be appointed from within the relevant profession can obviously be advantageous to both parties, because an expert arbitrator can circumvent the need for external consultancy, thereby reducing time and money.

In spite of these benefits, lawyers remain the preferred category from which arbitrators are chosen. This is also due to the particular relevance that the observance of correct procedures may have on the outcome of arbitration proceedings. Indeed, the Code of Civil Procedure (Section 829) indicates a list of circumstances in which an arbitral award can be challenged. Among other cases this happens when:

- the appointment of the arbitrator is invalid;
- the award contradicts either another award or a court decision that has already become *res judicata*;
- relevant legal rules are not applied in the correct way.

It is clearly important, therefore, that arbitrators should have a solid legal background in order to ensure their familiarity with legal procedures and avoid incorrect practices that may make the award challengeable or annullable. This is one of the main reasons why, in the vast majority of cases, the arbitrator is also a lawyer. Indeed, in general, Italian Chambers of Commerce tend to favour the appointment of candidates with a legal background, usually lawyers. This also derives from the assumption that the decision of a member of the legal profession will carry more weight than that of a non-lawyer. In any case, this notion seems to have become entrenched, and the tacit convention of appointing lawyers appears to be well-established.

3. The PRC Arbitration Law

The milestone of arbitration in China is represented by the Arbitration Law promulgated on August 31, 1994 and effective as from September 1, 1995 (Shuangyuan/Guomin 1996; Jin/Guomin 2001). The intent of the Chinese legislator was to adapt arbitration norms to international practices, by introducing some key principles that are internationally recognized.

3.1 Requirements for the appointment of arbitrators

One of the most interesting aspects regarding the field of arbitration is the appointment of arbitrators. As regards domestic arbitration, the legislation (Arbitration Law, art. 13) establishes both positive and negative conditions: it requires that the candidate be just and honest and also provides that an individual cannot be chosen as an arbitrator unless at least one of the requirements specified by the norm is met. The specific requirements introduce limitations as regards the possibility to resort to professional experts in fields different from the legal and the economic ones and are to be saluted favourably, given that they have a positive effect on the procedural regularity and on the correct interpretation of the cases. If we consider, for example, the Italian system, the reference norm as regards the qualifications of candidates is art. 812 Code of Civil Procedure, which does not mention anything concerning the characteristics of the training and experience of the individuals, except that they should at least have the legal capacity to act. The Italian legislation gives much more freedom to the parties, who may choose arbitrators among experts in a particular sector, which is, in practice, often crucial for the outcome of the cases. It may be objected that the introduction of 'technical experts' could threaten the fairness of the process making it less juridical, and above all more exposed to potential errors resulting from incomplete knowledge of the law. On the other hand, the assumption that legal knowledge is an essential component may encourage a move toward 'arbitigation', rather than arbitration as a non-legal practice.

Thus, the solution adopted in the arbitration system of China should be welcomed favourably. The only way for a subject without any specific legal training to be part of the arbitration panel is to meet the requirement indicated in Article 13: "at least eight years of work experience in arbitration". This seems to express a desire to balance the absence of legal training with a training period 'on the job'. What remains unclear is the rationale behind defining the time quantum in eight years in order to gain the necessary experience as an arbitrator. This choice seems illogical and completely arbitrary, but the issue of the time quantum is, in practice, a secondary problem. Indeed, the parties are unlikely to resort to a person without experience to settle their dispute. It is much more realistic to imagine that the new arbitrators work side by side with veterans for a period of training, in order to achieve the experience needed to manage future proceedings independently. However, where this cooperation has been tried, in actual practice it has sometimes encouraged exploitation of young and newly initiated arbitrators for a long time, resulting in senior practitioners acting as 'the old boys' club'.

Among other sources to consider in order to obtain a complete picture of the procedures for the appointment of arbitrators in case of domestic arbitration, one should refer, as regards arbitrations administered by CIETAC (Guillaumonde 2001; Moser/Yuen 2005; Chang 2001) to the *Stipulations for the Appointment of Arbitrators*. This document, promulgated by CIETAC and CMAC in 1995 and amended in 2000, is now in force in its most recent and updated version, that of 2005. In May 2008 CIETAC abolished the distinction between the list of arbitrators involved in the resolution of domestic cases and the list of arbitrators dealing with foreign-related cases. Thus, the parties involved in domestic cases are free to appoint, as their arbitrators, individuals coming from mainland China, Hong Kong, Macao, Taiwan or other countries.

One of the main requirements is the need to comply with the so-called *Ethical Rules*. The *Ethical Rules* were adopted on April 6, 1993 and are now in force, as amended on March 1, 2004, under the name of *Code of Conduct for Arbitrators*. A positive aspect is the requirement of independence and impartiality (Jin 2005; Hughes 1997; Articles 13 and 14 of the Arbitration Law; art. 24 of the CIETAC Rules), defined with specific reference to the facts, laws, international practices and principles of justice and fairness. The order in which the above sources are listed is not purely coincidental, but it is evidently an indication of their degree of importance. The reference to international practices is particularly important: although it is a residual source from a Chinese arbitrator's perspective, it definitely indicates a constant tension towards the affirmation of Chinese arbitration in the international arena.

Rightly, an arbitrator cannot represent a specific party in a case and must treat all parties equally. At first glance this requirement may seem almost useless, given that the Chinese system does not include the possibility of *ad hoc* arbitration, but only arbitrations administered by committees which have their own lists of professionals: in a similar system the risk of partiality on the part of an arbitrator should be basically nil. This danger is more relevant in the case of *ad hoc* arbitration, as it derives from the relationship of trust which actually exists between the party and the arbitrator chosen by it. In fact, this provision is very useful, given that there are several cases of corruption in a field that often involves very big economic interests (Georgiou 2011).

As regards the possibility for a judge to be appointed as an arbitrator, on 13.7.2004 the Supreme People's Court ruled:

> A judge's acting as an arbitrator and undertaking the arbitration work of cases is not consistent with the pertinent legal provisions, exceeds the functions of the people's court and the judges, and is disadvantageous to impartially protecting the legitimate rights and interests of the litigants according to the law. Thus, no judge may act as an arbitrator. Anyone who has been engaged by an arbitration commission to act as an arbitrator shall resign from his (her) position as an arbitrator and terminate the employment relationship. (<www.en.pkulaw.cn>)

This rule was confirmed by the decision of the Supreme People's Court on 24.2.2010. The issue of professionalism is very important in China: it is a well-known fact that one of the major problems of the Chinese judicial system, as well as one of the major obstacles for foreign entities to resort to Chinese courts, is the lack of professionalism. Consequently, it is required that the arbitrators constantly follow training sessions. Interestingly, such an important aspect refers to the ethics of arbitrators, as it is included neither in the CIETAC Rules nor in the Arbitration Law.

The seriousness of the commitment made by the arbitrators is expressed by the request for active participation in the organization of hearings, with the evident intent to safeguard speed and procedural fairness. As is well known, the most delicate and difficult moment to manage in the conduction of a case, keeping an ethically irreproachable conduct, is the oral hearing. CIETAC's aim (cf. art. 35) was to define the guidelines for the management of this phase of the case in order to reduce the practical problems related to bias and the failure to preserve the principle *audi alteram partem*. An arbitrator should not accept gifts from the parties during his service, or meet a party in private to discuss issues or accept material related to the case, except when the arbitrator meets the parties separately in accordance with the decision made by the arbitration panel during the mediation process. This aims at protecting the integrity of the evidence and is therefore a positive element. The arbitrators must ensure procedural fairness, which results in the protection of the parties through the respect of the principle *audi alteram partem*, which is indirectly mentioned through the reference to "adequate opportunity to present the case" (art. 35). It is strongly felt that procedural celerity should be guaranteed, as well as the avoidance of unexpected obstacles or incidents that may in any way undermine the interests of the parties involved.

Confidentiality must also be guaranteed. It is interesting to note that CIETAC (art. 38) has used the term *confidentiality* and not the term *privacy*, which is more common in other contexts. The choice does not seem accidental, but perfectly adherent to the cultural heritage of China. The term *privacy* refers to anything that falls within the personal sphere of the individuals, with regard to their interests and their ideas, and more generally what concerns the identity of a person. The term *confidentiality*, on the contrary, concerns relationships and the confidential management of relations. Confidentiality derives from the Latin expression *cum fides* meaning 'have faith' (i.e., reveal something to someone under the faith of secrecy), which presupposes the existence of a relationship. It is therefore clear that the use of the term *confidentiality* cannot be accidental but is motivated, first and foremost, by the relationship of trust that exists between the parties and the arbitrators and, secondly, by the cultural heritage of China that assigns a high level of importance to the notion of trust which underlies any relationship.

Good knowledge of the English language is required: in China one of the major obstacles is represented by difficulty in communication due to linguistic misunderstandings; few Chinese know English well, but even fewer foreigners are able to speak Chinese. It is therefore praiseworthy to attempt to create a class of competent arbitrators, able to communicate in English. What deserves to be censured is the possible exemption from the requirement of knowing the English language, according to which "for a small part of well-known personages or for those who have the knowledge of other foreign languages, the terms can be softened appropriately" (Stipulations for the appointment of arbitrators, art. 1.4). The unclear points are two: who are the subjects to whom this exception is applicable? What are the reasons and the boundaries of this exception? As for the first question, the subjects may be 'well-known' but certainly not to the reader, since there is no reference from which to infer, clearly, the people to identify. This exception may create a dangerous system that allows for the identification of subjects on a fully discretionary basis, which is detrimental to the objective of the rule itself, thus depriving the system of subjects able to communicate and work in English. Hopefully, the indiscriminate use of the exemption does not occur in practice, but exceptions should be made exclusively for the 'few' individuals, for whom it is in fact useful to waive from this requirement, given their high level of professionalism and their experience.

With reference to foreign-related arbitration, an arbitration commission (Arbitration Law, art. 67) may select and appoint the foreign arbitrators who possess specialized knowledge in the field of law, economics, trade, science and technology from its own roster. This is a general provision, which indicates the desire of the legislator to assign greater freedom to the parties with regard to international cases and demonstrates the extreme flexibility which the legislator envisaged. This indisputable simplicity is a fundamental strength of foreign-related arbitration, especially considering the central importance of the time of appointment. This procedure, in fact, plays a very important role for the success of arbitration and is, in practice, a significant element when the parties have to decide the place of arbitration, the institution, and the chances of a successful outcome according to the specific case. In general, it can be stated that the requirements for this type of arbitration are less restrictive than internal arbitration, in order to provide greater flexibility. What is required is a high level of professional preparation in some key fields, namely law, economics and trade, science and technology or maritime affairs. The strength of this provision is the lack of a specific indication of the professional level required, which is perhaps meant to provide greater freedom to the parties for the choice of arbitrators.

One needs to master the English language, which is essential when dealing with international issues, as well as Chinese language. In relation to the latter provision it should be noted that it is possible to make use of an interpreter in order to assist the arbitrators, but the presence of a third party would paradoxically lead to significant obstacles to full understanding. A third party would transpose the facts inevitably reinterpreted in the light of his personal understanding and perspective. Instead, an arbitrator who knew Chinese would hear directly what is reported. Nevertheless, interpreters are often vital, especially when dealing with a complex language such as Chinese. The possibility to waive this requirement exists, and it is provided that in any case, the terms can be properly loosened to some individuals well known within the field of international arbitration. However, it is not clear why the reference to "righteous and upright personality" (Stipulations for the appointment of arbitrators, art. 1.1) has been omitted as regards the need to respect the principle of independence and impartiality. The only plausible solution is to be found in considering this specification unnecessary, given that the principle of independence and impartiality necessarily presupposes a personality that is straight and spotless. It would be a contradiction in terms to imagine an arbitrator that is unfair but impartial, corrupt but independent.

3.2 Issues related to the non-fulfilment of the appointment requirements

It is now necessary to observe the possible issues that may occur when the designated arbitrator does not display the characteristics outlined above. On this point the Chinese arbitration system is well structured, since there are three tools available to ensure that the arbitrator does not continue his activity.

3.2.1 The abstention of arbitrators

The first tool is rightly reserved for the arbitrator and is based on his sense of responsibility: in certain circumstances, he "shall be withdrawn from his office" (Arbitration Law, art. 34), which is in line with the idea of abstention present in the Italian system. The arbitrator, at the time of the appointment or during the proceedings, must sign a declaration issued to the parties (CIETAC Rules, art. 31), which reveals any circumstances, existing or becoming known, that may determine a reasonable doubt about his impartiality or independence. If an arbitrator believes that he has an interest in a case and that may deprive him of the required impartiality, he/she will have to declare his relationship with the party in question: close family relationship, monetary/property relationship, or business/trade relationship, and he must apply for the withdrawal from the case voluntarily.

3.2.2 Challenge to the appointment of an arbitrator

The second remedy is represented by the fact that the parties are entitled to challenge the arbitrator when the arbitrator:

- is personally involved in the case or has a family relationship with the parties or their counsel;
- has a personal interest in the proceedings;
- has other relationships with the parties or with their lawyers that could affect an impartial decision of the case;
- meets the parties or their advocates privately or accepts gifts from them or attends banquets with the parties or their lawyers. (Art. 34 Arbitration Law)

The request for challenge is not enough, and in order to avoid an instrumental use of this remedy, the party must illustrate their reasons prior to the first hearing before the tribunal. If the reasons are known only after the first hearing, they must be declared before the end of the last hearing. The acceptance of the request for challenge implies the need to appoint a new arbitrator, for whose appointment the rules provided by the Arbitration Law must be followed.

As regards the activity carried out by the challenged arbitrator, the arbitral tribunal will decide whether the arbitration proceedings have to start over again. The challenge presented by one of the parties is necessary, but even if the parties agree, it will be up to the tribunal to decide whether the previous arbitration proceedings will have to be conducted again. This provision gives a strong discretional power to the arbitral tribunal which, according to the wording of the provision, is not required to justify its decision. In future, in order to ensure greater transparency, it would be preferable to introduce a mechanism to ensure, on the one hand, the rapidity of the procedure (which is clearly affected if the proceedings have be conducted again) and, on the other hand, greater protection for the parties. Rightly, even in the CIETAC Rules, the parties may initiate the procedure for the challenge after having received the statement from the arbitrator regarding the lack of existence of circumstances, existing or supervening, likely to lead to reasonable doubts as to his impartiality or independence if they believe they do not share the conclusion offered by the same arbitrator. The challenge may be submitted, in writing:

1. within 10 days of receipt of the statement made by the arbitrator, in accordance with art. 31. The term is expressly qualified as peremptory; therefore once the term has expired no complaint can be raised by the parties. It is required that the requesting party set out the facts and reasons on which the request is based, supported by the evidence.
2. within 15 days of notification of the formation of the arbitral tribunal or, if subsequent, within 15 days of the date when the party becomes aware of the reasons to challenge the arbitrator. In any case the challenge cannot be submitted after the conclusions offered in the last arbitration hearing.

In both cases the desire to protect different interests is evident: the protection of impartiality on the one hand and the need for speed and certainty on the other. These interests are protected by providing more opportunities to challenge the arbitrator, and by fixing a specific term (10 days or 15 days depending on the case). In both cases the requesting party must inform the other parties, the challenged arbitrator and the other members of the Arbitration Panel.

In order to discourage false statements by the arbitrators, there is a severe sanction if, following the challenge, the arbitrator himself decides to withdraw voluntarily or the other party accepts it: the arbitrator will no longer be part of the arbitral tribunal. This sanction is to be welcomed favourably, since it involves the full compliance with the law on the part of arbitrators and prevents situations that could adversely affect the arbitrator's impartiality and independence.

As for the challenge, the President of CIETAC must decide whether it is motivated or not. The provision that allows the President of CIETAC to decide without a reasoned decision should be eliminated, as the need for a motivation is an element that guarantees the transparency of the decision for the challenging party as well as the arbitrator. This provision attributes a discretionary power to the Chairman of CIETAC. It is also provided that the filing of the challenge shall not deprive the arbitrator of the power/duty to carry out the task assigned. This provision, on the one hand, discourages challenges that have a procrastinating objective and create a series of obstacles to the rapid continuation of the proceedings; on the other hand, it allows for the continuation of the arbitration proceedings, without any suspensions that would only lead to a lengthening of the timing. In future, the norm should be integrated as regards the consequences of the activity performed by the arbitrator against whom the request for recusal was subsequently upheld by the Chairman of CIETAC.

One may wonder: what happens in the period of time between the request for challenge and the decision made by the Chairman of CIETAC? Can the arbitrator continue to act during this period? And, if so, what happens to the action carried out if the challenge is accepted? Will this activity be carried out again in the presence of the new arbitrator? Will he simply continue the process by incorporating all the choices made by the previous arbitrator? The first solution damages the process in terms of speed and cost but is preferable in that it avoids a flawed judgment determined by previous decisions. CIETAC's Rules (art. 33) merely provide that in case of acceptance of the challenge, a new arbitrator will be appointed by the parties or, failing that, by the Chairman of CIETAC. Only after the appointment of the new arbitrator, the arbitral tribunal will decide if and to what extent the activities are to be carried out again.

3.2.3 Replacement of the arbitrator

In order to ensure the impartiality of the arbitrator an additional instrument was provided by the CIETAC Rules (art. 33). This is the power to replace the arbitrator with another person. The Chairman of CIETAC has the power to replace an arbitrator under the following circumstances:

- When the arbitrator is unable to carry out his functions;
- When the arbitrator does not perform his duties according to the CIETAC Rules or within the period specified in the Rules.

A good example is the case of a doubt about the impartiality of the arbitrator and the lack of trust in the arbitrator. In the cases outlined above it is always admitted that the arbitrator may voluntarily withdraw. This is a discretionary power: therefore the exercise thereof is entrusted solely to the Chairman of CIETAC. Discretion is unfortunately high, since, in this case, the decision made by the Chairman of CIETAC may be motivated or lacking motivation. In future, it would be preferable to change the rule in order to insert the obligation to motivate the decision, both in the interests of the arbitrator and the parties. Should the Chairman of CIETAC deem it appropriate to replace the arbitrator, the parties will appoint a new arbitrator and, if the parties fail to do so, the substitute arbitrator will be appointed by the Chairman of CIETAC. In case of replacement, the arbitral tribunal will decide if and to what extent the activities carried out in the presence of the arbitrator replaced will be conducted again. The Arbitration Law does not include a similar rule.

4. The Law on Mediation and Arbitration of Labour Disputes

The labour dispute arbitration system in China is the major Alternative Dispute Resolution (ADR) mechanism for settling conflicts outside labour litigation in court and has been advocated by practitioners and scholars in the areas of industrial relations and human resource management (Shen 2007a, 2007b; Mo 2000b; Thompson 2010). Labour arbitration exists outside the Arbitration Law of the people's Republich of China, whose purpose is to ensure fair and timely arbitration of economic disputes (Mo 2000a). In particular art. 77 of the Arbitration Law stated that arbitration of labour disputes and disputes taking place between members of collectives of farmers concerning contracts for the farming of collectively owned land was to be regulated separately.

Labour disputes can be settled upon request of one or both parties by means of conciliation, mediation or arbitration. In particular, this last system is not so well-known as commercial arbitration to people outside China. This is due to the fact that probably the government has generally been able to apply the administrative and judicial means to control and resolve labour disputes, and also to the fact that before choosing arbitration there are two other forms of ADR that parties can use to resolve labour disputes. Arbitration is considered a form of 'handshake diplomacy' (Shen 2007b: 523). Due to the complexity of litigation for resolving labour disputes, more reliance is placed on labour arbitration because this is the process by which two adversarial parties submit their claims to a third party – the arbitrator – who is supposed to be independent, disinterested and unbiased.

Labour arbitration is part of a wider framework of the evolution of Chinese labour legislation. In fact, in 1950, following the rise to power of the Chinese Communist Party, a Labour Arbitration System was established to regulate the establishment of arbitration commissions in municipalities and to govern the procedure. However, the transformation in the 50s of many private enterprises in state or public enterprises rendered this institution almost useless (the disputes were in fact resolved internally) and this system was abolished in 1957. It was with the labour reform of 1994 that the Chinese legislature intervened to reactivate this tool in order to minimize the risks of social disorder arising after the 70s. Subsequently, the legislature has produced the Law of the People's Republic of China on Labour-disputes Mediation and Arbitration, adopted at the 31st Meeting of the Standing Committee of the Tenth National People's Congress of the People's Republic of China on December 29, 2007 (valid from May 1, 2008), and the Law of the people's Republic of China on employment contract.

Labour arbitration plays a key role in finding a solution when workers claim that their rights have been abused. Labour disputes generally concern the interpretation of specific terms of employment, or particular conditions of work, or labour collective incidents. But a considerable number of labour disputes are brought to arbitration by employers as well (cf. Shen 2007a, in particular p. 56 and ff), concerning such issues as violations of contracts or deliberate damage to enterprise equipment.

4.1 The Arbitration Committee

Chapter 10 of the China Labour Act of 1994 deals with labour disputes (Sections 77–84). In particular, labour arbitration commissions are regulated by articles 79, 81–84. Section 81 is devoted to the composition of the Arbitration Committee. This committee is part of local governments and should consist of representatives of the relevant labour department, of the relevant workers' union and of the enterprise (employer). The provision does not indicate the size of the committee, but states that the number of the members must be odd. Also article 12 deals with the Arbitration Committee foreseeing that it should be established on the basis of geographical location. On this subject, Chapter 3 of the Law of the People's Republic of China on Labour-dispute Mediation and Arbitration of 2007 contains article 17 that specifies that Labour-dispute arbitration commissions shall be set up pursuant to the principles of overall planning, rational geographical distribution and meeting actual needs. The governments of provinces and autonomous regions are free to decide to set up such commissions in cities and counties, and where cities are divided into districts, one or more labour-dispute arbitration commissions may also be established.

Article 19 regulates the composition of arbitration commissions, stating that they are composed of representatives of the administrative department of labour, the trade unions and the enterprises. The duties of these commissions are specified as follows: (1) appoint and dismiss full-time or part-time arbitrators; (2) accept and handle labour-dispute cases; (3) discuss major or complicated labour-dispute cases; and (4) exercise supervision over arbitration. Moreover, article 20 specifies that labour dispute arbitration commissions will have to set up their own rosters of arbitrators.

4.2 The appointment of arbitrators

In China the system to appoint arbitrators for composing labour arbitration tribunals is unique (Zhenqi/Changshuo/Shangyuan 2003). Commissions are specific to this type of arbitration as they judge exclusively labour disputes. The arbitration panel normally consists of three arbitrators, but in the case of a simple dispute, one sole arbitrator can be appointed. The members of the labour arbitration tribunal must be chosen from the roster of arbitrators within five days from the date the application for arbitration is accepted.

As already mentioned, the arbitrator is required to be impartial in order to be able to play this role. Candidates must meet the requirements stated in Art. 20 of the Law on Mediation and Arbitration of 2007, which specifies:

(8) An arbitrator shall be fair-minded and upright, and meet one of the following requirements:
(1) having served as a judge;
(2) being engaged in legal research or teaching with a professional title at the intermediary level or above;
(3) possessing legal knowledge and having been engaged in human resources management, trade union work or other professional work for five full years; or
(4) being a lawyer, having been in legal practice for three full years.

The arbitrator must provide proof of possessing moral qualifications (i.e. of being righteous, upright, independent and impartial), as well as of a high level of professional qualification in law and other personal characteristics. Moreover, he must possess actual working experience in the object of the labour dispute, acquired in this particular field during a reasonable period of time. One of the major advantages of arbitration is that parties can appoint persons they consider honest, in whom they have confidence and who have the necessary legal and technical expertise for settling the dispute that often includes not only specific aspects of a labour relationship but also complex matters concerning highly specialized fields such as pension issues, medical fees, or work injury compensation.[8] However, it has been noted (e.g. Fan 2013) that it is often impossible and difficult to control the actual qualifications, experience and expertise of arbitartors because such information is not public.

In exercising his duties, the arbitrator will hear the parties and their respective claims, acquire the arguments and evidence submitted by the parties and issue a ruling in favour of one of the two. Indeed, when the parties agree to refer the matter to arbitration, they agree to accept the decision of the arbitrator as final and binding. If arbitration fails, the problem may be taken to a court.

Arbitrators may be part time or full time. Those who serve full time normally belong to a local administration. Those who serve part time must be chosen among professionals of the area of labour law, or among trade union officials, or professors of labour law, or attorneys experienced in labour law.[9] Arbitrators should also have adequate expertise and knowledge in order to deal with cases effectively and fairly. This is the reason why "the selection of the members of the arbitral tribunal is probably the single most important step in arbitration process, yet is one that can be fraught with unknown consequences" (McLaren 2003: 523).

The parties may be assisted by one or two lawyers or may be replaced by 'agents' who have been given specific proxy and can thus

8 See cases in Lu (2008), in particular notes 73, 78 and 80 on pages 260–261.

9 According to Shen (2007a: 113), "in 2005 there were 7,424 full time and 12,906 part time labour arbitrators nationally, 5,575 union officials had gained arbitrator licences (ACFTU 2005)".

present the case and participate in the sessions (art. 24 Law on Labour Dispute Mediation and Arbitration of 2007). The parties may stand in arbitration and reach an agreement that closes the procedure at any time. Third parties who have an interest in the dispute may participate in the arbitration procedure or can be notified to appear by the Commission (Art. 23 Law on Labour Dispute Mediation and Arbitration of 2007). With regard to participation in the procedure, Article 37 provides for the possibility to appoint an expert to examine particular specialized situations.

However, there are 'silences' in the law. For example, it does not stipulate that both men and women are eligible to be appointed as officers of the commission and that all officers must comply with a code of behavior or conduct. The law should also specify whether a person appointed as an officer/commissioner is empowered to undertake both conciliation/mediation and arbitration tasks, as well as provide information and advisory/training services to employers and workers.

4.3 The change of arbitrators

Art. 33 deals with the withdrawal of arbitrators. The article clearly specifies the cases in which this should take place:

(9) An arbitrator shall withdraw, and the parties also have the right to apply orally or in writing for his withdrawal, under one of the following circumstances:
(1) He is a party to the case in question or a close relative of a party or its agent;
(2) He has an interest in the case;
(3) He has other relations with a party to the case or its agent, which may affect impartial award; or
(4) He meets with a party or its agent without authorization or accepts invitation to dinners or gifts therefrom.

The labour-dispute arbitration commission shall, in a timely manner, make a decision on the application for withdrawal and notify the parties of the decision orally or in writing.

Therefore a party may challenge an arbitrator appointed by him, or in whose appointment he had participated, only for reasons of which he becomes aware after the appointment has been made. This is a very important provision, as a good arbitration system needs to be impartial, independent, immune and neutral. This means that an impartial arbitrator is one who is not biased in favour, or prejudiced against, a particular party or its case. It also means that an independent arbitrator has no close financial or professional relationship with a particular party or its counsel, and should be neutral in dealing with disputes.

On written request for recusal, the Commission must promptly decide, and notify the parties, verbally or in writing, of the composition of the Board of Arbitration within five days of acceptance of the case. In the event that the referee extorts or accepts bribes, engages in malpractices for personal gain, or perverts the law in making incorrect awards, revocation is made directly by the Commission (Art. 34).

In particular, article 34 specifies the cases in which arbitrators must be changed. The withdrawal can be requested by any members of the committee when there are the circumstances indicated in the article. The provision states that:

(10) Where an arbitrator is under the circumstances prescribed in Subparagraph (4) of Article 33 of this Law, or extorts for or accepts bribes, engages in malpractices for personal gain, or perverts the law in making awards, he shall bear legal liability in accordance with law. The labor-dispute arbitration commission shall dismiss him.

Similarly article 28 of the CIETAC Rules provides that any appointed arbitrator having a personal interest in the case has to disclose such interest to the Arbitration Commission and request to be withdrawn from his office. Some scholars may consider these requirements, imposed by Chinese legislation, as an improper restriction on party autonomy (Fan 2013: 65). But the majority of experts are convinced that when an arbitrator does not meet these characteristics or when he loses his qualities of independence, neutrality and impartiality, the fair resolution of the disputes may be at great risk.

5. Conclusion

The analysis of the two PRC laws on arbitration has highlighted that, from a juridical point of view, the intent of the Chinese legislature was to place arbitration in China in line with international practice, by introducing a few key, internationally recognized principles. Our study shows that this aim has been reached, as the requirements to become arbitrators are those that are generally recognized, that is, an arbitrator is required to settle the disputes between parties impartially, fairly, diligently and efficiently. The respect of the undelined features is guaranteed by three specific tools that are meant to avoid that the arbitrator continues in his official role if he does not meet the requirements prescribed.

Our investigation has also demonstrated that the procedures for the appointment and challenge of arbitrators may not always prove to be as smooth as Chinese arbitration norms indicate. Indeed, some of the requirements to be met by possible candidates in order to be appointed as arbitrators are quite subjective. Instead, in other systems, such as that of Taiwan, such constraints do not exist or are less binding: people who are willing to be appointed as arbitrators are not required to possess a specific background, but merely to be available to undergo some training 'on the job' in order to be included in the Taiwanese roster of possible arbitrators (Chen 2012).

As this study has highlighted, the issue of impartiality of arbitrators is a very complex matter, which needs to be regulated in a careful way in order to guarantee a smooth and fair resolution of both commercial and labour disputes. This requirement is particularly important in a dynamic context like that of China, in which the need for a well regulated, yet flexible, solution of commercial and labour disputes is crucial to the success of its economy.

References

Abrams, Stan 2007. Danone v. Wahaha: No Sympathy. At <http:// www. chinahearsay.com/danone-wahaha-no-sympathy/>.

Bartolini, Francesco / Delconte, Roberto C. (eds) 2001. *Il codice dell'arbitrato* [The Arbitration Code]. Piacenza: La Tribuna.

Bhatia, Vijay / Candlin, Christopher / Wei, Sandy 2001. *Legal Discourse in Multilingual and Multicultural Contexts: A Preliminary Study*. Research Group Report. Hong Kong: City University of Hong Kong.

Brown, Ronald 2010. *Understanding Labor and Employment Law in China*. New York: Cambridge University Press.

Chang, Sheng W. 2001. Cietac Amended Arbitration Rules 2000 Embrace the New Century. *Yearbook of Commercial Arbitration* 26, 366–375.

Chen, Wei-Jen 2012. Separate but Equal in Arbitration? An Analysis on Ad Hoc Arbitration of Taiwan and East Asia. *Contemporary Asia Arbitration Journal* 5/1, 107–132.

Corona, Isabel 2011. Arbitration Recontextualized. *World Englishes* 30/1, 129–140.

Fan, Kun 2013. *Arbitration in China. A Legal and Cultural Analysis*. Portland, Ore.: Hart.

Georgiou, Philip 2011. The Real Risk of Bias in 'Chinese Style' Arbitration. *Asian Dispute Review* 2, 89–91.

Guillaumonde, Robert 2001. *L'arbitrage en Chine*. Lyon: Adamas.

Horrigan, Brenda / Hess, Felix / Lin Mok, Siew [3]2011. Arbitration in China: Recent Developments. In Moser, Michael J. (ed.) *Business Disputes in China*. Huntington, NY: Juris, Chapter 5.

Hughes, Justin 1997. Foreign *lis alibi pendens*, Non-Chinese Majority Tribunals and Other Problems of Neutrality in Cietac Arbitration. *Arbitration International* 13/1, 63–84.

Jin, Chua Eu 2005. Arbitration in the People's Republic of China. *Asian International Arbitration Journal* 1/1, 18–28.

Jin, Huang / Guomin, Lu 2001. New Developments in Chinese Private International Law, 135.

Levant, Ezra 2007. Danone vs. Wahaha. At <http://ezralevant.com/ 2009/ 08/danone-vswahaha.html>.

Lu, Haina 2008. New Developments in China's Labor Dispute Resolution System: Better Protection for Workers' Rights? *Comparative Labor Law and Policy Journal* 29, 246–274.

McLaren, Douglas E. 2003. Party-appointed vs List-appointed Arbitrators: A Comparison. *Journal of International Arbitration* 20/3, 233–245.

Mo, John Shijian 2000a. Probing the Uniformity of the Arbitration System in the PRC. *Journal of International Arbitration* 17/3, 1–54.

Mo, John Shijan 2000b. Probing Labour Arbitration in PRC. *Journal of International Arbitration* 17/5, 19–83.

Moser, Michael J. / Yuen Peter 2005. The New Cietac Arbitration Rules. *Arbitration International* 21/3, 391–404.

Shuangyuan, Li / Guomin, Lu 1996. The law of International Civil Procedure in China. *Yearbook of Private International Law* 1, 135–156.

Shen, Jie 2007a. *Labour Disputes and their Resolution in China*. Oxford: Chandos.

Shen, Jie 2007b. Labour Arbitration in China. *Employee Relations* 29/5, 520–539.

Thompson, Clive 2010. Dispute Prevention and Resolution in Public Services Labour Relations: Good Policy and Practice. *Working Paper* 277, Geneva: ILO. <http://www.ilo.org/wcmsp5/groups/ public/---ed_dialogue/---sector/documents/publication/wcms_ 161204.pdf>.

Zhenqi, Wang / Changshuo, Wang / Shangyuan, Zheng 2003. *Labour Dispute Settlement System in China: Past and Perspectives*. IDE Asian Law Series 22. <http://www.ide.go.jp/English/ Publish/ Download/Als/ pdf/22.pdf>.

Focus on discursive practices

Tarja Salmi-Tolonen

How Do East and West Meet in Arbitration Discourse?

This chapter seeks to map out attributes of cultural similarities and differences concerning dispute resolution mechanisms and practices in the Western countries and Asian countries. It is a well-known fact that there has been a rush of Western companies to Asia over the past decades, whose aim is to profit from its economic growth. By analyzing surveys and dispute indexes, cases, and media coverage I try to discover both pragmatic and linguistic markers of similar or diverse attitudes towards the demands of global trading relationships both in partnership and conflict. The purpose of this chapter is also to try and find a methodology for a more detailed discursive and textual comparative study of arbitration approaches in the Western world and in Asia.

1. Introduction

Almost every facet of reality in matters of business, law and language hinges on contextual factors. This relationship is undoubtedly complex and involves an incessant interaction between context and law, business and language, which, for their part, have an impact on the context. This chapter looks at some issues that foreign firms face hoping to do business in Asia, in particular the cultural and legal differences that may cause problems. The purpose is first of all to try and find focal points that can be meaningful concerning attitudes and approaches to problem solving and hence also international commercial arbitration.

In recent years many companies have entered into joint ventures with Chinese and other Asian companies. Though many of these have been successful, it is the failures that have attracted most publicity and speculation. Therefore the failures are also more easily accessible to researchers.

International Commercial Arbitration (hereinafter, ICA) has become the obvious choice for solving disputes between international contracting parties not least because of its private and confidential nature. The initial hypothesis is that since ICA is international or trans-national by definition, national cultures or national legal cultures do not play a big role in it. However, as Karton (2013: 234) points out, the question remains whether ICA has developed and now possesses its own culture which interacts and competes with national legal cultures.

This observation aside, local or regional culture plays a role in business relations, and dysfunction in contractual relationships may be caused by different assumptions due to cultural understanding, and therefore lead to arbitration. Also presuppositions concerning business partnership may differ in ways that date far back in history. This chapter highlights some potential sources of misunderstanding particularly from the Western point of view.

2. Material and Methods

Traditionally research is organized around one discipline, but research topics such as international commercial arbitration require a multidisciplinary approach. In this chapter culture as a topic and research method in general is discussed. Then a summary of trends revealed by dispute indexes is presented. After that an autopsy of a real life case is discussed and finally opinions and research focusing on ICA are summarized. To conclude, a framework for the next phase of the comparative study will be proposed. The material studied for this chapter is composed of Dispute Indexes in the countries in Northern Europe, especially Denmark, Finland, Norway, Sweden. Reference is made to books on transnational dispute management written by researchers and practising arbitrators from the USA, Europe, Asia (China, Hong Kong, Singapore, Indian Subcontinent), journal articles on joint venture (JV) cases where parties are from European and Asian countries, or USA and Asian countries, interviews with arbitrators and lawyers (counsels). The interviews were collected within research projects led by Professor Vijay K. Bhatia on International Commercial Arbitration discourse.[1]

3. Culture

The *a priori* assumption here is that all communication to a large extent depends on culture. The challenge of communication arises from different legal and cultural backgrounds both in transnational business relations and dispute resolution. The processes involved in communication are deeply rooted in culture, emotion and education as Flader and Nappert (2010: 10) also note in their study on the psychology of persuasion in arbitration.

However, *culture* as a concept is at risk of theoretical blurring. While discussing international commercial arbitration it is necessary to consider culture at various levels. First of all there is the general culture of a certain community, the culture of business transactions and the legal culture of the parties. All these are naturally intertwined but can be discussed separately. Without a doubt, by preplanning and including an arbitration clause in a contract, parties to a contract aim at avoiding some of the cultural and legal differences in case a delivery is delayed, the goods are damaged, or the terms of the contract have been given different interpretations or where the language allows double meaning. People fail to cooperate when they do not have a common understanding of what has been agreed on (Salmi-Tolonen 2011: 86).

Because of the many-faceted character and fuzziness of the concept, it is difficult to find a widely accepted definition of culture. But as Professor Edward Dower (2010) quite aptly put it: "Culture is how

1 *Generic Integrity in Legislative Discourse in Multilingual and Multicultural Contexts* and *International Commercial Arbitration Practices: A Discourse Analytical Study*, both supported by UGC Research Grant Council Hong Kong.

we do things here!" This seems to be applicable to all three levels mentioned above.

Naturally, it is important to bear in mind that neither East nor West are monolithic cultures and what is understood by Western culture or Eastern culture depends very much on whether we are looking at it from the Eastern or the Western point of view. Asian sources referring to the West often seem to have North America or the USA in mind or more generally the English-speaking world. Today, Western sources referring to matters of business in Asia often have either China or the Indian subcontinent in mind whereas some time ago the focus was on Japan.

It is also important to bear in mind that we cannot help looking at cultural phenomena through the lens of our own culture, which filters our understanding of the foreign phenomena even if we do perceive them. On the other hand, we tend to take our own culture as given and do not necessarily even notice habits or practices that others find peculiar. We may need an outsider to point out the peculiarities. Contrastive or comparative studies both in law and linguistics have introduced the concept of a *tertium comparationis* for this purpose to represent a neutral yardstick (see e.g. Van Hoecke/Warrington 1998: 495; Jaszczolt 2003: 441). There are also many prototypical views which may lead us astray because they are generalizations and do not necessarily always apply. Inevitably the point of view in this chapter is based on Western culture and Western concepts. The non-Western phenomena are seen through Western eyes.

In this chapter, we focus on northern Asia representing the East (the Orient) and Europe and European-based cultures representing the West.

3.1 Directness v Indirectness

In the Western world a general assumption is that communication in Europe and Asia differs most in two respects, namely, directness *versus* indirectness and *politeness* and *face*. Since all these are essential in business relations, a few observations can be considered appropriate here. Westerners are generally thought to express themselves more directly and Asians more indirectly. Naturally there are scalar nuances within these two cultures as well.

3.2 Face

Face is a concept that often comes up when cultures are discussed. No one wants to lose face but it is generally considered to be taken more seriously in Asia than in the Western world. Face is defined as the public self-image every adult portrays, which must be attended to in interaction. A *face-threatening act* (FTA) is an act which deliberately threatens the face needs of others. It can take the form of a bald claim or a bald denial (Brown/Levinson 1987). Linguistic signaling of politeness is not necessarily signaled by specific words or phrases but "implicated by the semantic structure of the whole utterance" as Brown and Levinson (1987: 22) suggest.

3.3 Politeness

Politeness is described as a social norm, or a set of prescriptive social rules. The well-known politeness theory in linguistic pragmatics was first formulated by Brown and Levinson in 1978 and reissued ten years later in 1987. Politeness theory is relevant when trying to understand the similarities and differences in a communicative situation such as business negotiations, in particular, where the parties come from divergent cultures. Where politeness and indirectness are concerned, the more indirect or off-record a suggestion or request is, the more polite the utterance is perceived to be, and therefore this *saves face* more than a direct request.

The situation is complicated however by the fact that what is considered polite in one culture may be less so in another. Although the Eastern way of communicating is generally considered more indirect, a Western person working in China may get disconcerted by questions such as "How much money do you make?" or "How much do you weigh?" or other similar direct questions not usually considered appropriate to be put to a business partner or a mere acquaintance in

Europe.[2] The difference between direct or indirect seems to be rather subtle although Leech (2007: 167) contends that despite the differences, there is no East-West divide in politeness (see also views on Chinese requests in Chen/He/Hu 2013).

3.4 Guanxi

Guanxi as a term is less well known in the West although many know it as a concept. It is defined by *The Oxford English Dictionary* as "(in China) the system of social networks and influential relationships which facilitate business and other dealings."[3] The literal meaning according to Oxford dictionaries in Mandarin Chinese is 'connection' but is usually translated as 'relationship'. It seems to be a complex cultural concept and difficult for Westerners to comprehend. Consequently it is often misunderstood. It has been said that the importance of relationships in Chinese culture dates back even beyond Confucius, who was the one who reflected the society's values of his time and whose thinking was influential also in Japan (see Van Hoecke/Warrington 1998: 506 on Confucius and legal cultures).[4] The ideal society of non-litigation culture of China is also attributed to Confucius (see e.g. Zhang 2014).

4. Legal culture

What then are the characteristics of legal culture on which there seems to be some kind of an agreement? Bell (1995: 70) defines legal culture as "a specific way in which values, practices, and concepts are integrated into the operation of legal institutions and the interpretation of legal

2 PC Barbara Chaplin, a Canadian lawyer, who worked in China for ten years and studied Mandarin Chinese and culture. She also brought the concept of *guanxi* to my attention.

3 <http://www.oxforddictionaries.com/definition/english/guanxi>.

4 *The Analects of Confucius*. Translated by Arthur Waley. New York: Vintage Books, 1938.

texts". Law is more than just a set of rules or concepts. It is also a social practice within a legal community (Van Hoecke/Warrington 1998: 498). Sometimes *legal culture* and *legal tradition* are used in parallel, which indicates that legal culture is something old. This connotation presents a problem as some of the cultures are the result of very recent developments, such as, for instance, European legal culture (Van Hoecke 2007: 82) or the above-mentioned ICA culture.

In methodological studies of law, the concept of legal system seems to be challenged by the concept of legal culture. *Legal culture* is a ubiquitous catch-all expression especially when differences between legal orders or legal families are described. The meaning of this expression is far from unequivocal (Salmi-Tolonen 2011: 7). Karton (2013: 18) is also of the opinion that the word *culture* carries an analytical baggage which makes it problematic but that it is still the only word that encompasses "the various social factors that affect decision-making: standard practices, interests, values, goals and attitudes." On similar lines, comparatists generally agree that

> one must take account not only of legislative rules, judicial decisions, the 'law in the books', and also of general conditions of business, customs, and practices, but in fact of everything whatever which helps to mould human conduct in the situation under consideration. (Zweigert/Kötz 1998: 11)

The concept is wide and for it to function properly as an analytical tool for comparing legal cultures it has to be broken down into meaningful categories. Generally there are four distinguishable broad cultural families in the world: African culture, Asian culture, Islamic culture and cultures with European roots (Europe, America, Oceania) which is generally called the Western culture (Van Hoecke/Warrington 1998: 502).

4.1 Individual v collectivist

Where cultures and their way of communicating were above characterised as direct or indirect, legal cultures can be characterised as either *individual or collectivist*. Western legal culture has been characterised by individualism and rationalism. By individualism is meant a belief in the autonomy and total liberty of an individual in society. The counterpart for this conception is collectivism, which according to Van Hoecke / Warrington (1998: 503) is typical of non-Western legal cultures. The Asian collectivist approach was determined under the Confucian theory of the natural order of reality (see note 4 above and Van Hoecke/Warrington 1998: 506).

4.2 Rational v irrational

Another dichotomy used to characterise legal cultures is *rational v irrational*. Rationalism means the belief in infinite possibilities "available to human spirit to know, structure and master reality in an objective manner" (Van Hoecke/Warrington 1998: 503). The opposing concept (irrationalism) again "believes in a preponderance of sentiment and metaphysical elements, in order to know, structure and master the reality" (Van Hoecke/Warrington 1998: 503).

4.3 Discussion

A Chinese proverb says:

> It is better to die of starvation than to become a thief; it is better to be vexed to death than to bring a lawsuit. [5]

While corroborating the ideal of non-litigation in China, this old proverb seems to be in line with today's preferred tendency of referring disputes to arbitration, which is private, rather than to public courts (see e.g. Zhang 2014). Peaceful conflict resolution is sought after all over the world. After the introduction of the UNCITRAL Model Law on International Commercial Arbitration in 1985,[6] a number of developed jurisdictions adopted the model law or either reformed or amended their old

5 PC Ms Qian Chen 16.10.2014.

6 Amended in 2006, <http://www.uncitral.org/uncitral/en/uncitral_texts/arbitration/1985Model_arbitration.html>.

legislation in accordance with the model law (see generally Bhatia/ Candlin/Engberg/Trosborg 2003; Bhatia/Candlin/Gotti 2003). The model law has been adopted by 67 states in 97 jurisdictions. Arbitration as an alternative dispute resolution method is increasingly popular in international commercial disputes for various reasons not least because it is private and the parties have more control over the proceeding than they would in litigation. It also involves anticipation, planning ahead and taking initiative at the time the business contract is being designed; in addition, it is considered more effective and economical.

Factors that have impact on legal culture and legal discourse are:

- Historical
- Political
- Social
- Legal
- Linguistic

Historical for the obvious reasons that law and language have been developed over a long period of time. Language directs our cognitive processes, reshapes our values, reflects our social reality and constitutes reality. In addition, in most jurisdictions the statute book contains parts which date back a long time, hundreds of years in history. Political, because legislative bodies are elected on political grounds which means that laws are often a result of political compromises; furthermore the political system reflects on legislation and legal language. This is also the reality that has to be taken into consideration when studying international arbitration because arbitration is only possible in jurisdictions where the law enables parties in dispute to refer their case to arbitration, a private judicial procedure. Social factors determine the issues that are regulated. In welfare states, for instance, distributive laws are needed to provide for the benefits the citizens are entitled to receive and on what grounds. Linguistic factors arise first of all from the primacy of the constitutive function which constitutes the institutions. This, of course, requires collective intentionality. Furthermore there are the conventions characteristic of each language (Salmi-Tolonen 2008: 30).

These are the issues that need to be considered while comparing arbitration discourses.

5. International commercial arbitration culture

Culture, as a concept, is at risk of theoretical blurring, as was noted above. Nevertheless legal comparatists especially have found it appropriate to explain differences between jurisdictions as being due to legal culture. The vagueness of the concept may be a reason for its attractiveness, as Van Hoecke (2007) points out. In particular, researchers who discuss the tension emerging in the globalisation and harmonisation processes seem to find it convenient.

While discussing comparative law as a scientific tool, Sourgens (2007: 3) points out that the basic approach of scientific comparative law is rather intuitive and generally starts from a specific question and then moves on to larger contexts. One can start, for instance, from questions of legal procedure and analyze them in terms of legal principles and then look at the respective court systems. The interplay between the rules in application are then examined in the light of their place in the legal system in general. Finally, Sourgens (2007: 3) suggests that a comparatist puts the systems in perspective of their own historical, political and cultural environments. This view is also in accordance with Gessner/Hoeland/Varga (1996: 245), whose model I propose to use in the forthcoming analysis of arbitration in Asia. It involves legal norms, legal practice and the science of law, institutional actors: legal counsels, businesses, parties to a dispute where feasible. All these sectors contribute to the analysis of arbitration in particular where both Western and Asian parties are involved.

Karton (2013: 18) quite appropriately points out that there is no reason in principle why the ICA field could not possess its own, distinct culture. He is of the opinion that there is reason to believe that such a culture is already developing.

> Cultural theories can never provide the kind of deterministic explanation that science offers, but an impressionistic account of ICA that includes the essential variable of culture is preferable to a concrete-seeming account without it. (Karton 2013: 10)

Intergovernmental coalitions and globalisation in the world of business place pressure on national legal cultures. We no longer live in the confines of our own jurisdictions, and legislators, who once were autonomous, must now interact with other national legal cultures. In addition to the more formal means, model laws, and so on, harmonisation in the practice of international arbitration will no doubt be advanced by the practitioners in international arbitration facing similar cultural clashes, gaining and sharing experiences.

For comparing arbitration cultures I propose approaches similar to those that Gessner/Hoeland/Varga (1996: 245) propose for comparing legal cultures: legal theoretical and legal dogmatic comparisons, legal comparison, comparative implementation research, comparison of legal systems. While studying these we also need to consider the historical, political, and social and linguistic factors. This analysis and comparison will be done in the second forthcoming part of the Asian Arbitration Discourse research project.

Despite the analytical baggage the word 'culture' carries, as Karton (2013) notes, it is the best word to encompass both the specific instances of arbitral decision-making and the overall subject of this enquiry – the social context within which arbitrators decide disputes. Karton (2013: 40) further notes that culture is the only word that adequately encompasses the various social factors that affect decision-making: standard practices, interests, values, goals, and attitudes.

6. An autopsy of a joint venture

Next, a case of joint venture between a Chinese and a European company will be described. The purpose is to see if any lessons can be learnt from these experiences. The case description summarized below is by Dickinson (2007).

An Autopsy: Danone v Wahaha
The Facts
The Wahaha Joint Venture was formed in February 1996. At the start there were three participants in the JV. Chinese Hangzhou Wahaha Food Group Co. Ltd. (hereinafter Wahaha), Danone Group, a French corporation (hereinafter Danone) and Bai Fu Quin Ltd. a Hong Kong corporation (hereinafter Baifu). Danone and Baifu did not invest directly in the JV. Instead they formed Jin Jia Investment Co. Ltd. a Singapore corporation (Jinjia). Upon the formation of the JV, Wahaha owned 49% of the shares and Jinjia owned 51% of the shares. This structure led to immediate understandings between the participants. The 51%/ 49% ownership was not understood in the same way. Wahaha considered the ownership to be 49 Wahaha plus 25,5 Danone plus 25,5 Jinjia and that they were, from this point of view, the majority shareholder. Wahaha therefore felt comfortable enough to transfer their trademark to the JV. They felt further at ease because Jinjia was a Hong Kong company and therefore the Chinese partners outnumbered the foreign side.
Two years later in 1998, Danone bought out the interest of Baifu in Jinjia. Danone became a 100% owner of Jinjia and effectively the 51% owner of the JV and exercised legal control over the JV because they then had a right to elect the board of directors.
This was a shock to Wahaha because in China 49%/51% is practically the same as 50%/50%. Secondly because the trademark transferred to JV in this case belonged to the state not possible to transfer to a foreign company. Although from the legal standpoint the result was implied by the structure of the JV from the beginning it was clear Wahaha did not understand the implications. Therefore there was a lot of resentment and felt that they had been misled by Danone. The result, of course, was a cultural clash. Over 2007 both Danone and Wahaha filed for arbitration. Danone applied before Stockholm and California State court. Wahaha for their part before Hangzhou Arbitration Commission.
What are the lessons to be learned then? The legal proceedings were accompanied by bitter verbal attacks and the Chinese directors said it would be impossible to continue to operate in a joint venture with Danone. The dispute thus threatens to destroy a successful joint venture company in China. The 51% control of a joint venture may work in Europe or the USA but seldom in China especially if the control is gained over legal maneuvers. Commentators say that even though Danone acted within the strict requirements of the law, Wahaha did not see it this way.[7]

In a culture where relationship between business partners is considered highly important this should be anticipated and studied carefully

7 Dickinson in *China Economic Review* (2007). There is also an excellent analysis of this case by Isabel Corona (2011).

beforehand together with the financial and legal benefits and risks. What may work in one part of the world may not work in another. Had both parties been observant of the divergent cultural factors (direct v indirect, rational v irrational) and not only legal factors, there might be another story to be told. Generally speaking, it is not necessarily a lack of legal, technical or business expertise that causes the failure of a contract, it is more often than not a lack of communication. A recent press release announced a new JV between a Finnish company and a Chinese company:

> The joint venture between Metso and LiuGong will develop the Chinese track-mounted crushing and screening business
> *Metso Corporation's press release on February 17, 2014 at 10.00 a.m. EET*
>
> Metso and Guangxi Liugong Group Co., Ltd. (LiuGong) have obtained all necessary approvals from the Chinese authorities and the 50%–50% joint venture between the two companies has been officially established. [8]

In this case, the ownership shares are divided equally between the partners. There is no way of telling whether the other companies' past failures have had any effect on the decision but at least the starting point seems healthier than in the Wahaha Danone joint venture.

7. Surveys

It was mentioned above that international arbitration has increased over the recent years. In order to see whether they have changed and how they have changed, two surveys, one conducted in the UK and another in the Nordic countries will be analysed here. Surveys are conducted on a fairly regularly basis: the one in the Nordic countries every other year so that some tendencies can perhaps be detected. The surveys are

8 *China Daily* 18.2.2014 last visited Sep 8, 2014. <http://www.chinadaily.com.cn/business/2014-02/18/content_17289237.htm>.

conducted by Roschier,[9] one of the leading law firms based in Finland but which also operates in other Nordic countries. The other one is an independent academic survey conducted by the School of International Arbitration at Queen Mary University in London in 2013. The survey was financed by a world-wide consultant company PriceWaterhouse-Coopers, UK (hereinafter PwC),[10] who have commissioned several surveys on international arbitration over the years.

In the 2014 survey Roschier Disputes Index focused on the largest organizations in the four Nordic countries operating in the following industry sectors: real estate, construction, information, communications technology, engineering and machinery, energy, utility and other. The PwC survey, instead, focused on identifying differences in perceptions in three major sectors of the economy, namely, energy, construction and financial services. Construction and energy are the lines of industry which are shared by the two surveys.

The total number of companies in the Roschier survey was 133 and the response rate 74%. This means that it is statistically possible to draw conclusions related to the various industry sectors. The overall findings indicate that the dispute resolution market is relatively stable in the countries studied. Nevertheless some of the findings are really interesting. The survey shows that ADR, alternative dispute resolution methods, are more common in Norway than in Denmark, Finland and Sweden and that Finland and Sweden have a stronger preference for arbitration than do Denmark and Norway. Even if the Nordic countries have legislation and court systems very similar to each other so much so that in comparative law they are considered to form a legal family, the Nordic law, some differences can be found. The question then remains what causes these differences and – if the cause can be found – how this finding can be used when studying the preferences of ADR in other countries.

The PwC survey questionnaire was completed by 101 respondents and after completing the questionnaire 30 respondents were interviewed in order to gather qualitative information (PwC 2013: 24).

---

9 <http://www.roschier.com/sites/default/files/Roschier%20Disputes%20Index%202014.pdf>.

10 <http://www.pwc.com/arbitrationstudy>.

According to the Roschier survey, arbitration is the preferred dispute resolution method in the lines of industry studied with a 61% share. They point out that this figure is lower than that obtained in their 2010 and 2012 surveys. Then more than 70% of the respondents said arbitration was their preferred method. As was already noted Finland and Sweden still favour arbitration. Of the Finnish companies 74% preferred arbitration as opposed to Danish companies who reported 42% preference. If only Finnish and Swedish companies are considered, there is a slight increase in the preference of arbitration. An intriguing question then arises: what are the factors behind these differences?

According to the PwC's global survey, businesses continue to show preference for using arbitration over litigation for transnational disputes. The question put to the respondents was: Rank the following dispute resolution mechanisms in order of preference. The respondents then ranked arbitration, court litigation, adjudication / expert determination and mediation. Arbitration ranked first more often than any of the other methods. It was preferred by 52% of the respondents. The survey also confirms that arbitration is more popular in some industry sectors (2013: 4, 6).

The Roschier survey then looked into the factors for the choice of arbitration. It is worth comparing the lists of the decisive factors behind the preference of arbitration and the preference of litigation. The survey was conducted so that preferences were given points based on importance. In Table 1 only the order of importance is given, not the points. Interestingly the topmost decisive factor for the choice of litigation is lower cost. This seems to be against the general belief that arbitration is cost effective. On the arbitration side cost is only on the fourth place. In addition the respondents also commented on the heavy procedure of arbitration and the extended length of time. This means that the efficiency that is sought after is not always achieved in reality. Efficiency is the second most decisive factor of choosing arbitration in this survey. If the procedure is time-consuming it cannot be effective which also means that the costs increase.

The second factor in favour of litigation is that the judgment can be appealed whereas the opposite, impossibility of appealing an award, works in favour of arbitration and is on the fifth place. No doubt this preference is very much dependent on the case and the line of business. Enforceability is favoured by the respondents in both arbitration and litigation. This property is one that these two dispute resolutions methods share as against the other alternative methods, such as mediation or conciliation.

	Arbitration	*Litigation*
1	Non-public nature of procedure	Lower costs
2	Efficiency of procedure	Judgment can be appealed
3	Expertise of arbitrators	Public nature of procedure
4	Cost	Efficiency of procedure
5	Not possible to appeal	Subject matter of the dispute
6	Enforceability of award	Level of complexity
7	Predictability of result	Enforceability of the judgment
8	International nature of dispute	Neutrality of decision maker
9	Complexity of dispute	Dispute value
10	Subject matter of the dispute	Expertise of judges
11	Flexibility of procedure	Predictability of results
12	Neutrality of arbitrators	Domestic nature of dispute
13	Dispute value	Flexibility of procedure
14	Domestic nature of dispute	International nature of dispute

Table 1. Decisive factors for choice according to the Roschier survey (2014: 8).

When the different countries were singled out, respondents from Finland and Sweden were more likely than the others to identify the long duration of the proceedings as disadvantages of litigation. Although one cannot draw too far-reaching conclusions from these results, as the survey also notes (Roschier 2014: 9), it nevertheless signals cause and effect between the efficiency of public courts and the preference of arbitration. One general remark against litigation deserves to be highlighted here, namely that a public court is hardly "the place for sensible environment for a business solution" (Roschier 2014: 9).

In the PwC survey several of the respondents who were interviewed are reported to have mentioned 'fairness' above all other considerations when asked what they look for in a dispute resolution mechanism (PwC 2013: 7). The researchers who conducted the survey do not say how they would explain this opinion. Perhaps one can try and explain it bearing in mind that arbitration was preferred particularly in transnational cases. Companies may find that court litigation might not be fair when considered globally.

Both surveys show that the line of industry is a strong variable for choosing the preferred dispute resolution mechanism. Both surveys single out the construction sector where arbitration is more popular (PwC 2013: 7; Roschier 2014: 13). The Roschier Index (2013) combines real estate to construction and energy to utility but otherwise the surveys seem to be compatible and point to the same direction.

These kinds of surveys help us see that although the preference for arbitration over litigation has increased, it has not increased unequivocally in all the studied countries or industry sectors. In spite of the fact of what the respondents say are the reasons for choosing arbitration rather than litigation, one thing is clear: there is a direct reverse relationship between whether the court procedures are considered effective and the preference for ADR. Therefore, as was proposed above, a comparison should combine different sections of legal practice and also that even if the overall result of a survey points to one direction it may not be applied evenly to different jurisdictions in the survey.

To conclude, the surveys show that parameters such as speediness and lower cost are no longer seen as the reality in international arbitration. Companies are generally very concerned about the rising costs of arbitration; furthermore public courts are seen in some cases to be more effective and less costly. Instead the decisive factors for choosing arbitration over litigation or other dispute resolution methods seem to depend on the line of industry which has a strong link to 'the enhanced technical nature' of the dispute which favours arbitration as opposed to 'the legal nature' in e.g. the financial sector which consequently prefers litigation (PwC 2013: 7). Also jurisdiction and the efficiency of the court system and the businesses' trust on the court system play a part particularly in transnational disputes.

8. ICA in common law v civil law countries

Contractual interpretation in civil law and common law jurisdictions is based on fundamentally different perspectives. International arbitrators may be called to interpret contracts under principles of law that are not known to all parties although it can be said that at least one civil law view is well-known, namely,

> that it is the *intention* of the promisor which counts and the common law view is that priority is given to the external phenomenon of expression. The internal will of the promisor is treated as significant "only so far as it coincides with the normal objective meaning that a reasonable person would attribute to its expression". (Zweigert/Kötz 1998: 401)

The following quote from one of the eminent Law Lords supports what was said by Zweigert/Kötz (1998: 401):

> The meaning of words is a matter of dictionaries and grammars; the meaning of the document is what the parties using those words against the relevant background would reasonably have been understood to mean. (UKHL 38[16] 2009, speech of Lord Hoffman)

The case described below also shows that it is possible that common law judges do not always strictly interpret the expression of the contract but interpret according to the meaning a reasonable person would give to it and this narrows the gap between the interpretations of the two legal families.

In 2009, in *Chartbrook v Persimmon Homes*, the House of Lords (UK) reaffirmed the ban on consideration of prior negotiations as evidence of what the parties understood the contract to mean, except for purposes of rectification or estoppel by convention. This was so even though the contractual terms at issue in *Chartbrook*, if interpreted "in accordance with ordinary rules of syntax, makes no commercial sense". (UKHL 38[16] 2009, opinion of Lord Hoffman; Karton 2013: 10; cf. also Salmi-Tolonen 2014: 332)

The division between civil law and common law does not coincide with our thinking of the East and the West. In the West the division is usually between the English-speaking world and the others. In other words, of the countries discussed here, the Nordic Countries and the continental European countries, belong to the civil law tradition going back to Roman law. Of the Asian countries China, except for Hong Kong, and Japan have adopted the civil law tradition. Apart from the contract interpretation approaches, namely, what the parties intended to mean, what the civil law jurisdictions have in common is that they generally find robust cross examination disconcerting. Cross examination in the common law tradition is a rule and it seems to have colonized international commercial arbitration practices.

Of the Asian countries relevant to our study the Indian Subcontinent, Singapore and Hong Kong belong to the common law family together with the UK and the USA in the West. What they have in common is first of all the prohibition of exclusionary rules, the interpretation of contracts is literal and a lot of emphasis is laid on cross examination. Arbitrators whose background is in either of these traditions bring their background to ICA practices. This became evident in the interviews conducted for the purposes of the research projects on arbitration discourse in several countries.

9. Conclusion

The title of this chapter asks how East and West meet in arbitration discourse. It was suggested that in order to answer this question several aspects need to be considered because of the multifaceted nature of international commercial arbitration. The approach will inevitably have to be multidisciplinary for the answer to be as accurate as possible. Next, attention should be paid to the historical, political, societal and linguistic contexts of the arbitration events and their participants. We saw that the cultural, legal, and geographical dividing lines are not the same. Where general culture may be very similar, legal culture may, for historical reasons, stem from a different legal family. A case in point is mainland China and Hong Kong. Furthermore, all arbitrators are inescapably part of their professional community and training. It was pointed out that arbitrators from the common law tradition pay a lot of attention to cross-examination whereas their civil law colleagues shy away from robust cross-examination techniques.

Arbitration is a creature of contract, and contract, as is often said, is a meeting of the minds (see e.g. Sussman 2010; Karton 2013). It was pointed out above that juxtaposing cultures and jurisdictions based on the geographical East v West thinking is not enough. Up to a point we can see differences in the European-based and Asian culture and attitudes. But considering legal cultures the dividing line is not the same because some big countries in Asia are civil law countries and some are common law countries depending on their legal history: mainland China belongs to the civil law tradition and Hong Kong to the common law tradition. They both have big arbitration centres.

At this point of the project I would say that having looked at literature written by experienced law professors (e.g. Karton 2013) and arbitrators (e.g. Hwang 2013) and studied the interviews with arbitrators and media coverage on joint ventures plus arbitration surveys available, three main points of difference have emerged: First of all when entering a business relationship where both Asian and Western companies are involved and especially, if the domicile of the joint venture is in an oriental country, one should be aware of general cultural traditions and differences to one's own culture. It is best to avoid 'legal tricks' even if there is no doubt about their legality as demonstrated by the case Danone v Wahaha.

Secondly, attitudes towards arbitration differ. The two arbitration surveys studied showed that there is a clear connection in attitudes towards arbitration if the public courts are considered to work expeditiously. This probably also has repercussions on international arbitration and on the willingness to include an arbitration clause into the contract. Therefore it is suggested here that the public court systems and attitudes toward them should be studied as well as how conflicts are perceived in general.

Thirdly, the clearest differences can probably be found in the legal traditions of the arbitrators and perhaps also arbitration centres. The interpretation of contracts will be dependent on the training and experience of the members of tribunals either in civil law or common law, and the underlying doctrines remain irreconcilable. As Karton (2013: 197) put it, if a contract is the meeting of the minds then civil law emphasizes the 'minds' and common law the 'meeting'.

References

Bell, John 1995. Comparative Law and Legal Theory. In Krawietz, Werner / MacCormick, Neil / von Wright, Georg Henrik (eds) *Prescriptive Formality and Normative Rationality in Modern Legal Systems: Festschrift for Robert Summers*. Berlin: Duncker and Humblot, 19–31.

Bhatia, Vijay K. / Candlin, Christopher N. / Engberg, Jan / Trosborg, Anna (eds) 2003. *Multilingual and Multicultural Contexts of Legislation. An International Perspective.* Bern: Peter Lang.

Bhatia, Vijay K. / Candlin, Christopher N. / Gotti, Maurizio 2003. *Legal Discourse in Multilingual and Multicultural Contexts. Arbitration Texts in Europe.* Bern: Peter Lang.

Brown, Penelope / Levinson, Stephen C. 1978. Universals in Language Usage: Politeness Phenomena. In Goody, Esther (ed.) *Questions and Politeness: Strategies in Social Interaction.* Cambridge: Cambridge University Press, 56–310.

Brown, Penelope / Levinson, Stephen C. 1987. *Politeness: Some Universals in Language Usage*. Cambridge: Cambridge University Press.

Chen, Rong / He, Lin / Hu, Chunmei 2013. Chinese Requests: In Comparison to American and Japanese Requests and with Reference to the 'East-West Divide'. *Journal of Pragmatics* 55, 140–161.

Corona, Isabel 2011. Arbitration Recontextualized. *World Englishes* 30/1, 129–140.

Dickinson, Steven M. 2007. Danone v. Wahaha: Lessons for Joint Ventures in China. Accessed on 28 January 2015, at <www.chinalawblog.com/DanoneWahahaLessons.pdf>.

Dower, Edward 2010. Reflections on American Arbitration – 35 Years of Savoring the Evidence. Plenary lecture at Law and Language in International Partnerships and Conflicts Conference, Rovaniemi, Finland, March 18, 2010.

Flader, Dieter / Nappert, Sophie 2010. The Psychology of Persuasion in International Arbitration – A Project. *Transnational Dispute Management* 7/1, 1–30. <www.transnational-dispute-management.com>.

Gessner, Volkmar / Hoeland, Armin / Varga, Csaba (eds) 1996. *European Legal Cultures*. Aldershot: Dartmouth Publishing.

Hoffman, Lord 2009. Opinions of the Lords of Appeal for Judgment in the Cause. Chartbrook Limited (Respondents) v Persimmons Homes Limited and others (Appellants) and another (Respondent). House of Lords, Session 2009–09 [2009] UKHL 38. 2–28. Available at <http://www.bailii.org/uk/cases/UKHL/2009/38.html>.

Hwang, Michael 2013. *Selected Essays on International Arbitration*. Singapore: Academy Publishing.

Jaszczolt, Katarzyna M. 2003. Tertium Comparationis in Contrastive Semantics and Pragmatics. In Jaszczolt, Katarzyna / Turner, Ken (eds) *Meaning Through Language Contrast*, Vol. 2. Amsterdam: John Benjamins, 441–462.

Karton, Joshua J.D. 2013. The Culture of International Arbitration and the Evolution of Contract Law. *Oxford Scholarship Online* May 2013. DOI: 10.1093/acprof: oso/9780199658008.

Leech, Geoffrey 2007. Politeness: Is there an East-West Divide? *Journal of Politeness Research* 3/2, 167–206.

Oxford English Dictionaries <http://www.oxforddictionaries.com>.

Salmi-Tolonen, Tarja 2008. *Language and the Functions of Law: A Legal Linguistic Study*. Turku: Painosalama.

Salmi-Tolonen, Tarja 2011. Proactive Law and Alternative Dispute Resolution Mechanisms. In Sorsa, Kaisa (ed.) *Proactive Management and Proactive Business Law: A Handbook*. Turku University of Applied Sciences Course materials 66. Erasmus Curriculum Development Project. Tampere: Juvenes Print, 85–109.

Salmi-Tolonen, Tarja 2014. A Respected Neutral Expert: Arbitrator Profile in Focus. In Bhatia Vijay K. / Garzone, Giuliana / Salvi, Rita / Tessuto, Girolamo / Williams, Christopher (eds) *Language and Law in Professional Discourse*. Newcastle upon Tyne: Cambridge Scholars.

Sourgens, Frédéric Gilles 2007. Comparative Law as Rhetoric: An Analysis of the Use of Comparative Law in International Arbitration. *Pepperdine Dispute Resolution Journal* 8/1, 1–24. Available at <http://heinonline.org>.

Sussman, Edna 2010. Why Arbitrate: The Benefits and Savings. *Transnational Dispute Management* 7/1, 20–24.

The Analects of Confucius 1938. Translated by Arthur Waley. New York: Vintage Books.

Van Hoecke, Mark 2007. European Legal Cultures in a Context of Globalisation. In Gizbert-Studnicki, T. (ed.) *Law and Legal Cultures in the 21st Century*. Plenary paper presented at the IVR World Conference, August 1–6, 2007. Krakow, 81–99. Available at <http: //biblio.ugent.be/record/1060884>.

Van Hoecke, Mark / Warrington, Mark 1998. Legal Cultures, Legal Paradigms and Legal Doctrine: Towards a New Model for Comparative Law. *International and Comparative Law Quarterly* 47, 495–536. DOI:10. 1017/S0020589300062163.

Zhang, Liping 2014. Linguistic Politeness in Lawyers' Petitions under the Confucian Ideal of no Litigation. *The International Journal of Speech, Language and the Law* 21/2, 317–342.

Zweigert, Konrad / Kötz, Hein 1998. *Introduction to Comparative Law*. Translated by Tony Weir. Oxford: Clarendon Press.

Surveys

PriceWaterhouseCoopers 2013. Corporation choices in International Arbitration: Industry perspectives. Available at <http://www.pwc.com/gx/en/arbitration-dispute-resolution/assets/pwc-international-arbitration-study.pdf>.

Roschier Disputes Index 2014. Available at <http://www.roschier.com/sites/default/files /Roschier%20Disputes%20Index%202014.pdf>.

Cases

Chartbrook v Persimmon Homes. UKHL 38[16] 2009. Available at <http://www.bailii.org/uk/cases/UKHL/2009/38.html>.

Joanna Jemielniak

Exploring Med-Arb and Arb-Med Discourse in China: Challenges and Prospects

1. Introduction

Hybrid processes, combining arbitration with mediation or conciliation, while long known to the Western legal tradition, have never enjoyed popularity comparable to their Chinese counterparts. According to recent empirical data, as much as 30–40 percent of cases before the China International Economic and Trade Arbitration Commission (CIETAC, currently the busiest arbitration centre in the world) are being resolved by the means of arb-med.[1] Furthermore, 50 percent of recently inquired Chinese arbitrators declared that they forwarded conciliatory options to the parties in over 90 percent of arbitration cases they have handled (Kun 2013a).

As discussed in this chapter, this firmly established national and regional trend can be explained by a number of historical and cultural factors, which affect the modern-day functioning of hybrid processes. Consequences of their popularity in East Asia, however, extend beyond the limits of the region and affect a growing number of parties and legal professionals worldwide. As the trade exchange between Chinese and Western business partners grows, so does the number of related commercial contracts, as well as controversies resulting from such transactions. As a consequence, the group of stakeholders from different

1 Interview with Tang Houzhi, Honorary Secretary Gen. of the CIETAC, in Beijing (Mar. 27, 2007), conducted by Gabrielle Kaufmann-Kohler and Fan Kun, during a research trip in 2007 as part of a research project on Arbitration in China (led by Kaufmann-Kohler, funded by the Swiss National Science Foundation).

countries and legal traditions, directly exposed to hybrid processes, expands quickly.

This chapter examines legal, cultural and discursive particularities of this unique phenomenon. It also explores methodological aspects of research on this issue in regard to existing studies, as well as postulated ones. It discusses how the presence of 'soft', conciliatory components in hybrid processes makes the results of a legal doctrinal, text-oriented analysis incomplete, as many of the key aspects of arb-med proceedings remain oral. It is also argued that the existing quantitative studies of this subject should be supplemented by qualitative ones, so as to allow for an in-depth, comparative interpretation of various regional types of hybrid processes, of the functions they fulfill and of their legal and social consequences. A study approaching hybrid processes on the level of specific proceedings, but also in a broader, regional context, as well as with regard to global arbitration trends, is thus proposed.

The chapter examines historical accounts of the use of hybrid processes in imperial China, as well as in the Western legal tradition since antiquity. It aims at unveiling the historical roots and determinants of modern-day approaches to arb-med and med-arb. Confucian background and the amalgam character of the traditional extrajudicial dispute resolution in China are considered. The following investigation of Western sources discloses strong presence of conciliatory components in the arbitral process over the course of several epochs, subsequently lost during the period of decline of arbitration in the 17th–19th centuries.

The historical background is further used as a basis for an attempt at assessing current significance of arb-med and med-arb in arbitration. The development of arbitration after World War II is discussed, in particular the accommodation of another strong regional trend, characterized as the 'American wave' in the 1990s and 2000s, and the accompanying proceduralization of international commercial arbitration. The status of hybrid processes as a possible conciliatory counter-trend to this tendency is explored. The existing empirical studies on the frequency of use of hybrid processes by practitioners with different primary legal backgrounds, and the issue of correlation between national culture and propensity for recourse to such mechanisms, are then analyzed.

Qualitative empirical studies on relations between national culture and approaches to dispute resolution are in turn consulted in order to achieve a fuller picture of the reasons for the existing national and regional discrepancies, evidenced by quantitative research. The information so acquired is then used for an examination of framework conditions for the postulated, multimethod comparative study, to be specifically dedicated to the issue of hybrid processes in a cross-regional and cross-cultural perspective. In this part, the chapter examines how the particularities of legal discourse in hybrid proceedings pose challenges to investigators, and how they might be addressed through a proper selection and calibration of research methods. The findings of the chapter are then recapitulated in concluding remarks.

2. Hybrid processes in a historical perspective

Hybrid processes, often indicated as highly typical of the Chinese approach to dispute resolution (largely influenced by the Confucian tradition) have also been known and practiced in Western legal traditions since antiquity. A closer look at the historical background discloses a number of facets of this phenomenon, which still significantly affect its modern-day functioning. The discrepancies between ostensibly similar procedural solutions adopted in both traditions, as well as their sources and consequences will also be examined.

2.1 Chinese legal tradition

The orientation of traditional legal culture in China towards avoidance of open disputes and their harmonious social absorption by amicable, possibly informal means, has been widely commented upon (Kun 2013b). This dispute-aversive approach, characterized by reliance primarily on local social groups such as clans, guilds and villages, and not on external institutions administering justice, permeated the commercial sphere as well. It affected also commercial relations with non-Chinese parties, which resulted in the relatively limited significance of adjudicatory mechanisms (arbitration and litigation) in such cases.

Furthermore, even in those controversies which were resolved by the means of arbitration (according to some rules of guilds and clans, which adopted this mechanism), it took a form significantly different from its Western counterpart. The dissimilarities included the non-voluntary character of arbitration (being not an option available to the parties, but a mandatory stage to be exhausted before they could turn to formal litigation); the role of the clan or guild leader (which was much closer to one of a conciliator, facilitating settlement, than that of an adjudicator); and finally, the non-binding character of the outcome of the proceedings (as the parties still could have further complained to the authorities (Hsiao 1879; MacCormack 1996; Kun/Jemielniak forth.).

Similarly, mediation in imperial China did not strictly resemble the Western version of this process. Again, its commencement before the group leaders was mandatory in 'trivial' matters before seeking recourse to official mechanisms under the sanction of corporal punishment. Guild/clan/village leaders were predetermined to act as mediators, but also empowered to decide the controversy in case of a lack of agreement between the contestants. Consequently, the disputants were not free to abide by the result of the process, but it could have been imposed upon them due to the authority of the elders or leaders within the group (Kun 2013c).

Hence it is difficult to provide a clear delineation of roles, in which the persons guiding the process of dispute resolution acted. In particular, application of the Western concepts of arbitration and mediation (based on voluntary submission of a case, as well as selection of arbitrators or mediators by the contestants) is not fully adequate. The adoption of specific roles was rather an expression of the general legitimacy to act, ascribed to local group leaders as the 'first instance' dispute resolution facilitators in the Chinese society. The enforcement stage, while outwardly voluntary, was marked by high presence of social pressure and obedience due to honorary reasons, largely considered to be much more efficient than any legal sanctions. The conciliatory phase of proceedings before the group leaders (with repeated attempts at reaching settlement) frequently preceded the more formal one, with examination of evidence and final decision-making. The latter, however, was also aimed at finding the possibly compromising solution.

This process can be characterized as mediation, which in case of failure of repeated settlement attempts was being turned into arbitration – with reservations as to the strict adequacy of those terms, as highlighted above. The limits between the two types of proceedings were vague, and dispute resolution under such circumstances can be seen as driven by the specific structure of the traditional Chinese society, in which direct personal bonds and authority of the leaders served an important role in the preservation of social harmony and avoidance of escalation of conflicts. This deeply and widely internalized social norm of adopting a gradual approach to the means of dispute resolution (resembling the med-arb procedural sequence), can be seen as an important predecessor of the modern-day hybrid processes.

2.2 Western legal traditions

Whereas the Chinese traditional approach blended conciliatory components with the elements of arbitral process without a clear separation between the types and stages of proceedings, in the Western legal tradition hybrid processes were adopted with a marked distinction between the mediation and arbitration phases. In the context of the contemporary rather scarce use of med-arb and arb-med, it might seem somewhat surprising that hybrid processes have indeed a very long, rich and successful history in Western arbitration.

Multiple records of use of combinations of arbitration with mediation, found in ancient Greek sources, offer an abundant documentation of the widespread practice of arbitration (frequently additionally strengthened by inclusion of religious components, Tod 2003). Its high popularity in trade-related disputes has been connected with intense development of Mediterranean maritime commerce and with proliferation of uniform customs, shared by the Greek, Phoenician and Egyptian sea merchants (as restated e.g. in the first Rhodian Sea Law;[2] cf. Domke 2003).

Arbitration as a common method of addressing commercial cases (in particular maritime trade-related ones) was since its very origins frequently combined with amicable mechanisms. As indicated by Roebuck (2007: 106):

> in the ancient Greek world, including Ptolemaic Egypt, arbitration was normal and in arbitration the mediation element was primary. However formal the procedure, mediation was attempted first and a mediated settlement was preferred, so that even an adjudication might, where possible, be incorporated in an agreement. Conversely, a settlement might be converted into an award, for easier enforcement. The processes of mediation and arbitration often intermingled, but they were conceptually distinct, as shown by the precision of terminology and the formal step of swearing an oath before moving to adjudication.

The following significant decrease of recorded uses of hybrid processes in ancient Roman sources has been commented upon as a result of proliferation of standardized and affordable arbitration proceedings. This culture of arbitration (used in two main forms: an officially administered one; and *ad hoc* and private) was however lost in the early Middle Ages along with the rapid decline of commerce following the fall of the Roman Empire. The next historical period, in which arbitration and hybrid processes started gaining popularity anew, was the medieval revival of cities, including the reestablishment of their position as trade centres in the tenth and eleventh centuries. Arbitration became a default method of addressing commercial controversies, endorsed by the guilds of craftsmen and merchants in major European cities (Ogilvie 2011). As Gelderblom (2011) notes, popularization of professional merchants' tribunals in main trade fair centres, accompanied by the proliferation of uniform customs of trade (*lex mercatoria*), between the twelfth and sixteenth centuries, had been officially endorsed by the town magistrates in such countries as Italy, Germany, Spain and England, vitally interested in benefits brought by the flourishing trade exchange. Specialized sea trade tribunals were also created besides the general commercial ones.

---

2 A maritime code with rules dating back to the third century B.C. and later reapplied in the Middle Ages as official sea trade standards by the Italian city of Pisa.

The combination of arbitration with mediation was very common in the Middle Ages and in early modern Europe, to the extent that legal historians characterizing dispute resolution facilitators use the terms 'arbiters' and 'mediators'. The parties had easy access to two basic forms of arbitration: to a formal and legalistic one, with court-appointed arbitrators, and to services offered by professionals, described in the Dutch sources as *goede mannen* or *amiable compositeurs* and being appointed by the parties. The latter form was characterized by 'soft touch' and extensive inclusion of conciliatory components and enjoyed wide popularity (Gusbers 1999). Similarly, in Elizabethan England, arbitration was 'omnipresent' (Roebuck 2015), with its hybrid form being a standard, and the mediation and arbitration phases carefully delineated.

The period of rapid expansion of hybrid processes was followed by a steep decline of arbitration between the 17th and 19th centuries, resulting from the consolidation of modern nation States and centralization of dispute resolution functions through State-related systems of administration of justice. The 20th century, post-WWII intense revival of arbitration, discussed below, did not bring an accompanying renaissance of hybrid processes, and inclusion of conciliatory components into the arbitral process has not been strongly represented in the mainstream Western arbitral practice. The arbitration boom of the last decades of the 20th century was thus largely a revival of arbitration as an adjudicatory mechanism of dispute resolution (with arb-med and med-arb remaining rather niche solutions). This tendency has been strengthened by the trend of judicialization of arbitration, or its 'colonization by litigation' (Nariman 2000), which was interpreted as further disconnecting Western arbitration from its roots as a flexible and informal 'merchants' justice' (Dezalay/Garth 1996). This phenomenon, its consequences and most recent developments in the discussed field are examined in the following section.

3. Current significance of hybrid processes in arbitration

3.1 Regional influences and the global culture of arbitration

The historical data shed a new light onto the recent revival of interest in hybrid processes in the arbitration practice worldwide, and help to interpret this phenomenon in the context of new, strong regional developments, as well as with regard to the emerging global culture of arbitration. The issue of global versus regional influences in arbitration (or its globalization versus glocalization) is thus one of the key vectors of the proposed analysis of hybrid processes. The rekindled interest in arb-med and med-arb will also be considered against the background of development of contemporary (post-World War II) arbitration, and in particular the absorption of regional trends – which might offer an indication as to how the global arbitral landscape was changing under their influence in recent times. The account of 'regional waves' in modern-day arbitration may thus serve as a second vector, guiding the analysis. Finally, the broader historical perspective, offered in the preceding section, should offer a background for identifying sources of present cultural differences, observable in regional approaches to hybrid processes.

The unprecedented, worldwide growth of international commercial arbitration (ICA) in the post-WW2 decades has, in the field of cross-border commercial disputes, gradually led to arbitration largely eliminating national courts as a default procedural option (Lalive 1987; López Rodriguez 2003). Due to the widespread adoption of the New York Convention through subsequent waves of accessions, the proliferation of arbitration has been secured by guarantees of enforceability of awards. As a result, in the area of international commercial disputes, national courts have been to a large extent replaced by a private, global, highly competitive, expert-based network of arbitral centres and services offered *ad hoc*. This process, commented upon as the 'phenomenal boom' (Kaufmann-Kohler 2006) of arbitration, has been interpreted as signaling an emergence of arbitration as an autonomous, transnational legal order (Gaillard 2010).

These developments have been followed by a trend described as processualization and judicialization (Brower 1994; Nariman 2000) of arbitration – an increased saturation of the regulatory framework of ICA with standardized, complex procedural solutions. This tendency has often been connected with an 'American wave' in ICA in the 1990s and early 2000s (Newman 2001), as the quickly increasing number of cases in which US parties were involved turned out to be a global game changer for arbitration, traditionally perceived as a European method of dispute resolution, largely influenced by the civil law tradition. The influx of US-related cases, in which important actors were counsel primarily trained in the highly adversarial, American-style procedure, posed new demands for arbitrators dealing with the task of accommodating the processual needs of the parties.

The accompanying proceduralization and judicialization of the arbitral procedure has been characterized as a departure from the original concept of arbitration as an informal 'merchants' justice' (Bühring-Uhle/Kirchhoff/Scherer 2006). This phenomenon has been however interpreted by some commentators as a sign of progressing autonomization of arbitration. According to Dezalay and Garth (1996), commercial arbitration has reached a stage of maturity, in which its social legitimization as a flexible, efficient alternative to the overly formalized domestic litigation is no longer necessary. According to this stance, as international commercial arbitration has already achieved a largely self-sufficient, independent standing, it no longer needs to distinguish itself from the national courts. Moreover, the judicialization trend cannot merely be a simple consequence of procedural habits of the US litigators joining the arbitration game, but a sign of a more complex phenomenon of consolidation of arbitration and its readiness to accommodate large, complex cases on a regular rather than exceptional basis, as well as of responsiveness of the arbitration community to the multicultural character of the field (hence the comments on arbitration becoming neither Americanized nor civilized, but increasingly harmonized: cf. Helmer 2003).

As Bergsten (2006) remarks, the experience of the American wave, being accommodated by the global arbitration practice (originally shaped as the European 'Grand Old Men's' game), can be compared to the situation of migrants, who adapt to their new country, but the country is also changing under their influence. However, a prominent regional tendency towards the rapid rise of East Asian arbitration centres can be currently observed. As evidenced by the statistics on cases accepted annually, three of these institutions have over the past years consistently held top positions among the ranks of global leaders: China International Economic and Trade Arbitration Commission (CIETAC, currently the arbitration centre with the largest caseload in the world),[3] Hong Kong International Arbitration Centre (HKIAC) and Singapore International Arbitration Centre (SIAC). CIETAC and HKIAC are Chinese centres, with HKIAC being traditionally selected by Western parties.

In the practice of East Asian – particularly Chinese – centres, a trend opposite to processualization can be observed. The parties increasingly seek recourse to hybrid proceedings and depart from the strictly adversarial model. A recent empirical study shows that 50 per cent of the Chinese arbitrators surveyed have proposed mediation to the parties in over 90 per cent of the cases when they act as arbitrators (Kun 2013a). This phenomenon has been explained by the "conflict aversive culture of the region, where negotiated deals are preferred to formal dispute settlement" (Nakagawa 2007: 863). It has also been recently accompanied by signs of renewed interest in the, previously not popular (Kun/Jemielniak forth.), hybrid processes at leading Western arbitration centres, such as the International Chamber of Commerce (ICC) (Morek 2013) and the American Arbitration Association (Philips 2010).

The rekindled interest in hybrid processes in Europe matches the unprecedented expansion of commercial exchange between business partners from the EU and China (Greenberg/Kee/ Weeramantry 2010). The parties to such contracts are increasingly likely to have their disputes resolved by the means of hybrid processes – their proper understanding is thus an economically and legally vital issue for a quickly growing number of stakeholders. Especially the European parties and their counsel might not be sufficiently prepared for such proceedings, and not fully aware of regional particularities of ostensibly similar procedural mechanisms.

---

3 International Arbitration Cases Received – statistical compilation by HKIAC. Available at <http://www.hkiac.org>, last visited in October 2014.

However, proliferation of hybrid processes, due to its current wide social impact, demands not only a purely doctrinal insight. As a complex cultural phenomenon, it also calls for an in-depth interpretation in the context of general development of ICA. Are hybrid processes merely a token of regional legal culture – prominent, but strongly determined by local circumstances? Or can they be seen as symptoms of an 'Asian wave', comparable to the 'American' one, which can affect global trends in ICA?

3.2 Quantitative data on inclusion of conciliatory components into the arbitral process

An attempt at assessing current significance of hybrid mechanisms in arbitration, and examination of their cultural foundations, requires an overview of empirical accounts of this phenomenon. Three major existing studies on inclusion of amicable components into arbitral processes can be mentioned in this regard.

First, pioneering research conducted in two stages (in 1994 and 2004) by Christian Bühring-Uhle on arbitration and mediation practitioners will be mentioned. The study took a form of a quantitative survey based on a standardized questionnaire. In 1994, the researcher distributed around 150 questionnaires, and received 91 completed responses from professionals from 17 countries. 67 of them (from eight countries) were approached through personal interviews and the remaining ones submitted their replies in writing (Bühring-Uhle/Kirchhoff/Scherer 2006). In the second survey, conducted between 2001 and 2004 by means of the same methodology, 53 questionnaires were completed by respondents from 14 countries (including 20 interviewees from the US, 8 from Germany, 11 from other continental European countries, and 11 from other common law countries; Bühring-Uhle/Kirchhoff/Scherer 2006). The results of both surveys offer valuable evidence of national varieties, present in the behaviour of practitioners involved in commercial dispute resolution in regard to hybrid processes, with the most notable divergence disclosed between the behavioural patterns of the German and American practitioners.

As demonstrated by Bühring-Uhle, the respondents were generally expressing the view that facilitation of a settlement is an integral part of the arbitral process (83% of interviewees in the first survey and 86% in the second). However, whereas this opinion was in the second survey unanimously shared by 100% of the German and of the non-US common law respondents, 26% of the Americans and 15% of interviewees from the non-German civil law countries disagreed with this statement.

Furthermore, in terms of settlement rate, the study evidenced an overall 43% share of cases being concluded by amicable means before issuance of an award. Again, a notable divide between the German and US practitioners was disclosed. Whereas the former notified the researcher about the settlement rate at the level of 69%, their American counterparts reported respectively only 33% of cases as settled. The interpretation of this discrepancy, proposed by Bühring-Uhle, points to the essential difference in perception of the role of an adjudicator in both legal systems. Whereas German judges are obliged to undertake settlement attempts, their US colleagues are culturally and procedurally established as non-intervening, 'detached and impartial' decision makers.

The second empirical study, offering important data on arbitrators' approaches to hybrid processes, was conducted by Shahla Ali and was based on the Bühring-Uhle's standard questionnaire. In particular, Ali's survey brought valuable evidence of behavioural patterns of Asian arbitrators. The focus of Ali's 2006–2007 study was primarily on East Asian practitioners (77 respondents), with the remaining 26 interviewees coming from the US and European countries (Ali 2011). In response to the question on facilitation of settlement as an integral part of the role of an arbitrator, 82% of the East Asian practitioners (and 62% of their Western counterparts) replied affirmatively. The question on the settlement rate revealed a particularly high diversity among the respondents (with reported percentages ranging between 5% and 85%, with an average of 35%). The disclosed settlement rate was also, surprisingly, lower in total in East Asia (30%) than among the European and US practitioners surveyed (48%). The author explains it as an effect of much more intensified settlement efforts at the pre-arbitration stage of the dispute in East Asia than in the West (with 38% of East Asian respondents convinced that amicable options were exhausted before commencement of arbitration, as opposed to 28% of their Western colleagues).

An area in which regional variations turned out to be the most prominent in Ali's study was propensity of arbitrators to become actively involved in different forms of settlement interventions. Whereas all surveyed practitioners perceived such activity as generally appropriate, offering suggestions of settlement negotiations on a regular basis was declared by over 40% of East Asian respondents and only 16% of their Western counterparts. Regular engagement into settlement negotiations with the parties was reported by over 30% of interviewees from East Asia and by 16% of the Western ones. Having separate meetings with the parties for the discussion of a settlement was employed by 26% of East Asians and only 8% of the Western respondents. Offering a settlement formula regularly to the parties was reported by 17% of East Asians and by only 4% of the Western practitioners.

The third empirical study, providing evidence of influence of national background onto arbitrators' pro-active stance towards settlement of the dispute, is an analysis of awards by consent issued by the ICC tribunals in 2002–2005. In the research, conducted in 2008, Gabrielle Kaufmann-Kohler and Victor Bonnin examined a sample of 63 out of 136 awards by consent, issued in the targeted period. The study disclosed patterns in national composition of the tribunals rendering awards by consent (Kaufmann-Kohler/Bonnin 2007). They were most commonly issued by Swiss arbitrators (tribunals in analyzed cases had 15 chairmen or sole arbitrators, and 17 co-arbitrators of Swiss origin). The next most popular nationality was German (6 chairmen or sole arbitrators and 14 co-arbitrators), followed by English (6 chairmen or sole arbitrators and 9 co-arbitrators). As the investigators emphasized, this trend is even more striking when the standard composition of the ICC tribunals is taken into account (with English arbitrators being much more commonplace than their German colleagues in ICC arbitrations). The study also offers further evidence of high propensity of German and German-speaking Swiss arbitrators to get actively involved in settlement facilitation, as compared to their English and US colleagues.

These empirical studies thus demonstrate the existence of a correlation between the national and regional background of the arbitrators, and the approaches towards hybrid processes which they adopt. These valuable sets of quantitative data form a solid starting point for further analysis of the sources and consequences of this correlation and of the specific forms it might take. However, such an analysis cannot be completely conducted by the means of quantitative tools and – as argued in detail in the following sections – the use of qualitative methods is further called for.

4. Empirical evidence of impact of national culture onto approaches to dispute resolution

The existing cross-cultural studies on workplace organizations and on sets of socially shared values determined by national cultures shed an additional light on the discussed correlation, confirmed by quantitative studies on hybrid processes. In particular, Geert Hofstede's Value Survey Model offers tools for extracting these aspects of culturally determined behavior, which are relevant to commercial dispute resolution and the practice of hybrid processes (Hofstede/Hofstede/Minkov 2010). Hofstede originally identified five main dimensions of national cultures, observable in social actors' behavior: Power Distance Index (PDI), Individualism versus Collectivism (IDV), Masculinity versus Feminism (MAS), Uncertainty Avoidance Index (UAI) and Pragmatic versus Normative (PRA), later supplemented by Long-Term Orientation (LTO) or Confucian work dynamism (in reaction to criticism of the overly Westernized character of his model).[4] He further measured the levels of presence of social actors' behavior determined by each of these dimensions in different states. Based on the application of his model, cultural profiles of 76 countries have been created.

4 LTO was added to the model in 1991 based on research by Michael Harris Bond, supported by Hofstede and conducted in collaboration with Chinese academics.

Three of these dimensions can be identified as bearing particular relevance to dispute resolution (Kun/Jemielniak forth.): IDV (which characterizes the level of interdependence between society members); PDI (which tests the degree of social acceptance for unequal distribution of power by the less entitled members of organizations and institutions); and LTO (which measures the societies search for virtue, inclination for perseverance, and interest in saving and long-term investment rather than in quickly achievable goals).

As demonstrated by Hofstede in terms of IDV, low individualism and high collectivism scores strongly influence social approaches to communication and dispute resolution. In collectivist cultures, the pervasive styles of communication are the indirect ones, with the actors avoiding explicit expression of their individual goals and needs. This further translates onto lower tendency to adopt a directly confrontational position in case of a dispute (Jandt 2013). In the PDI dimension, societies with high scores tend to accept hierarchical structures and do not contest authority or demand its additional justification. In terms of approaches to dispute resolution, in cultures with high PDI, considerations of distributive justice prevail over those of procedural justice, as the authority is already highly accepted and does not require additional, externalized support through procedures (Tyler/Lind/Huo 2000).

Finally, in cultures with a high LTO index, perseverance and thrift rather than quick achievement of one's short-term goals are indicated as highly esteemed social values. Adoption of such a stance results in the area of dispute resolution in acceptance of the Confucian ideal of persuasion as the preferred means of handling controversies (which should rather bc mitigated than decided):

> Lead them by political maneuvers, restrain them with punishments: the people will become cunning and shameless. Lead them by virtue, restrain them with ritual: they will develop a sense of shame and a sense of participation.[5]

Lawsuits and adversarial approach to dispute resolution, as a distortion of social harmony, are, as a consequence, highly undesirable – in part because of their superficial character (as they can merely mend the

5 *The Analects of Confucius*, translated by Simon Leys. New York: Norton and Company, 1997.

external symptoms of wrongful behavior, whereas the true goal lies in inner ethical transformation). Based on confrontation between extreme positions of the parties, litigation also contradicts the Confucian ideal of the middle way (Lawless 2008). This doctrine finds a natural realization in amicable and conciliatory ways of resolving disputes; hence mediation and conciliation enjoy a strong cultural support in countries with high LTO scores.

In the dimensions discussed above, the scores in the three main arbitration jurisdictions in East Asia have been recorded as follows:

- IDV: China (20), Hong Kong (25), Singapore (20), world average (40);
- PDI: China (80), Hong Kong (68), Singapore (74), world average (56.5);
- LTO: China (118), Hong Kong (96), Singapore (48), world average (45).[6]

All three analyzed jurisdictions have a level of individualism which is about twice lower than the global average, and are thus decisevely collectivist societies. All three discussed countries/territories also score remarkably high on the PDI scale, which is an indicator of a strong social support for the authority and lesser focus on procedural justice. In terms of LTO, only Singapore displays a level of this index close to the world average, whereas both PRC and Hong Kong have record scores, which more than double it. The resulting profiles of national cultures for the three analyzed jurisdictions display a combination of socially shared values, which provides a strong cultural support for adoption of a conciliatory approach to dispute resolution, rather than the adversarial one.

The impact of national cultural background onto business relations and professional settings was also the topic of another empirical study, conducted by Fons Trompenaars, and further developed in collaboration with Charles Hampden-Turner (Trompenaars/Hampden-Turner 1998). A key finding of Trompenaars's research, particularly relevant to the sphere of dispute resolution, is the distinction between specific and diffusive cultures. In the former, the same social actors enter into interactions without intermingling them, so their actions in

6 Source : <http://geert-hofstede.com/countries.html>.

one of the spheres of life do not necessarily have a direct spillover effect onto the other ones. In diffusive cultures the social perception is complex as the actors are seen as interacting on multiple levels at the same time. As a consequence, their behavior in one social sphere has a direct effect onto relations with the same persons in the remaining ones. As evidenced by Trompenaars, whereas the US is an exemplary country with a specific culture, the highest levels of diffusiveness have been recorded in the East Asian professional environments, with China as the most diffusive society.

The characterization of a particular culture as specific or diffusive has far-reaching consequences for the sphere of conflict management and dispute resolution. In a specific culture, business or workplace-related controversies do not necessarily radiate directly onto other spheres of interactions and life of the involved actors and onto their future relations. The effects of a conflict taking a clearly adversarial form are thus significantly less harmful on the social, as well as on the individual level, as the parties can relatively successfully extract and separate the dispute from their other interactions. On the other hand, the perception of a dispute in a decidedly diffusive culture tends to be much more one of a serious social disturbance. Such personal feelings as anger and offence are also much more likely to be developed.

Somewhat paradoxically, a conflict is thus much more likely to get dangerously escalated in a diffusive culture than in a specific one, as it is much more difficult to keep it contained within a single, strictly business-related sphere and a particular set of circumstances. This is the reason why in diffusive cultures maintenance of social harmony is a value with highest priority, and why the open conflicts are considered a danger that should be carefully avoided. As Trompenaars demonstrates, the correlation between a conciliatory (and not adversarial) approach to dispute resolution and a high level of social diffusiveness is thus not only a matter of historical traditions, but a very current issue, distinctly present in modern-day corporate cultures and in approaches to business disputes, adopted by social actors.

As demonstrated above, the existing quantitative studies on hybrid processes, as well as qualitative research on the divergences between national approaches to dispute resolution, reveal a strong correlation between the national legal tradition and propensity of seeking recourse to conciliatory mechanisms. National culture in this regard is also historically determined, with the shared traditional perceptions of social fabric and interactions still influencing contemporary strategies, adopted in the commercial context. A full examination of these factors and an in-depth interpretation of the discussed trend would require a comparative, cross-regional and cross-cultural analysis of hybrid processes.

The postulated, cross-cultural study would also allow for uncovering such links, interrelations and tensions, shaping arbitral discourse, that exist between components drawn from different sets of values (cultural orders of different kind), sometimes also placed on different levels of functioning of hybrid processes. A prominent example of such a clash in the Chinese context involves the demands of a regional conciliatory culture of dispute resolution (strongly present at the meso- and micro levels) being confronted with the cosmopolitan professional culture of arbitration practitioners (Kauppi/Madsen 2013; Jemielniak 2014) present at the macro level. As for the arbitration counsel, the duty to best represent their clients in a specific case might occasionally require an adoption of a strongly adversarial (rather than conciliatory) strategy, which leads them to find themselves at odds with cultural pressure for adopting an amicable position. This causes professional frustration, but also raises a question about the strategies adopted by legal practitioners on the micro level, aimed at solving this dilemma.

5. Discursive particularities of hybrid processes and perspectives for future research

Research on hybrid processes, approaching them as a unique social practice and aimed at unveiling its different aspects, calls for an adoption of a carefully designed combination of quantitative and qualitative components. The legal doctrinal and comparative methods, based on documentary analysis are not fully adequate for capturing the 'soft' components of such proceedings, largely happening in action and not reflected in written records. The existing legal literature focuses largely on the procedural framework for these processes in the context of specific jurisdictions, without offering a wider comparative angle. It is also to a large extent rather oriented at legal practice than at providing a thorough interpretation of hybrid proceedings (Bartel 1991; Peter 1997; Ross/Conlon 2000; Houzhi 2005; Spencer/Brogan 2006; Alibekova/ Carrow 2007; Sussman 2009).

On the other hand, the existing empirical studies on hybrid processes, as discussed in the preceding chapters, have a primarily quantitative focus. They offer highly valuable evidence of the correlation between the national and regional background of arbitrators and their inclination to endorse or to actively forward amicable settlement of arbitrated disputes. However, detailed information on the nature of such interventions, motivations for making them, and their exact consequences, could be collected by the use of qualitative means (Kun/ Jemielniak forth.). Furthermore, a comparative study combining quantitative and qualitative components would provide empirical material allowing for a broader interpretation of this phenomenon not only on the micro level of functioning of hybrid processes (regarding strategies adopted in specific cases), but also on the meso (regional) and macro (global) one. As a consequence, a comparative, multimethod cross-regional and cross-cultural analysis of hybrid processes is postulated, in order to capture these factors and to offer an in-depth interpretation of the discussed trend.

A systematic, cross-cultural investigation on the practice of hybrid processes and the particularities of the arbitration discourse in this area poses several challenges to the investigator. The postulated qualitative research, to be conducted by a variety of methods (from semi-structured and focus interviews to in-depth ethnographic case studies) would allow for capturing different aspects of this phenomenon. The existing empirical studies, discussed above, besides their quantitative orientation, relied only on *post factum* accounts of the hybrid processes practice, filtered through the memory, recapitulations and post-rationalization strategies of the surveyed practitioners (or, in case of Kaufmann-Kohler and Bonnin's study, on arbitral awards, being secondary materials in terms of access to knowledge on conduct of the examined procedures).

Hence the inclusion of qualitative methods into investigation, and broadening its scope so as to encompass direct, non-participant, real-time observation, would significantly enrich the picture of the investigated field. It would be the more desired, as the examined practices are – as discussed above – strongly determined by cultural factors, which are difficult to grasp and interpret by the means of quantitative tools, and call for a multimethod examination, extensively including qualitative components. Whereas undoubtedly beneficial for the state of the art and broadening knowledge of the complex, unique phenomenon of high legal and economic importance, such a study would face a number of issues, which would need to be carefully addressed.

Accessibility of the field is the first of them. The reputation of arbitration as a notoriously opaque legal area has been widely commented upon in literature and has always posed challenges to empirical investigations. Confidentiality of arbitration has been frequently indicated as one of the key advantages of this method of dispute resolution, attracting commercial parties who seek to avoid the public character of litigation. The opinions as to its practical significance differ though, ranging from the view that it is "perhaps one of the fundamental, if not the most compelling, of reasons for which the parties choose to arbitrate" (Noussia 2010: 1) to the claims that for the parties selecting a preferred method of dispute resolution it is a consideration of secondary importance (as argued by Richard Naimark and Stephanie Keer (2003) in their interpretation of data from an empirical study on AAA arbitration participants and counsel).

Motivations of the parties notwithstanding, the confidential character of arbitration is well-established in practice, and can be found in two procedural aspects (Brown 2001). First, confidentiality *sensu stricto* functions as an obligation not to disclose information about arbitration to the external actors. Second, privacy of ICA is a practice of excluding third parties from the arbitral proceedings. These two aspects of confidentiality, while not unanimously accepted by commentators as mandatory standards forming an integral part of the arbitration process, have been nevertheless largely observed in the arbitration practice

(Rogers 2006). Pragmatic reasons, offered for the *de facto* adoption of this rule, cover a number of issues, including the intent of the parties to avoid publicizing particular types of sensitive allegations (as misrepresentation or bad faith); aversion to disclosing loss to the general public; and protection of confidential business information and trade secrets (Buys 2003). Combined with limited publicity of arbitral awards, such a procedural model largely operates on a basis of the *de facto* presumption of non-transparency.

All these considerations are not only present, but further augmented in arb-med and med-arb, due to their hybrid nature. A highly closed and informal character of mediation is accompanied by the very private status of its outcomes: whereas the number of arbitral awards being published is but a fraction of their total amount, the settlements concluding a successful mediation phase of hybrid processes are by definition an agreement meant to remain private. Broad inclusion of 'soft', mediation-related components into the arbitral process blurs the formality of proceedings and provides the parties with non-official mechanisms of facilitation of settlement. Based, as an ideal model, on trust and direct cooperation between the mediator and the parties, the mediation phase by definition lacks the decision-making rigidity of arbitration, as it is oriented at consensus, unlike arbitration which aims at the delivery of the externalized (issued by an empowered neutral) outcome based on the provisions of the law. Even though the difficulties with clear distinction between both roles, when performed by a single med-arbitrator/arb-mediator are often pointed to as drawbacks of hybrid processes, the procedural goals of the two phases are essentially different.

The closed character of the field due to confidentiality concerns, even more intensely present in hybrid processes than in regular arbitrations, as well as extensive inclusion of soft components (which decreases standardization and predictability of the course of proceedings), are thus the elements that largely determine particularities of legal discourse in this field as opposed to adjudicatory methods of commercial dispute resolution. The third key element is high saturation of the discourse of hybrid processes with oral components, due to the usual dynamics of the mediation phase, largely based on direct interactions between the parties and the dispute resolution facilitator (whereas in classical arbitrations the organization of hearings might be limited or not even necessary). Notably, it can be discussed to what extent the professional discourse of hybrid processes can still be characterized as a variation of legal discourse – since in the case of proceedings dominated by mediation components and/or concluded by the means of settlement, the presence of legal arguments and discursive strategies might be suppressed by extralegal ones.

These characteristics make it even more difficult for investigators to inquire on the actual functioning of hybrid processes on the basis of *post factum* accounts and official documents, than in the case of standard arbitrations. Arb-med and med-arb happen largely 'in action', due to the very wide scope of procedural discretion allocated with the facilitator, and the proceedings being based on personal interaction, with extralegal factors being considered besides the legal ones. As a consequence, an in-depth analysis of this phenomenon calls for the study of the course of proceedings rather than of their recollections. Overcoming the difficulties with access to the proceedings in real time, to be examined by the means of observation-based methods, for the purposes of conducting ethnographic and discourse analytical studies, is thus of key importance.

6. Conclusions

The outreach of hybrid processes is growing as the volume of trans-regional trade increases quickly and more and more parties are being directly exposed to this mechanism of dispute resolution. Hence explorations of this practice are not only academically desired – as a study of a complex, deeply historically and culturally rooted and regionally diversified phenomenon – but also most timely. Proper understanding of the sources, goals, types, functions and consequences of arb-med and med-arb in a comparative perspective is, as argued in this chapter, vital not only on the micro level of specific cases, on which particular dispute resolution strategies are adopted, and discursive identities are being displayed by the participants of the proceedings (cf. Bhatia/ Candlin/ Engberg 2008; Bhatia/Candlin/Gotti 2012). It is also crucial for an interpretation of this social and legal phenomenon in a broader perspective: in the context of regional determinants of its popularity and adoption of specific forms (the meso level), as well as in the light of the emerging global culture of arbitration (the macro level).

In regard to the latter, the signals of procedural convergence can be examined, in particular in the context of the earlier experience of the 'American wave' and its interrelation with the processualization and judicialization trend in arbitration. As discussed above, the accommodation of the 'American wave' by the arbitral practice and the resulting popularity of compromising solutions (aimed at addressing the justified procedural needs of both parties) may serve as a point of reference for the current growing popularization of soft approaches. Hybrid processes, enjoying a special position in Chinese arbitration for a number of cultural, as well as institutional reasons, already affect stakeholders outside East Asia, because of the high number of Chinese-Western commercial contracts and resulting controversies.

Whether this phenomenon might exert an enduring, broader effect onto global trends in arbitration remains to be seen, and it can be explored in the light of the theory of legal glocalization (Robertson 1994; Kun 2013c), focused on interrelations, mutual influences and conflicts between local and global elements in globalized legal phenomena. However, as historical analysis demonstrates, while hybrid processes have not so far been popular throughout the post-WWII revival of arbitration, they are indeed deeply rooted in the Western tradition of arbitration (although in the forms different from their Chinese counterparts, mostly due to the fully voluntary character and clear distinction between the med-arb phases).

What is already observable in the current functioning of hybrid processes, are the clashes between demands stemming from different sets of arbitration-related values, such as the pressure for conciliatory orientation of proceedings (rooted in Confucian culture, dominant on the meso level) and the recommendations of the globalized professional culture of arbitration practitioners (according to which interests of the client may be served best through the adversarial means of dispute resolution). Reconciliation of such clashes, and the resulting adaptation of specific discursive strategies in particular cases calls for an empirical study, postulated in this chapter.

As argued here, such a study would face challenges related to particularities of legal discourse in hybrid proceedings. Such factors as limited accessibility of the field (increased even in comparison with the, already opaque, standard arbitration), more informal course of communication due to extensive inclusion of soft components into the process, and largely oral character of proceedings, require careful preparation and relevant calibration of research methods. These features, however, also make the area of hybrid processes an object of study as interesting, as it is demanding, that calls for an in-depth inquiry.

References

Ali, Shahla 2011. *Resolving Disputes in the Asia-Pacific Region: International Arbitration and Mediation in the East Asia and the West*. New York: Routledge.

Alibekova, Anita / Carrow, Robert 2007. *International Arbitration and Mediation – From the Professional's Perspective*. Salzburg: Yorkhill Law Publishing.

Bartel, Barry C. 1991. Med-Arb as a Distinct Method of Dispute Resolution: History, Analysis, and Potential. *Willamette Law Review* 27/3, 661–691.

Bergsten, Eric 2006. The Americanization of International Arbitration. *Pace International Law Review* 18/1, 289–301.

Bhatia, Vijay K. / Candlin, Christopher / Engberg, Jan 2008. Concepts, Contexts and Procedures in Arbitration Discourse. In Bhatia, Vijay K. / Candlin, Christopher / Engberg, Jan (eds) *Legal Discourse across Cultures and Systems*. Hong Kong: Hong Kong University Press, 3–32.

Bhatia, Vijay K. / Candlin, Christopher / Gotti, Maurizio 2012. *Discourse and Practice in International Commercial Arbitration: Issues, Challenges and Prospects*. Farnham: Ashgate.

Brower, Charles N. 1994. Introduction. In Lillich, Richard B. / Brower, Charles N. (eds) *International Arbitration in the 21st Century: Towards 'judicialization' and uniformity?: Twelfth Sokol Colloquium*. Leiden: Martinus Nijhoff, iv-ix.

Brown, Alexis C. 2001. Presumption Meets Reality: An Exploration of the Confidentiality Obligation in International Commercial Arbitration. *American University International Law Review* 16/4, 969–1025.

Bühring-Uhle, Christian / Kirchhoff, Lars / Scherer, Gabriele [2]2006. *Arbitration and Mediation in International Business*. Antwerp: Kluwer Law International.

Buys, Cindy G. 2003. The Tensions between Confidentiality and Transparency in International Arbitration. *American Review of International Arbitration* 14/121. <http://ssrn.com/abstract=1330243>.

Dezalay, Yves / Garth, Bryant G. 1996. Fussing about the Forum: Categories and Definitions as Stakes in a Professional Competition. *Law & Social Inquiry* 21/2, 285–312.

Domke, Martin 2003. *Domke on Commercial Arbitration (The Law and Practice of Commercial Arbitration)*. Eagan, Minn.: Callaghan.

Gaillard, Emmanuel 2010. *Legal Theory of International Arbitration*. Leiden: Martinus Nijhoff.

Gelderblom, Oscar 2011. The Resolution of Commercial Conflicts in Bruges, Antwerp, and Amsterdam (1250–1650). In Ma, Debin / van Zanden, Jan Luiten (eds) *Law and Long-Term Economic Change: A Eurasian Perspective*. Stanford, Cal.: Stanford University Press, 244–276.

Greenberg, Simon / Kee, Christopher / Weeramantry, J. Romesh 2010. *International Commercial Arbitration: An Asia-Pacific Perspective*. Cambridge: Cambridge University Press.

Gijsbers, Wilhelmina Maria 1999. *Kapitale ossen. De internationale handel in slachtvee in Noordwest-Europa 1300–1750*. Hilversum: Verloren.

Helmer, Elena V. 2003. International Commercial Arbitration: Americanized, 'Civilized', or Harmonized?. *Ohio State Journal on Dispute Resolution* 19, 66–67.

Houzhi, Tang 2005. Combination of Arbitration with Conciliation – Arb-Med. In Van den Berg, Albert J. (ed.) *New Horizons in*

International Commercial Arbitration and Beyond. Antwerp: Kluwer Law International, 89–124.

Hofstede, Geert / Hofstede, Gert Jan / Minkov, Michael 2010. *Cultures and Organizations: Software of the Mind.* New York: McGraw-Hill.

Hsiao, Kung-Chuan 1970. *Compromise in Imperial China.* Seattle: University of Washington Press.

Jandt, Fred E. [7]2013. *An Introduction to Intercultural Communication: Identities in a Global Community.* London: Sage.

Jemielniak, Joanna 2014. *Legal Interpretation in International Commercial Arbitration.* Farnham: Ashgate.

Kaufmann-Kohler, Gabrielle 2006. Foreword. In Park, William W. (ed.) *Arbitration of International Business Disputes: Studies in Law and Practice.* Oxford: Oxford University Press.

Kaufmann-Kohler, Gabrielle / Bonnin, Victor 2007. Arbitrators as Conciliators: A Statistical Study of the Relation between an Arbitrators' Role and Legal Background. *International Court of Arbitration Bulletin* 18, 79–85.

Kauppi, Niilo / Madsen, Mikael Rask 2013. *Transnational Power Elites: The New Professionals of Governance, Law and Security.* London: Routledge.

Kun, Fan 2013a. An Empirical Study of Arbitrators Acting as Mediators in China. *Cardozo Journal of Conflict Resolution* 15, 777–811.

Kun, Fan 2013b. *Arbitration in China: A Legal and Cultural Analysis.* Portland: Hart Publishing.

Kun, Fan 2013c. Globalization of Arbitration: Transnational Standards Struggling with Local Norms through the Lens of Arbitration Transplantation in China. *Harvard Negotiation Law Review* 18, 175–219.

Kun, Fan / Jemielniak, Joanna (forthcoming). *Ethnographic Methods in the Study of Hybrid Proceedings in Arbitration: the Chinese and Western Perspectives.*

Lalive, Pierre 1987. Transnational (or Truly International) Public Policy and International Arbitration. In Sanders, Pieter (ed.) *Comparative Arbitration Practice and Public Policy in Arbitration.* Antwerp: Kluwer Law International, 257–318.

Lawless, Niall 2008. Cultural Perspectives on China Resolving Disputes Through Mediation. *Transnational Dispute Management* 4, <www. transnational-dispute-management.com/article.asp? key=1294>.

López Rodríguez, Ana M. 2003. *Lex Mercatoria and Harmonization of Contract Law in the EU*. Copenhagen: Djof Publishing.

Mac Cormack, Geoffrey 1996. Assistance in Conflict Resolution: Imperial China. *L'assistance dans la résolution des conflits* 1, 109–153.

Morek, Rafal 2013. What's 'New' in the New ICC Mediation Rules? *Kluwer Mediation Blog*, 09 Dec 2013.

Naimark, Richard W. / Keer, Stephanie E. 2003. What Do Parties Really Want from International Commercial Arbitration?. *Dispute Resolution Journal* 57/4, <http://www.jurispub.com/cart.php?m =product_detail&p=16004>.

Nakagawa, Junji 207. No More Negotiated Deals?: Settlement of Trade and Investment Disputes in East Asia. *Journal of International Economic Law* 10/4, 837–867.

Nariman, Fali S. 2000. The Spirit of Arbitration: The Tenth Annual Goff Lecture. *Arbitration International* 16/3, 261–278.

Newman, Lawrence W. 2001. International Arbitration – Unfinished Business. *New York Law Journal* April, 3.

Noussia, Kyriaki 2010. *Confidentiality in International Commercial Arbitration: A Comparative Analysis of the Position Under English, US, German and French Law*. London: Springer.

Ogilvie, Sheilagh 2011. *Institutions and European Trade: Merchant Guilds, 1000–1800*. Cambridge: Cambridge University Press.

Peter, James T. 1997. Med-Arb in International Arbitration. *American Review of International Arbitration* 8/83, 83–94.

Philips, Gerald F. [2]2010. Same-Neutral Med-Arb: What Does the Future Hold?. In *American Arbitration Association Handbook on Mediation*. <http://www.jurispub.com/cart.php?m=product_detail&p=8244>.

Robertson, Ronald 1994. Glocalization: Space, Time and Social Theory. *Journal of International Communication* 1/1, 33–52.

Roebuck, Derek 2007. The Myth of Modern Mediation. *Arbitration: the Journal of the Chartered Institute of Arbitrators* 73, 105–116.

Roebuck, Derek 2015 *The Golden Age of Arbitration: Dispute Resolution under Elizabeth I.* Oxford: HOLO Books.

Rogers, Catherine A. 2006. Secrecy and Transparency in Dispute Resolution: Transparency in International Commercial Arbitration. *Kansas Law Review* 54, 1301–1344.

Ross, William H / Conlon, Donald E 2000. Hybrid Forms of Third-Party Dispute Resolution: Theoretical Implications of Combining Mediation and Arbitration. *Academy of Management Review* 25/2, 416–427.

Spencer, David / Brogan, Michael 2007. *Mediation Law and Practice.* Cambridge: Cambridge University Press.

Sussman, Edna 2009. Developing an Effective Med-Arb/Arb-Med Process. *NYSBA New York Dispute Resolution Lawyer* 2/1, 71–74.

Tod, Marcus N. 2003. International Arbitration amongst the Greeks. In Varady, Tibor et al. (eds) *International Commercial Arbitration: A Transnational Perspective.* Ithaca, NY: Cornell University Press, 270–271.

Trompenaars, Fons / Hampden-Turner, Charles 1998. *Riding the Waves of Culture: Understanding Diversity in Global Business.* New York: McGraw Hill.

Tyler, Tom / Lind, E. Allan / Huo, Yuen J. 2000. Cultural Values and Authority Relations: The Psychology of Conflict Resolution Across Cultures. *Psychology, Public Policy, & Law* 6/4, 1138–1163.

Ulisse Belotti / Mariacarla Giorgetti[1]

Critical Aspects of Arbitration Practices: Narratives from Singapore

1. Introduction

The expansion and globalisation of cross-border investment and trade has led to increased and ever more complex commercial relationships between businesses, investors and states. When disputes arise, parties may decide, among various options, to resort to arbitration to resolve their disputes. This was particularly true in the industry sector (construction, commodities, shipping and insurance) where the arbitrators' technical expertise was highly valued. Over the last few decades, arbitration has been increasingly embraced by the international community, with many recognising its importance as the primary means of resolving complex, transnational commercial disputes, even though the process is becoming more and more complex, especially in the case of multiple-party arbitrations. In general terms, it seems that arbitration is being pulled in separate and diverging directions. On the one hand, effort is made so that arbitration becomes more predictable and reliable. This process, known as judicialization of arbitration, results in arbitration proceedings which are very similar to those found in litigation. On the other hand, dissenters of the judicialization of arbitration contend that arbitration should remain a different and alternative type of dispute resolution and provide awards without the high costs and destructive results sometimes experienced in litigation.

1 The authors would like to acknowledge the assistance given by the following advocates, whose precious collaboration has made this study possible: Raja Bose, Samuel Chacko, Steven Y.H. Lim, Kah Cheong Lye, Paul Sandosham, Kabir Singh, Francis Xavier, Jimmy Yim.

In the Asian context, Singapore has been one of the countries that has greatly profited from the opportunities offered by the 'arbitration market'. This small country, which gains economic return by providing high quality services, has produced consistent law reforms with the aim of both strengthening Singapore as an investment-receiving country and attracting international arbitration (Pryles 2010).

Singapore legal background is still highly dependent on English law since the latter applied not only during colonial rule but also after independence in 1965. As far as arbitration is concerned, it seems relevant to underline the fact that, as observed by Schaefer (2000: 300), the "International Arbitration Act was not enacted to emancipate from the colonial legal tradition but rather to equip Singapore with a modern legislative infrastructure". Conveniently located between China and India, Vietnam and Indonesia, the Middle East and the Far East, Singapore has become a well-known arbitration hub. The reasons for this internationally recognized success lie in an arbitration regime that is characterized by maximum party autonomy, minimal judicial intervention and very supportive judiciary (Cheng 2011). In addition, the setting up of the Singapore International Arbitration Centre (SIAC) in 1991 marked a significant change from the past. One of the most important novelties that ensued was that foreign lawyers were allowed to represent parties in arbitration proceedings (Boo 2003), thus making Singapore an attractive site for international law firms and arbitration practitioners from other countries. A further incentive to arbitration experts to work in Singapore was represented by the fact that the income derived from arbitration work done in Singapore was exempted from taxes. Moreover, the International Arbitration Act (enacted in 1994, revised in 2002 and amended in 2012) adopted and gave force to the UNCITRAL Model Law on International Commercial Arbitration (Pillay 2004). Even though ad-hoc arbitration counts are not known, the number of institutional arbitrations held in Singapore is on the increase as stated by SIAC, which handled 259 new cases in 2013, reaching a value of over 24 million Singapore dollars. It is also interesting to note that 86% of new cases filed with SIAC were international in nature, with India and

China on top.[2] Moreover, in 2010 SIAC was the first international arbitration institution based in Asia to introduce emergency arbitration in which an arbitrator is appointed to deal with requests for urgent interim relief. This allows parties to apply for interim relief without having to go to court or to wait until the arbitration tribunal is appointed.

2. Arbitration in Singapore

Arbitration in Singapore is governed by two sets of regulations, one for domestic and the other for international arbitration (Tan 2005; Chan 1995). Domestic arbitration is disciplined by the 2002 Arbitration Act (AA). This applies to all arbitration that takes place in Singapore and which is not classified as International Arbitration. It conforms broadly to the UNCITRAL Model Law on International Commercial Arbitration.

International arbitration is disciplined by the International Arbitration Act (IAA). Arbitration is considered international when:

(i) at least one of the parties has its registered head offices in a state other than Singapore; or
(ii) the state in which arbitration takes place is different from that in which the parties have their registered head offices; or
(iii) the state in which an essential part of the obligation that is the object of the dispute or where the asset is held that is the object of the dispute, is different from that in which the parties have their registered head offices; or
(iv) the parties have expressly agreed to this effect.

In international arbitration, the role of the national judge is extremely limited and these limits are expressly marked out by the law. Similarly, the possibilities of challenging a foreign award before a domestic judge are limited.

2 Information and statistics concerning arbitrations managed by SIAC have been retrieved from <http://www.siac.org.sg/> (December 2014).

2.1 General discipline of arbitration

Arbitration in Singapore may follow ad hoc rules or it may be administered by an arbitration court. The Singapore International Arbitration Centre (SIAC) is the only arbitration court in Singapore. The SIAC usually conducts its arbitrations in accordance with its specific Rules of Arbitration, though the parties are free to choose any other rules, including the 1976 UNCITRAL Arbitration Rules. The SIAC has its own Panel of accredited arbitrators, divided into a regional Panel and a Panel of international experts, from which the Deputy Chairman of the SIAC usually selects the arbitrators, though the faculty remains of appointing arbitrators *ad hoc*, not necessarily members of the above Panels. According to the SIAC Rules of Arbitration, the parties are required to pay an administration fee, proportional to the value of the dispute. However, when appointment of the arbitrators is delegated exclusively to the SIAC, only an appointment fee is due, which is calculated on a fixed basis. At present (2015), the maximum amount of the administration fee is $ 60,250.00. According to the SIAC rules, the parties may also be represented by persons other than lawyers, or by lawyers not qualified to practice law in Singapore, even when the applicable law is that of Singapore.

2.2 The arbitration process

2.2.1 The arbitration agreement

Whether arbitration has been chosen on the strength of an arbitration submission agreement or an arbitration clause, it must nevertheless arise from an agreement concluded in writing and signed by both parties, in which the wish to resolve the dispute by arbitration is unequivocally stated [Sect. 4(1), Arbitration Act.; Sect. 4(2), Arbitration Act.; Sect. 4(1) and (2) of the Arbitration Act correspond to Art. 7(1) of the Model Law; Sect. 4(3), Arbitration Act. This provision is similar to that in Art. 7(2) of the Model Law].

Arbitrators in Singapore have the power to rule on the merits of the existence of their jurisdiction and on the validity of the arbitration agreement (whether it is an arbitration submission agreement or an arbitration clause). When the arbitration panel rules that a case comes under their jurisdiction, this decision can be challenged in the High Court and, in certain cases, at the second level before the Court of Appeal. If the arbitrators rule that the case does not come under their jurisdiction, however, this decision cannot be appealed against and the case automatically goes to the ordinary court [Art. 16(1) Model Law, IAA; Sect. 21(3), Arbitration Act.; PT Asuransi Jasa Idonesia (Persero) v. Dexia Bank SA [2007] 1 SLR 597 (CA), reversing the decision of the High Court in PT Asuransi Jasa Indonesia (Persero) V. Dexia Bank SA [2006] 1 SLR 197(HC).]

If one of the parties, violating the arbitration agreement, opens proceedings before the ordinary court, the other party may request that these proceedings be stayed, and a term granted within which the arbitration award is to be made. In such a case, in the framework of international arbitration, the civil judge will have no margin of discretion with which to assess his/her own jurisdiction, provided that the appellant party has not so far begun to defend its case before the ordinary court. Unless the arbitration agreement is null and void, the stay must of necessity be granted and the parties must submit to the arbitration procedure.

2.2.2 Appointment of the arbitrators

According to the International Arbitration Act, anyone can be appointed as an arbitrator, including a foreign citizen [Art. 12(2) Model Law and Sect. 14(3)(b) Arbitration Act.; Art. 11(1) Model Law, IAA]. Many of the arbitrators are members of the Singapore Institute of Arbitrators and/or the Chartered Institute of Arbitrators, London, although membership in such institutions is not a condition for acting as arbitrator.

In any case, in arbitration proceedings governed by the SIAC regulations, arbitrators are required to disclose any conflicts of interest or any circumstance that may affect the independence of their judgement. The appointment of the arbitrator may be contested exclusively where there exist 'serious doubts' concerning his/her impartiality and independence and/or where he/she does not possess the professional requisites agreed upon in the arbitration agreement [Sect. 14(1),

Arbitration Act.; Rule 9.2, SIAC Rules; Art. 12 Model Law, IAA; Sect. 14(2), Arbitration Act, Art. 12(1), Model Law, IAA. See also Rule 2.1 of Code of Ethics for an Arbitrator of SIAC.; Sect. 14(3), Arbitration Act, Art. 12(2), Model Law, IAA.].

The number of arbitrators is freely agreed between the parties. In the absence of such an agreement, the choice of a single arbitrator is presumed. An even number of arbitrators is not prohibited, but for obvious reasons the parties usually prefer a single arbitrator or a panel of three. If the parties have chosen an even number of arbitrators and a stalled decision results, there is no specific regulation for overcoming this. If the parties insist on an even number of arbitrators, therefore, it is advisable for them to include in their arbitration agreement a specific clause governing an impasse of this kind [Sect. 12(2), Arbitration Act; Sect. 9, IAA and Rule 5, SIAC Rules. Note that Sect. 9, IAA modifies Art. 10(2) Model Law].

If the parties cannot agree upon the appointment of the single arbitrator, this is referred to the Deputy Chairman of the SIAC. Where there is no agreement upon the choice of an arbitration panel, on the other hand, each party is free to appoint an arbitrator of their choice, while the third will be chosen by the Deputy Chairman of the SIAC. An appointment made by the Deputy Chairman in lieu of a decision by the parties is not open to appeal [Sect. 13(3)(b) Arbitration Act, Art. 11(3)(b) Model Law, IAA read with Art. 6 Model Law and Sect. 8(2) IAA; Rules 5, 6 and 7 SIAC Rules].

2.2.3 Procedure

In Singapore the parties are always free to choose the arbitration procedure. If they fail to agree, the decision is delegated to the arbitration panel itself [Sect. 23(1), Arbitration Act; Art. 19(1) Model Law, IAA]. The parties are normally assigned a term within which to appear before the arbitration court and file their defence statements. In general, the claimant has a term of thirty days from the constitution of the arbitration panel in which to file the claim and serve it upon the defendant. The latter then has a similar term within which to join suit by filing the defence statement. The panel will subsequently draw up a memorandum of issue. This is a statement of the factual and legal questions it is asked to investigate. The panel may, at its discretion, assess whether or not to hold one or more oral hearings, or whether a written procedure is preferable, based on the filing of claims and counterclaims [Art. 19(2), Model Law, IAA; Sect. 23(3), Arbitration Act].

There is no obligation in arbitration procedures to comply with court rules concerning evaluation of the evidence, since the so-called Evidence Act, applicable to all ordinary procedures need not be applied here. All assessments concerning whether or not each single piece of evidence is admissible, relevant and probative, depend exclusively on the discretion of the arbitration panel [Sect. 28(2), Arbitration Act]. The IAA confers powers upon the arbitration panel similar to those of an ordinary court, including those of issuing orders during the procedure and/or adopting precautionary measures [Set out in Sect. 12, IAA]. Guarantees may be requested, such as an escrow account, bank and/or insurance guarantees or other forms of guarantee. According to the SIAC, the arbitration panel also has the power to order *in rem* precautionary measures, such as seizures, impoundment and/or forced sale, regarding the assets that are the object of the dispute [Sect. 12(1)(g), IAA and Sect. 12(1)(e) IAA]. There is no similar power for arbitrators under the Arbitration Act. Only the High Court has the power to grant interim injunctions and/or any other interim measures or order to secure the amount in dispute [Sect. 31(1)(b) and (d), Arbitration Act].

Compulsory execution of such orders requires the issue of formal authorization by the High Court, in order to become fully enforceable. With regard to such measures, Singapore legislation recognizes, in any case, the overlapping jurisdiction of the arbitration panel and the High Court. The parties are therefore free to request the issue of such orders both from the panel and from the High Court. The dispositions of the arbitration panel prevail, however, where they overlap with those of an ordinary judge.

2.2.4 The arbitration award

The arbitration award is defined by the IAA as "a decision by the arbitration panel regarding the right and/or the asset which is the object of the dispute and also includes any partial, *ad interim* or interlocutory decision" [Sect. 2(1), IAA; Sect. 2(1), Arbitration Act; Sect. 28,

Arbitration Act and Sect. 12, IAA]. Expressly excluded from this definition are any dispositions assumed as part of the procedural regulation of the arbitration, as well as any decisions that do not have the power to modify the legal status of the right and/or asset which is the object of the dispute.

Any award other than the final and definitive one is deemed to be *ad interim*. Decisions concerning the applicable law or the jurisdiction, etc., are considered *ad interim* awards. Partial awards are those which do not totally cover the object of the dispute. Interlocutory awards are those which, for example, pronounce on the merits of the claim but reserve the right to quantify the damage later, which will be decided in the definitive award [Sect. 46, Arbitration Act; Sect. 19, IAA]. As indicated above, any award, whether final, partial or interlocutory, can be subject to enforcement, once this has been authorized by the High Court.

The IAA does not envisage a term within which the arbitration panel must pronounce the award, whereas the SIAC regulations indicate a term of forty-five days from the date on which the procedure is concluded. However, this term may be extended if requested by the parties. If an arbitrator acting under the Arbitration Act fails to use reasonable dispatch in making the award, he risks being removed by the court, provided it can be shown that the delay causes substantial injustice to the party applying for the removal [Sect. 16(1)(b), Arbitration Act].

The award must be drawn up in writing and must be signed by the arbitrators, indicating clearly the date and place where it was written. In the case of an arbitration panel, it is sufficient for the IAA if the award is signed only by a majority of the arbitrators. However, those abstaining must state their motives. This obligation may be waived if the parties have specifically agreed to this effect [Art. 31(1), Model Law, IAA; Sect. 38(1)(b), Arbitration Act; Rule 27.4, SIAC Rules; Sect. 38(2), Arbitration Act; Art. 31(2), Model Law, IAA.; Art. 31(3), Model Law, IAA; Sect. 38(3), Arbitration Act].

According to the SIAC regulations, the award must be sent to the registry office of the Chamber of Arbitration, which will issue authenticated copies. These copies will then be transmitted to the parties, provided they have paid all fees. In practice, where the award involves parties from different jurisdictions, a certificate of authentication is attached to the award to facilitate enforcement under the New York Convention 1958. In all cases, the registry office of the SIAC provides the service of registration and issue of arbitration awards made as part of arbitration proceedings taking place in Singapore.

Once the award has been registered, it is fully valid and effective for the parties. No further action is needed to render it effective, apart from the remedies envisaged by the law which will be illustrated below [Sect. 19B(3) IAA, and Sect. 44(3), Arbitration Act provide that the award is made when it is "signed and delivered" in accordance with Art. 31 Model Law and Sect. 38 Arbitration Act respectively; Sect. 44(1), Arbitration Act; Sect. 19B, IAA]. It remains understood that, if the award is not put into effect by the losing party, it may be subject to enforcement in the manner described below.

2.3 Contesting the award

2.3.1 Correction, interpretation and additional award

In any arbitration performed in Singapore, the arbitrators are authorized to correct errors of calculation, typing, typography or spelling contained in the award. Such corrections may be made at the direct initiative of the arbitrators or at the request of one of the parties, within a term of thirty days from service. This term may be extended at the request of a party [Art. 33(1) and (2), Model Law; Sect. 43(1), Arbitration Act; Rules 28.1 and 28.2, SIAC Rules]. Similarly, the parties may request the arbitrators to provide an authentic interpretation of one or more parts of the award [Art. 33(1), Model Law, IAA; Sect. 43(2), Arbitration Act]. Corrections and interpretations must be made by the arbitrators within thirty days of the request.

If the award has not pronounced on one or more of the questions which are the object of the dispute, and without prejudice to any agreement to the contrary, the parties are entitled to file, within thirty days of pronouncement of the award concerned, a specific petition, requesting the arbitrators to complete the award already issued with a suitable additional award. This must be issued within 45 days according to the

SIAC regulations, within 60 according to those of the IAA [Art. 33(3), Model Law, IAA; Sect. 43(4), Arbitration Act; Rule 28.3, SIAC Rules].

2.3.2 Appealing against the award

Theoretically, and subsequently to agreement by the parties, it is possible to appeal against an arbitration award before another arbitration panel, which will act as appeal arbitrators. In practice, however, this is never done in Singapore. It is possible to appeal against an arbitration award before a civil judge, but only where the award was issued in the context of domestic arbitration. In the case of international arbitration, this is ruled out and the only possible challenge is the so-called setting aside [Sect. 49, Arbitration Act. No appeal is permitted under the IAA].

2.3.3 Setting aside the award

The so-called 'setting aside' is the only possible means of challenging an international arbitration award in Singapore. This may take place under the following conditions [Sect. 48, Arbitration Act]:

(i) incapacity of one of the parties;
(ii) invalidity of the arbitration agreement under the law to which this same is submitted (or that of Singapore if the parties have not expressly indicated a different choice);
(iii) failure to notify one of the parties correctly concerning the introduction of the arbitration procedure;
(iv) issue of an award that has as its object a dispute not included in the submission agreement or the arbitration clause, or one which cannot be settled by arbitration, or that contains decisions that exceed the scope of the said arbitration. In the latter case, the excess part will be removed if this is possible; otherwise the entire award will be set aside;
(v) failure to comply with the agreement between the parties concerning the composition of the arbitration panel or the arbitration procedures to be adopted, except where this agreement envisages procedures contrary to mandatory IAA rules or SIAC regulations;
(vi) an award that is the result of fraud or corruption;

(vii) presence of serious procedural infringements during the arbitration procedure, such as may prejudice the parties' rights;
(viii) an award that is contrary to public order.

In the case of a petition for setting aside an award, the Court of Appeal has jurisdiction. The appointed judge, however, may not reconsider the award from the point of view of facts, rights or interpretations of the law. His role is limited to assessing whether at least one of the above requisites is present. Generally speaking, the Court of Appeal is inclined towards protecting the validity of arbitration awards. Setting aside is envisaged only in the case of the most serious and relevant infringements.

2.4 Enforcement of the arbitration award

2.4.1 Enforcement of an award issued in Singapore

The necessary condition for enforcement of an arbitration award issued in Singapore, whether in the domestic or the international context, is authorization by a civil judge [Sect. 46(1), Arbitration Act; As for procedure, see Order 69 and Order 69A, Rules of Court (2006 Rev Ed)]. A petition for enforcement must be presented before the judge having jurisdiction, identified in the High Court, within six years of the issue of the arbitration award. At the end of this term the award becomes null. In cases of particular urgency, a procedure may be implemented that will lead to the issue of authorization *inaudita altera parte*. The party subject to enforcement retains the right to subsequently petition under the law against this enforcement.

If authorization is not granted, the party concerned has a term of one month from the pronouncement of rejection to petition against it before the Court of Appeal.

Authorization for enforcement is a court order to all effects and must be served upon the party affected according to the law. If the order is issued *inaudita altera parte*, the party in question has a term of 14 days from the date of service to petition against the order before the High Court, or else to pay. At the end of this term, the order may be enforced as of law [Order 57, Rule 4, Rules of Court (2006 Rev Ed)]. In the case of a petition against the order before the High Court, enforcement of the order is suspended, but if the petition is rejected, the award will become executive once more. It is possible to plead against rejection of the petition, this time before the Court of Appeal. The term for this is thirty days, but the filing of such a plea does not, in itself, suspend the executive status of the award [Order 57, Rule 15, Rules of Court (2006 Rev Ed.);Sect. 36(1), Supreme Court of Judicature Act Cap. 322].

Nevertheless, the Court of Appeal, in response to a plea by the debtor party and the provision of a suitable guarantee, may suspend enforcement of the award where there are concrete risks of irremediable prejudice to the said party [Para. 254 of Michael Hwang and Andrew Chan's Singapore Chapter in Moser (2008)]. With regard to the premises for a legitimate rejection of the plea for enforcement, the IAA envisages that this may take place only in the presence of the same circumstances as would justify setting aside the award in question (including grounds on the existence of fraud, corruption and the breach of natural justice, these being additional grounds to set aside the award under the IAA).

2.4.2 Enforcement of a foreign award in Singapore

In order to enforce in Singapore a foreign arbitration award issued by a member country of the New York Convention, the procedure established by the IAA may be followed, since Singapore has signed the reciprocal agreement as of Art I (3) of the Convention. Such awards may therefore be enforced in Singapore, following authorization by the High Court. Such authorization also has the value of recognizing the award as fully valid and effective under the Singapore judicial system. The said award will therefore be binding upon the parties to whom it is issued and may be used by either party as the basis of a plea for enforcement in any civil court of Singapore. Where an action arises out of an award on a salvage award or a claim under a charter party, it falls within the Admiralty jurisdiction of the High Court and an action *in rem* could be brought [See Alexander G Tsavliris & Sons Maritime Co v. Keppel Corp Ltd (1995) 2 SLR 113; Sect. 19, IAA read with Sect. 29 of the IAA].

A plea for enforcement of a foreign award made under the New York Convention must be filed no later than six years from the date of the award. The plea for enforcement must be filed together with an affidavit containing the agreement and the arbitration award (either the original or an authenticated copy), identification of the parties and a formal declaration that the award has not been executed [Sect. 6(1)(c), Limitation Act Cap. 163]. This procedure is usually completed *inaudita altera parte.* Once the award has been recognized, it is served on the debtor party who has the normal term of 14 days to comply or to petition against enforcement. At the end of this term, the award may be enforced by law.

The court which hears the plea for recognition of the award may not enter into the legal merits of the dispute, but it may refuse recognition on the basis of the principles as of Sect. 31(2) of the IAA, which are identical to those under V of the New York Convention. Decisions of this kind by the High Court may be pleaded against before the Court of Appeal. It is also possible to enforce an award issued under the International Convention for the Settlement of Investment Disputes between States and Nationals of Other States (ICSID Convention), according to the criteria envisaged by the Rules of Court. As of today, however, this has never been done.

Arbitration awards issued in the United Kingdom or other member countries of the Commonwealth have access to special procedures, on the basis of reciprocal recognition agreements. In practice, in view of the simplified procedures envisaged under the New York Convention, the normal procedure is generally preferred even for arbitration awards issued in these countries [Reciprocal Enforcement of Commonwealth Judgments (Extension) (Consolidation) Notification NI, 1999 Rev. Ed. lists the territories to which the Act extends. For Australia, see Declaration under Sect. 5 (Cap. 264, Declaration 1) (24 September 1993)].

2.4.3 *Enforcement of an award outside Singapore*

A party wishing to enforce abroad an arbitration award issued in Singapore must comply with the procedure envisaged under Art. IV (1) of the New York Convention and file a plea before the foreign court with jurisdiction for enforcement. Judges in different countries may interpret differently the procedure set out by the New York Convention. They may, for example, require compliance with specific formalities.

Awards issued by the SIAC are certified and authenticated by the SIAC Registry Office if requested by the parties. Awards thus authenticated are recognized and accepted in a large number of states. There is, in any case, no public body in Singapore for the certification and authentication of arbitration awards issued outside the SIAC. This function has been entrusted to the SIAC, provided the award was issued in Singapore during the previous three months, is duly signed by a single arbitrator or at least one member of the arbitration panel, and is accompanied by the arbitration submission agreement or the arbitration clause.

3. Research on arbitration narratives

Narrative is considered a universal mode of verbal expression (Barthes 1977; Bruner 1986) and narrative analysis has been conducted according to an array of approaches. For example, language acquisition, processing and pathology have been investigated by psycholinguists, whilst sociolinguists have analysed narratives in social contexts. On the other hand, linguists have focused on various aspects of narratives, such as the concept of evaluation (Labov/Waletzky 1997), the notion of footing (Goffman 1986) and that of voicing (Bakhtin 1981). Narrative analysis has also been employed to investigate different domains such as clinical ethics and human identity (Jordens/Little 2006), but also literature (Voloshinov 1971; Banfield 1982), news reporting (Fairclough 1992; Waugh 1995) and academic discourse (Swales 1990; Thompson/Ye 1991; Hunston 1993).

As far as arbitration discourse is concerned, research has explored a variety of features, ranging from the analysis of the linguistic and discoursal characteristics of international arbitration laws enacted in different countries, cultures and socio-political backgrounds (Bhatia *et al.* 2003) to the investigation of the influence that litigation practices and discourse have had over arbitration as a method of resolving international commercial disputes (Bhatia *et al.* 2010; Bhatia 2011; Gotti 2011). More specifically, oral arbitration narratives have received less attention, probably because arbitration practitioners are very busy people and are often reluctant to be interviewed.

Nonetheless, within the international project entitled *International Commercial Arbitration Study,*[3] a corpus of interviews to Italian arbitration practitioners was collected in order to analyse the state of the art of arbitration in Italy and investigate the linguistic realizations that these experts, mainly counsels and arbitrators, had employed using English as a lingua franca (Belotti 2012a, 2012b). As regards the Singapore arbitration context, useful insights have been provided by Kathpalia (2012), who investigated the relationship between international commercial arbitration (ICA) and litigation through a survey which was distributed to arbitrators and legal practitioners in Singapore. Kathpalia's findings show that these practitioners were concerned about a number of issues, including, among others, the escalation of costs, appeals and enforceability of arbitration awards.

4. Data and Methods

This study is based on eight interviews with professionals involved in arbitration practice, carried out in Singapore between 21st and 26th July 2014. The respondents were all law-firm professionals, based in Singapore, mainly acting as either counsels to the parties or arbitrators in arbitration proceedings. The interviewees were all but one native speakers of English[4] and they all agreed that interviews would be conducted in English. The corpus comprises eight audio files amounting to 4 hours 19 minutes of recorded interviews which were transcribed (288,648 words) using SoundScriber (2004). Even though the number of interviews is limited, it seems worth pointing out that the interviewees were all members of the 2014 panel of arbitrators of the SIAC.

---

3 The *International Commercial Arbitration Practice: A Discourse Analytical Study* project was funded by the Research Grants Council of the Government of HKSAR [Project No. 9041191 (CityU 1501/06H].

4 As regards the issue of considering Singapore English as one of the varieties of English, see Silver (2005), Bolton (2008), Crystal (2008), Ghim/Chew (2014).

5. Critical aspects of arbitration

Respondents were asked to rate aspects and considerations for preferring arbitration to litigation and then they were also asked to rate areas of concern which, in their view, were likely to make ICA less attractive as an instrument of alternative dispute resolution. This study identifies and explores some of most critical issues, i.e. arbitration clauses, confidentiality and privacy in arbitration proceedings, costs and duration of arbitration. Moreover, cross-examination and the perception that arbitration has become similar to litigation have also been investigated together with some of the linguistic realizations that respondents have employed to deliver critical speech acts.

5.1 Arbitration clauses

Since the foundation of ICA lies in its consensual nature, the parties to an international contract are entitled to design the manner in which the arbitral proceedings are conducted, the drafting of the arbitration clause being one of the most important steps. Whether the companies opt for a clause drafted by an arbitration institution or decide to draft their own arbitration clause, there are a few mandatory requirements that must be met and provisions that are to be included. It should also be noted that an arbitration clause aims not only to provide a possible way out of disputes which may arise, but also to avoid litigation in the other party's 'home' court (Hunter 2000). Indeed, arbitration clauses may come in various shapes and sizes. Some are very detailed and try to illustrate the steps the parties are expected to take before they resort to arbitration.

These steps may include amicable settlement which, in case of failure, is to be followed by formal mediation. Others are quite concise and may simply hint at a generic commitment of resolving the disputes arising between the parties. Since it is customary that arbitration clauses are inserted in the contract the very last moment, they are also termed *midnight-clauses* or *airport-express-bus-clauses*. Indeed, this is likely to produce arbitration clauses that are pathological (Townsend 2003; Liu 2006) not only in terms of legal criteria but also from a linguistic point of view (Frade 2010), especially when drafters are not fully aware of the linguistic risks connected to ready-to-use standard model clauses.

When arbitration clauses are poorly drafted, problems arise over an array of aspects such as the seat of the arbitration, the language, the number and the method of selecting arbitrators, the applicable law(s), the appointing authority, the confidentiality clause and even the scope of the dispute. As observed by Debattista (2005: 240), it is worth noting that "These clauses are intended by commercial parties to assist them in resolving existing disputes, not to raise another dispute as to how to resolve those disputes." As far as our corpus is concerned, interviewees identified five different reasons why arbitration clauses are badly drafted, as shown in the following extracts.

5.1.1 Poor or incomplete knowledge of the arbitral procedure

(1) Yes (.) yes we've had quite a few instances that we encountered (.) very badly drafted clauses and you know invariably it's put down to the eh (.) lawyers who are involved at the drafting stage of the contract (.) how much or how little they know about the arbitral process (.) and in fact I think that's probably one of the great weaknesses because the people who actually conduct the arbitrations and experience the ups-and downs and the difficulties (.) are the dispute resolution lawyers but the lawyers who draft them are the transactional or corporate lawyers (.) *many of whom may not have ever seen the inside of an arbitration chamber* (laughs). (AAD[5] 2014: I4)

Extract (1) highlights the problem of arbitration clauses which are drafted by lawyers who are often more qualified as litigators than arbitrators, which leads to flaws in the arbitration clauses themselves. The clause *many of whom may not have ever seen the inside of an arbitration chamber* clearly signals that badly drafted arbitration clauses are those drawn up by corporate lawyers.

5 Throughout this chapter, AAD 2014 refers to the interviews based on the questionnaire administered to Singapore arbitration practitioners (cf. Appendix 2); the numbers refer to the individual interviews. As regards transcription conventions, cf. Appendix 1. In all quotations emphasis has been added.

5.1.2 Arbitration clauses are either crammed with unnecessary details or lack something which is deemed to be relevant

(2) Well (.) nine times out of ten ahm (.) they will have something in their contract which they shouldn't eh (.) it makes a number of basic mistakes ehm (.) either because they omit something that needs to be there or for the most part it includes unnecessary details (.) and we generally prefer and our advice is .stick with the model clause of the institution. (AAD 2014: I7)

(3) They can be quite a nightmare (laughs) … recently I was dealing with an American company which has templates agreements and their arbitration clauses are (slight intake of breath) very confusing (.) and to the extent that they are going into such much detail (.) it creates opportunities for ambiguity and disputes arising (.) and the other problem was you know you had Singapore experts of the substantive dispute (.) parties actually being based in the US and in different states in the US so there were issues of where the arbitration was to be held which state … which state law was to apply and the US … you know … they came up with a clause which is rather hodge-podge and everything (.) ah so we had a sort of sit down and *tell them* (.) *if **you** really **want** to avoid disputes and **you want** a clean arbitration (.) **you may want** to simplify all of this (.) pick an arbitral institution whether it is Singapore or the US (.) **specify** their procedure (.) **specify** your seat* (throat clearing) *and then leave the rest to the arbitrator in terms of procedure which is not covered under the rules of that specific institution.* (AAD 2014: I8)

As exemplified in (2), one of the most frequent flaws in arbitration clauses is the presence of unnecessary details, which make the clause lengthy and verbose. On the other hand, it may happen that these clauses do not contain details which are deemed to be relevant thus the suggestion of drawing on reliable clauses drafted by an arbitral institution. In extract (3), the interviewee's oral narrative includes a stretch of direct speech embedded in his narrative which is signaled by the use of the verbal phrase *tell them* where *them* is likely to refer to the American company representatives. From a linguistic point of view, this is an example of self-quotation. Here, the respondent is manifesting his own concern about the fact that the arbitration clause may not be as effective as hoped and provides advice on how to proceed. In this case, suggestions are made stronger by the repetition of the same verbal phrases *you want* (repeated three times) and *specify* (repeated twice). Grammatical parallelism serves not only the function of making the narration cohesive but also helps the speaker to stress the idea that an arbitration procedure works well on certain conditions.

5.1.3 Arbitration clauses are too lengthy

(4) people tend to get longer arbitration clauses and they think that the longer the better (.) I hold the opposite view (.) my view is (.) ***if you indulge … go the website of the <tribu> of the institution … pick out their clause … you're probably in very safe cans*** (.) because it's got the essential elements eh … and again problems … said to say with my colleagues on the transaction practices is (.) they come with an arbitration clauses that are one and a half page long …
Interviewer: Which has to be interpreted
Which is fine but one and half page long also remember (.) gives your counter-party in a dispute a lot more opportunity to find problems with it (.) and so ***we always say to them look … yes it may look very nice at the beginning but when things go wrong ah*** … we … (AAD 2014: I6)

The whole corpus comprises 58 instances of direct speech acts, which are irregularly distributed across the sections of the questionnaire. As far as the respondents in our corpus are concerned, the data show that seven out of eight interviewees reported utterances of others in their narratives. Three respondents were particularly at ease with reported speech and used it quite extensively. In particular, one of the interviewees used reported speech 32 times, showing how this rhetorical device was considered particularly suitable as a frame for the construction of his narrative. Data in our corpus also show that narrators incorporated reported speech into narratives by using not only reporting verbs but also signalling devices, such as discourse markers and silent or filled pauses. Excerpt (4) contains two examples of direct speech acts embedded in the narrative. In the first one, the respondent suggests that downloading arbitration clauses from arbitral institutions websites would be a reasonable way of having reliable and ready-to use clauses while the second highlights the risks of using lengthy arbitration clauses.

5.1.4 Cut-and-paste techniques

(5) but I think ehm the common problem that we see is people do a cut and paste approach (.) so ***they don't think about*** what dispute they're dealing with ***they don't think*** about the value of the claim ***they don't think about*** the subject matter ***they don't think about*** the location of the parties ahm ***they don't think about*** which institutional rules may be better for them ehm … they simply say … ok this company A and company A uses SIAC and we will always use SIAC and may not be the case and may not be favourable for you … so I think that's the common problem we see (.) (AAD 2014: I6)

In (5), talking about how arbitration clauses may be badly drafted, one of the interviewees uses a number of negative remarks directed to 'people' who are entrusted with the drafting of arbitration clauses. The negative verbal phrase *they don't think about* signals overt criticism of a modus operandi which is likely to cause problems to the whole arbitration procedure. The content of these critical speech acts reveals that these 'people' do not take into account aspects which are considered vitally important, such as the nature of the dispute, the value of the claim, the subject matter, the location of the parties and the rules of the arbitral institution. From a linguistic point of view, it is worth pointing out that the critical claim *they don't think about* is repeated five times without any hedging devices which conveys the idea that this grammatical parallelism, besides providing cohesion to the narration itself, makes it clear that some arbitration clauses are drafted without considering the basics, thus causing serious problems to arbitration itself.

5.1.5 'Home-made' arbitration clauses

(6) Well (.) I mean it really depends on whether that clause is properly drafted (.) I mean if it works (.) then … the reason the clients wonna go with that … is that they are comfortable with it (.) they are familiar with it (.) they know what to do if a dispute arises (.) and to some extent it is tried and tested (.) I mean my surprise … ahm … in dealing with a lot of these cases is that (.) despite the ease of adopting a standard template on the website which you can take from SIAC or ICC (.) people still try and draft their own piece of arbitration agreements and that's where the problems arise …
Interviewer: *Home-made*
Yea home-made and I don't understand why they don' just grab something off (.) I mean clients come to us and say (.) *look why didn't you grab something off*

the web site from ICC because that's tried and tested you know it works why do you need to come up with some ***funky or unusual things*** *(.) unless you have some unique circumstance which requires that* (.) but even then most standard templates can address those issues. (AAD 2014: I3)

(7) we're doing a case at the moment where we act for eh … an American oil company and they have a dispute with a eh … Korean contractor (.) in relation to a gas-pipeline in Myanmar (.) ***the arbitration clause was taken from something that Koreans had used in Korea↓ and they just … changed the word Korea to London ah but the institution that they referred to doesn't exist in London*** … you know so the Korea I think … centre for international arbitration (.) KCA and they just said the London centre for … so there is no such corresponding institution in London (.) and also was they could have … it didn't make sense why they were choosing to go to London to arbitrate a dispute … it could be much more sensible for them to choose Singapore or Hong Kong (.) ehm luckily for us in that case … we ahm (.) we were able to persuade them … why don't we sign a fresh arbitration agreement choosing Hong Kong and a single arbitrator (.) instead of going to London with three arbitrators (.) forcing the LCIA to accept and run the risk that somebody runs to court and challenges it … and say … I'll never come to this so … eh … (AAD 2014: I7)

In extract (6), the respondent highlights one of the problems that may arise when the parties decide to draft their own arbitration clauses. This may lead to situations in which disputes arise over the interpretation of the arbitration agreement resulting in the fact that the award itself may be unenforceable. In (7), the 'home-made' arbitration clause provides the name of an arbitral institution which does not exist (*there is no such corresponding institution in London*) thus causing a number of problems.

5.2 Costs of arbitration

With the general trend towards cost-cutting within organizations, the rising costs in international arbitration is a cause for concern. Packed schedules and the difficulty in matching the schedules of counsel and the tribunal means more tranches of hearing and this results in higher costs (Aksen 2007; Stipanovich 2008). However, it should be noted that costs are not the primary concern of commercial parties in deciding to arbitrate, which is in line with the results from the survey on arbitration conducted in 2013 by Queen Mary University of London (School of International Arbitration) and PricewaterhouseCoopers. When asked to indicate whether arbitration is more or less expensive than litigation, one of the interviewees replied that what really matters is not how the dispute is going to be resolved but how relevant the stakes are.

(8) I mean whether it is litigation or arbitration ahm (3) it is not so much a question of whether it is litigation or arbitration (.) it's more the question of whether how important are the stakes here (.) right↑ (.) and and how much each party is prepared to put in to fight it out (.) (AAD 2014: I4)

One of the findings in Kathpalia's (2012: 270) work was that "a significant number of respondents (63 per cent) indicated that ICA is as expensive as transnational litigation for medium/smaller cases but better value for more complex cases". In our corpus, one of the respondents argued that it is not just a matter of comparing small/medium cases with more complex cases in arbitration but comparison should be made between arbitration and litigation costs:

(9) Complicated question↓ (.) because when we compare the cost of ah.. international arbitration (.) we always have to compare it against litigation costs (.) if you had gone to court and that immediately begs the question which court (chuckle) … so for example if … you're comparing a three tribunal member arbitration going on in Geneva for two weeks and you're comparing <u>THAT</u> against … let's say a high court hearing for two weeks in Malaysia↑ … I'm pretty sure that Geneva (laughs) arbitration is going to come out as more expensive but if you would compare it against eh … a court of a different country (.) you know … let's say we are all in the English commercial courts with very expensive English commercial Queen's Counsels and juniors arguing it … then perhaps the Geneva ah. arbitration would be a better value (.) ahm but (.) let me see what I can say (.) which is objective (2) no matter which national court we are comparing international arbitration against (.) the <u>SAVING</u> that international arbitration makes in terms of costs (.) is the <u>REDUCTION</u> in the appeals … and so ah … with international arbitration you get your (.).I adopt the phrase .your first instance decision which is your award … right … but once you get that award it's more or less unshakable the the you know … you don't have all these appeal mechanisms (.) but if you had (.) you're comparing to a national court (.) you may get your first instance decision shall we say relatively cheaply (.) <u>BUT</u> depending on the system the layers of appeal that you have to get at the end of it ah … you know it could end up costing a lot more and I think that's what we can say <u>OBJECTIVELY</u> without having to go into detail exactly which court am I comparing against … (AAD 2014: I5)

Other respondents pointed out that costs for high value cases are higher than those applied by courts, as clearly indicated in the following extract:

(10) I mean … some people have the idea that it should be … cheaper it goes back to the idea that arbitration should be less formal … faster and cheaper but I don't think that is necessarily the case … certainly not for the kind of high value disputes that that people see now … in arbitration and I think actually … to be perfectly honest … that arbitration for high value cases is probably more expensive than litigation going on in court. (AAD 2014: I1)

From a linguistic point of view, this stretch of speech contains the parenthetical phrase *to be perfectly honest*, a device which is used by the speaker to express his stance on the belief that arbitration is cheaper, faster and less formal than litigation. The position of this parenthetical phrase, placed between the verbal phrase *I think* and the relative clause *that arbitration … is probably more expensive than litigation going on in court*, indicates overt criticism of those who think that arbitration is better value in complex cases.

Another interesting point was made by one of interviewees who offered his view in terms of legal costs recoverability in Singapore where parties are in a more favourable position if they decide to resolve disputes through arbitration, rather than resort to litigation:

(11) in the Singapore context … your recoverability of legal cost is much better in arbitration than it is in litigation so if you're looking at it from that perspective yes you may be paying your lawyers five million dollars in legal fees but at the end of the day if you win … ahm … you may get four million dollars or four and half million dollars from the arbitrator so that's quite good recovery … whereas in litigation … at least in the Singapore context … if you pay five million dollars you may get back one million dollars. (AAD 2014. I6)

5.3 Confidentiality

Even though the Singapore International Arbitration Act does not expressly provide for arbitral confidentiality, the 2013 SIAC international arbitration rules, largely consistent with those of the LCIA, provide a specific rule that states that "The parties and the Tribunal shall at all times treat all matters relating to the proceedings and the award as confidential" (SIAC Rules 2013, Rule 35). Before considering interviewees' ideas and comments on confidentiality, it seems relevant to distinguish between privacy and confidentiality since the former usually applies to preliminary conferences or hearings and means that third parties are unable to attend, while the latter is concerned with the obligation not to disclose information relating to the content of the arbitration (Trakman 2002; Kouris 2005).

The issue of confidentiality, rated as second cause for concern by interviewees, is one of the most important factors behind the choice of arbitration as a dispute resolution mechanism. The main reason is that large and well-known corporations, banks and financial institutions among others, do not wish to air their dirty laundry in public. What arbitration may offer is a confidential means to settle disputes without affecting their public image. In actual fact, the companies involved in litigation might be forced to disclose confidential information concerning their internal operations and customer relationship, which provides a further reason for choosing arbitration. In terms of linguistic realizations, extract (12) provides a further example of direct speech:

(12) in Singapore when when we sell it to a domestic client the client's first question is … *why do I need arbitration when my courts are so efficient.. I can get a judgment in court within twelve months or eighteen months at a decent cost … so what's the draw in arbitration …* as a practitioner I need to say to him *if you have a dispute … arbitration allows you keep it confidential.* (AAD 2014. I6)

When a narrator reports somebody else's words, the original intent is usually that of repeating exactly the actual words spoken but what is produced is just an attempt to recall what the original speaker said. What narrators try to do, when using quotations, is to give a general picture of what the reported people meant. Another important use of quoted direct speech is to provide what Labov (1972) has termed embedded or internal evaluation, which occurs when the point of the story is conveyed through the narration itself, including the remarks of another person. Here, the other person is represented by a prospective client whose doubts about choosing arbitration instead of litigation are voiced by the respondent. The function of embedded evaluation is one of the most frequent uses of quoted direct speech, presumably because responsibility for the remark is clearly attributed to someone other than the speaker. It is interesting to note that the interviewee replies to the client's doubts by performing his own role. In this particular case, the speaker is not reporting past events but he is providing an answer that is likely to have been given in that situation.

In extract (13), the respondent maintains that confidentiality is not to be taken for granted in arbitration and that the parties should get to an agreement in order to include confidentiality in the arbitration agreement. From a linguistic point of view, the grammatical parallelism *it depends on the rules* (.) *it depends on the seat* serves the function of conveying the idea that confidentiality is still dependent on an array of factors, all of which are to be taken into account if one wants to keep the whole arbitration procedure confidential and not just private.

(13) if you take ICC arbitration the privacy is not automatic (.) if you take SIAC arbitration and some other introductions yes it becomes private because of the rules so you have to (.) exercise care to make sure that your arbitration is private (.) *it depends on the rules (.) it depends on the seat* ... but you can't make it private just by making sense so in your clause (.) but again ... because of the tendency to have you know *I did this way last time I do the same thing* ... people are not paying attention so a lot of arbitrations are not private ... people are shocked (chukle). (AAD 2014. I2)

5.4 Cross-examination

> It seems to me that at the arbitration, it is the cultural attributes of counsel that are often more crucial than that of the client. [...] We all see cases where the background of the lawyers determines the nature of the arbitration. If they come from the same background, they know the ground rules. Fascinating and difficult situations arise when they come from different backgrounds and these differences have not been adequately addressed at an early stage. (Kaplan 2002: 255)

Neil Kaplan, one of the most distinguished professionals in the arbitration arena, highlights one of the main difficulties arbitration practitioners experience when dealing with colleagues coming from different legal backgrounds. These cultural differences tend to permeate the whole arbitration process and become apparent when parties are involved in cross-examination. Indeed, cross-examination of witnesses by a counsel for the opposing party, which derives from the common law, has become 'standard practice' in international arbitration proceedings even for legal practitioners from civil law countries in which cross-examination is not a feature of domestic litigation. The diversity in the national and legal backgrounds of the lawyers leads to situations in which international commercial arbitration practitioners are likely to come to cross-examination with very different levels of experience and comfort. For example, "some arbitrators may not be familiar with common-law style cross-examination or may even have a negative view of cross-examination" (Kent 2006: 1). In addition, the preparation of witnesses for testimony is precluded in civil law jurisdictions (e.g. Italy, France, Switzerland, Belgium), but considered an obligation in common law jurisdictions (Moses 2012), where witnesses are carefully instructed on how to behave and what to say in the course of a cross-examination. Arbitration practitioners who practice in multiple jurisdictions have the challenge of adjusting to these varying rules, and the situations may get even more challenging because there are no written rules of cross-examination for arbitration proceedings (Cymrot 2007). In extract (14), the respondent confirms that cross-examination is a well-established practice in the Singapore context and that the principal objective of cross-examining witnesses is twofold: *to destroy their credibility of the stand (.) to destroy the veracity of the evidence.* It is worth noting that the speaker used the verb *destroy* twice in order to stress that cross-examination, as indicated elsewhere (Schneider 2009), is primarily aimed at discrediting the witnesses from the opposing side. The speaker also points out that the so-called 'chess-clock approach' is gaining in popularity. This particular approach is explained as follows: *we will take an arbitration and will say ok we have got two weeks for the hearing (.) whether you have five witnesses or eight witnesses (.) you are going to be given three days (.) you finish your cross-examination.* From a linguistic point of view, the interviewee makes use of direct speech embedded in his narration. Here the speaker plays the role of the arbitrator / arbitral tribunal fixing a time limit for cross-examining witnesses, irrespective of their number. When this approach is taken, the likely objective is to reduce the length of the arbitration proceedings.

(14) Again for the arbitrations that we've been involved in here it's almost a default (.) you will have cross-examination and eh as a lawyer we look to that as a very important part of the process because it's the only time that you get to challenge the other side witnesses (.) you get to (.) you know (.) make an attempt to destroy their credibility of the stand (.) to destroy the veracity of the evidence so I think it's quite an important part of the process ahm at least in the Singapore context again in the UK context as well (.) if you look at the top arbitration practitioners who are well regarded (.) some of them are (.) some of the very best cross-examiners (.) because they will actually bring a particular barrister in (.) only to look at cross-examination and they will take him out (.) and for that he can charge a few hundred thousand dollars because he's that good (.) so it's quite an important part of the process here but I think ahm much will depend on also the background of the tribunal (.) if you have a very civil law centric tribunal (.) they may not appreciate ah too much cross-examination and it is getting increasingly common now to have what is called the chess-clock approach (.) we will take an arbitration and will say ok we have got two weeks for the hearing (.) whether you have five witnesses or eight witnesses (.) you are going to be given three days (.) you finish your cross-examination so you (.) I think you are not going to find people giving you that kind of liberty (.) (AAD 2014: I6)

Cross-examination does not exist as a procedure for assessing evidence in civil law jurisdictions because the evidential process in civil law countries tends to be conducted primarily in writing and oral testimony has a limited role, thus there is no real need for the cross-examination procedure with the result that cross-examination of witnesses is virtually non-existent in civil law countries. This leads to difficult situations for law counsels involved in international commercial arbitrations, as exemplified in the following extracts.

(15) (.) so more than half the world ***does not*** *cross-examine (.) they* ***don't know*** *what cross-examination is … they* ***haven't been taught*** *cross-examination … they* ***have not been*** *on their feet cross-examination* and cross-examination is like any skill (.) I can read five hundred books on swimming (.) but the guy who doesn't read any of these books and jump into the water is a better swimmer than me so there is a real problem (.) now what would you do (.) the other problem is this (.) there are different levels of competence and eh sophistication in the arbitration award (.) so you'll get arbitrators like Dub Jones (.) who is literally a walking encyclopedia of arbitration (.) Neil Kaplan and I can name you many names and you can tell me many names yourself (.) you know (AAD 2014: I2)

The interviewee, talking about civil law counsels engaged in cross-examination, expresses his overt criticism towards those civil law practitioners who are involved in arbitration proceedings without having the necessary knowledge. Here, direct criticism is expressed by the unmitigated forms *they don't know what cross-examination is ... they haven't been taught cross-examination ... they have not been on their feet cross-examination* in which the negative auxiliary *haven't* is repeated twice in order to stress the speaker's distance from a condition which is deemed to be critical for a proper management of the arbitration itself.

In excerpt (15), the speaker refers to an arbitration in which a civil law counsel agreed to cross-examine witnesses even though she lacked the necessary knowledge of how cross-examination works in reality. The verb phrase *they didn't understand* is repeated three times serving the function of highlighting the fact that the lack of knowledge about cross-examination inevitably leads to a complete failure. The use of parallelism seems to follow a route in which the initial idea SHE ... *didn't understand what cross-examination was* is being expanded as the flow of argumentation proceeds. In fact, the second verbal phrase *she was so disadvantaged*, then modified into *they were very disadvantaged*, contains a remark in which the adjective disadvantaged is pre-modified by *very* thus envisaging the negative conclusion which is likely to happen.

(16) Yea I mean it's ... it's ... I mean the question you ask me was actually a real life example that I had (.) where the counsel for the claimant was a common law (.) practitioner and ... the counsel for the (.) respondent wasn't (.) but they had agreed to this procedure but I think the counsel for the respondent (.) SHE ... ***didn't understand*** what cross-examination was and she was so ***disadvantaged*** because every time she asked the questions the witness (.) just said yea but she ***didn't seem to understand*** what she was supposed to get OUT of the witness then ultimately (.) they lost but I think ***they were very disadvantaged*** (.) they agreed to a process which ***they didn't really understand what it entailed*** (.) so it's I think it's it's a problem (.) and I don't know whether what the right answer is in terms of what's the middle ground where (.) the civil law and common law meet halfway and come up with a process where the evidence can be tested (.) the other way is perhaps (.) the tribunal should be more interventionist (.) right↑ (.) they should ask questions more rather than leaving it in the hands of the entirely in the hands of counsels (laughs). (AAD 2014: I3)

5.5 Amicability has nothing to do with arbitration

The original foundation of arbitration consisted in having an expert decide a dispute (Nariman 2000; Aksen 2007) but this seems to be something relating to the past. International trade has become so complex and the values at stake so huge that the resolution of disputes has given rise to a market in which an array of players (courts, lawyers, law-firms, arbitrators, mediators etc.) compete to attract customers, i.e. companies, conglomerates and multinationals. The vast majority of respondents agreed on the fact that international arbitration is rarely amicable since parties are represented by counsels who adopt an adversarial stance. They also claimed that the appointment of lawyers as arbitrators may contribute to making the proceedings more formal and litigious. However, most respondents said that experienced lawyers sitting as arbitrators are likely to maintain the neutrality and justice of the arbitral process thorough the control they exercise over the proceedings.

According to the 2013 PricewaterhouseCoopers survey, corporations are very much concerned about the judicialisation of arbitration. This means that the control over the arbitration process is moving towards law firms and away from arbitration users, that is, the companies themselves. Arbitration practitioners from Singapore provided reasons, exemplified in the following extracts:

(17) I think (.) I think ehm … this change is not just a cultural change within arbitration (.) this change is a change that has affected the whole world (.) the concept of gentlemanly behavior (.) I'm sure you all watched the last world cup ***right*** … you saw how they (.) they knocked each other I mean ferociously … ***right*** I mean (.) you've lived long enough to remember football twenty years ago ***right …*** they wouldn't do those things ***right*** … there's too much at stake now you know to be (.) to be … the winner … comes with so much more than to be second and so I think in that sense people have I think become a lot more … a lot more … how do you say … anxious about securing a win … so this … ah …. amiable compositeur does not apply anymore … anymore (AAD 2014: I4)

(18) I have not in my twenty-seven years of experience seen a single arbitration resort to an amiable compositeur route … it is not different from a state court litigation except the paradigm is different … that's all … so I think that's really a relic of the past. (AAD 2014: I2)

From a linguistic point of view, extract (17) contains an example of how the discourse marker *right* has been used by one of the respondents. This stretch of speech contains four of the 34 instances of *right* that this interviewee used through the whole interview. Research has shown that people involved in an interaction use discourse markers to mark their stances in the interaction itself. Two categories of stances are noticeable for the use of *right*: the epistemic stance and the interpersonal stance where the former can be considered a shorthand for the verbal phrase *is that right* (when a participant is aligning epistemic stances) and the latter as a shorthand for *do you agree with me that I am right*, which shows a more evaluative component. In extract (17) the first and the third occurrences of *right* are clear examples of epistemic stance (*I'm sure you all watched the last world cup / you've lived long enough to remember football twenty years ago*) in which the speaker is both affirming the common experience and requesting confirmation.

On the other hand, the second and the fourth occurrences are examples of interpersonal stance. If we consider the function they perform, we see that the evaluative component is salient. In particular, if we focus our attention on the second occurrence of *right* (*you saw how they knocked each other I mean ferociously … right)* we see that the speaker, while expressing disapproval of unfair play from some of the participants in the world cup, seeks confirmation from the interlocutor by using the discourse marker *right*. It is also interesting to note that this stretch of speech also contains another discourse marker *I mean*, repeated twice, which encapsulates the discourse marker *right* in what may be termed a cluster of markers, in which three discourse markers have been used out of four words. A further aspect, which deserves a more careful investigation, relates to the way in which focus shifts from the speaker, when he uses *I mean*, to the interlocutor when the same speaker uses the discourse marker *right*.

6. Conclusion

This study has shown that arbitration in Singapore is still considered a viable way of resolving international commercial disputes, even though a number of critical aspects have been detected. Some of these drawbacks, such as poorly drafted arbitration clauses, excessive costs, delays in rendering the awards and cross-cultural differences in managing cross-examination, are connected to arbitration per se and do not seem to be greatly influenced by the surrounding socio-cultural background, with the exception of the Singapore judiciary that is considered to be very supportive of arbitration. The majority of interviewees agreed that arbitration will continue to be one of the preferred methods for resolving disputes, also because the quality of court judgments in neighbouring countries (India, Thailand, Vietnam, Malaysia etc.) is deemed to be inconsistent, thus favouring arbitration in more reliable contexts, such as Hong King and Singapore. From a linguistic point of view, the analysis has highlighted some of the realizations that respondents used in the course of the interviews, with a particular focus on the use of grammatical parallelism, critical claims and how interviewees used direct speech acts embedded in their narratives not only to report other people's thoughts (clients, parties, counsels, arbitrators etc.) but also to express evaluation and to add credibility to their narratives. The limited number of interviews does not allow us to draw definite conclusions on the state-of-the-art of arbitration in Singapore but these findings may be used to investigate differences and similarities in arbitration practice in a civil law country vs a common law country.

References

Arbitration Laws of Singapore 2008. In *Singapore International Arbitration Centre*, Special edition. <http://www.siac.org.sg/images/stories/documents/singarb/2009/singarb-200912-Se.pdf>.

Arbitration Rules of the Singapore International Arbitration Centre 2013. <http://www.siac.org.sg>, accessed December 2014.

Aksen, Gerald 2007. Reflections of an International Arbitrator. *Arbitration International* 23/2, 255–259.

Banfield, Ann 1982. *Unspeakable Sentences. Narration and Representation in the Language of Fiction*. Boston: Routledge and Kegan Paul.

Bakhtin, Michail 1981. *The Dialogic Imagination*. Austin, Texas: University of Texas Press.

Barthes, Roland 1977. *Image-Music-Text*. Glasgow: Fontana.

Belotti, Ulisse 2012a Arbitration in Italy: A Two-headed Janus? In Bhatia Vijay K. *et al.* (eds), 239–261.

Belotti, Ulisse 2012b. *Dispute Resolution Narratives. A Linguistic Analysis of Arbitration Practices*. CERLIS Series, Vol. 2. Bergamo: CELSB. <http://hdl.handle.net/10446/27256>.

Bhatia, Vijay K. 2011. Interdiscursive Colonisation of International Commercial Arbitration Practice. *World Englishes* 30/1, 76–80.

Bhatia, Vijay K. / Candlin, Cristopher, N. / Gotti, Maurizio (eds) 2003. *Legal Discourse in Multilingual and Multicultural Contexts. Arbitration Texts in Europe*. Bern: Peter Lang.

Bhatia, Vijay K. / Candlin, Cristopher N. / Gotti, Maurizio (eds) 2010. *The Discourses of Dispute Resolution*. Bern: Peter Lang.

Bhatia, Vijay K. / Candlin, Cristopher N. / Gotti, Maurizio (eds) 2012. *Discourse and Practice in International Commercial Arbitration. Issues, Challenges and Prospects*. Farnham: Ashgate.

Bolton, Kingsley 2008. English in Asia, Asian Englishes, and the Issue of Proficiency. *English Today* 24, 3–12.

Boo, Lawrence G.S. 2003. The Law & Practice of Arbitration in Singapore. *ICCA-International Handbook on Commercial Arbitration*. Supplement 38, 165–187.

Bruner, Jerome S. 1986. *Actual Minds, Possible Words*. Cambridge (MA): Harvard University Press.

Chan, Helena H,M. 1995. The Legal System of Singapore. *Alternative Dispute Resolution in Singapore*, <http://www.singaporelaw.sg/sglaw/arbitration-adr/arbitration-adr-in-singapore>.

Cheng, Charles L.A, 2011. The Developmental Life Cycle of International Arbitration Legislation – Singapore IAA Case Study. *Asian International Arbitration Journal* 7/1, 1–28.

Commentary on the Rules of SCMA, in <http://www.scma.org.sg/pdf/rules_commentary.pdf>.

Crystal, David 2008. Two Thousand Million? *English Today* 24, 3–6.

Cymrot, Mark A. 2007. Cross-examination in International Arbitration. *Dispute Resolution Journal* 62/1, 52–65.

Debattista, Charles 2005. Drafting Enforceable Arbitration Clauses. *Arbitration International* 21/2, 233–240.

Fairclough, Norman 1992. *Discourse and Social Change*. Cambridge: Polity Press.

Frade, Celina 2010. Linguistic Pathologies in Arbitration Clauses. In Bhatia, Vijay K. *et al.* (eds), 145–164.

Ghim, Phyllis / Chew, Lian 2014. The Role of English as a Lingua Franca in Institutions of Higher Education in Singapore. *The Asian Journal of Applied Linguistics* 1/1, 28–35.

Goffman, Erving 1986. *Frame Analysis: An Essay on the Organization of Experience*. Boston, MA: Northeastern University Press.

Gotti, Maurizio 2011. Litigational Influence on Italian Arbitration Discourse. *World Englishes* 30/1, 81–91.

Hunston, Susan 1993. Projecting a Sub-culture. The Construction of Shared Worlds by Projecting Clauses in Two Registers. In Graddol, David *et al.* (eds) *Language and Culture*, Clevedon: BAAL and Multilingual Matters, 98–112.

Hunter, Martin 2000. International Commercial Dispute Resolution: The Challenge of the Twenty-first Century. *Arbitration International* 16/4, 379–392.

The International Arbitration Act of Singapore, <http://www.scma.org.sg/pdf/rules_iaa.pdf>.

Jordens, Cristopher F.C. / Little, Miles 2006. 'In this scenario, I do for these reasons': Narrative, Genre and Ethical Reasoning in the Clinic. *Social Science & Medicine* 58, 1635–1645.

Kaplan, Neil 2002. Arbitration in Asia. Developments and Crises. *Journal of International Arbitration* 19/3, 245–259.

Kathpalia, Sujata 2012. Is Arbitration Being Colonized by Litigation? Practitioners' Views in the Singapore Context. In Bhatia, Vijay K. *et al.* (eds), 263–281.

Kent, Rachael D. 2006. An Introduction to Cross-Examining Witnesses in International Arbitration. *Transnational Dispute Management* 3/2, 1–9.

Kouris, Steven 2005. Confidentiality: Is International Arbitration Losing One of Its Major Benefits? *Journal of International Arbitration* 22/2, 127–140.

Labov, William 1972. *Sociolinguistic Patterns*. Philadelphia: University of Pennsylvania Press.

Labov, William / Waletzky, Joshua 1997. Narrative analysis: Oral Versions of Personal Experience. *Journal of Narrative and Life History* 7/14, 3–38.

Liu, Xiaohong 2006. Achieving Effectiveness of Arbitration Clauses – A Practical Survey from a Chinese Legal Perspective, *US-China Law Review* 3/6, 33–41.

Moser, Michael ^{4}2012. *Arbitration in Asia*. Huntington, NY: Juris.

Moses, Margaret L. 2012. Ethics in International Arbitration: Traps for the Unwary. *Loyola University Chicago International Law Review* 10/1, 73–80.

Nariman, Fali S. 2000. The Spirit of Arbitration. *Arbitration International* 16/3, 261–278.

Pillay, Mohan R. 2004. The Singapore Arbitration Regime and the UNCITRAL Model Law. *Arbitration International* 20/4, 355–386.

Pryles, Michael 2010. *Singapore: the Hub of Arbitration in Asia*. Singapore Arbitration Centre. Online at <http://www.siac.org.sg/>, accessed 15 December 2014.

Queen Mary University of London / PricewaterhouseCoopers 2013. *Corporate choices in International Arbitration. Industry Perspectives*. Online at <http://www.arbitration.qmul.ac.uk/docs/123282.pdf>, accessed 15 December 2014.

Schaefer, Jan K. 2000. Leaving the Colonial Arbitration Laws Behind: Southeast Asia's Move into the International Arbitration Arena. *Arbitration International* 16/3, 297–332.

Schneider, Michael, E. 2009. *Twenty-one Theses about Witness Testimony in International Arbitration and Cross-examination*. Geneva, 27 January. Available at <http://www.lalive.ch/documents/Conference_paper.pdf>.

Silver, Rita E. 2005. The Discourse of Linguistic Capital: Language and Economic Policy Planning in Singapore. *Language Policy* 4, 47–66.

SoundScriber 2004. Regents of the University of Michigan. Online at <http://www-personal.umich.edu/~ebreck/sscriber.html>, accessed December 2014.

Stipanovich, Thomas J. 2008. *Arbitration: The 'New Litigation'*. Online at <http://microlib.cc.utexas.edu>, accessed December 2014.

Swales, John 1990. *Genre Analysis. English in Academic and Research Settings*. Cambridge: Cambridge University Press.

Tan, Kevin Y.L. 2005. *A Short Legal and Constitutional History of Singapore, Essays in Singapore Legal History*, at 29.

Thompson, Geoff / Ye, Yiyun 1991. Evaluation in the Reporting Verbs Used in Academic Papers. *Applied Linguistics* 12/4, 365–382.

Townsend, John M. 2003. Drafting Arbitration Clauses: Avoiding the 7 Deadly Sins. *Dispute Arbitration Journal* 58/1, 1–8.

Trakman, Leon E., 2002. Confidentiality in International Commercial Arbitration. *Arbitration International* 18/1, 1–18.

Voloshinov, Valentin Nikolaevich 1971. Reported speech. In Matejka, Ladislav / Pomorska, Krystyna (eds) *Readings in Russian Poetics*. Ann Arbor, MI: Michigan Slavic Publications, 149–175.

Waugh, Linda R. 1995. Reported Speech in Journalistic Discourse. The Relation of Function and Text. *Text* 15, 129–173.

Websites

<http://statutes.agc.gov.sg/aol/search/display/view.w3p;orderBy=relevance;query=Content%3Aarbitration;rec=0;resUrl=http%3A%2F%2Fstatutes.agc.gov.sg%2Faol%2Fsearch%2Fsummary%2Fresults.w3p%3BorderBy%3Drelevance%3Bquery%3DContent%253Aarbitration;whole=no>

<http://www.lawsociety.org.sg/forMembers/ResourceCentre/ArbitrationScheme.aspx>

<http://www.lawsociety.org.sg/Portals/0/ResourceCentre/ArbitrationScheme/pdf/Frequently%20Asked%20Questions%20on%20LSAS.PDF>

<http://www.singaporelaw.sg/sglaw/singapore-legal-system/singapore-jurisdiction-law>

<http://www.singaporelaw.sg/sglaw/singapore-legal-system/2013-01-28-11-14-34/ supreme-court>

<http://www.singaporelaw.sg/sglaw/singapore-legal-system/2013-01-28-11-14-34/ state-courts>

<http://www.singaporelaw.sg/sglaw/arbitration-adr/arbitration-adr-in-singapore>

<http://www.singaporelaw.sg/sglaw/arbitration-adr/arbitration-adr-institutions/ singapore-international-arbitration-centre>

<http://www.singaporelaw.sg/sglaw/arbitration-adr/arbitration-adr-institutions/ singapore-mediation-centre>

<http://www.singaporelaw.sg/sglaw/laws-of-singapore/overview/chapter-1>

<http://www.singaporelaw.sg/sglaw/laws-of-singapore/overview/chapter-2>

<http://www.singaporelaw.sg/sglaw/laws-of-singapore/overview/chapter-3>

<http://www.singaporelaw.sg/sglaw/laws-of-singapore/overview/chapter-4>

<http://www.singaporelaw.sg/sglaw/laws-of-singapore/overview/chapter-5>

<http://www.singaporelaw.sg/sglaw/laws-of-singapore/commercial-law/chapter-8>

<http://www.singaporelaw.sg/sglaw/laws-of-singapore/commercial-law/chapter-10>

<http://www.singaporelaw.sg/sglaw/laws-of-singapore/commercial-law/chapter-16>

<http://www.siac.org.sg/faqs>

<http://www.siac.org.sg/model-clauses>

<http://www.siac.org.sg/images/stories/articles/rules/Singapore_IAA_with_2012_Amendments.pdf>

<http://www.siac.org.sg/images/stories/articles/rules/SIAC-Rules-2013_English_ 31072014.pdf>
<http://singaporeinternationalarbitration.com/faqs/>
<http://www.scma.org.sg/pdf/rules_iaa.pdf>

Appendices

Appendix 1: Transcription conventions

The audio recorded materials in the corpus have been transcribed according to the following conventions.

Symbol	*Represents*
(.)	Micro-pause (< 0.2 seconds)
(1.8)	Timed pause
< ? >	Unintelligible speech
a::nd	Colons represent lengthened vowel sound
<u>RIGHT</u>	Underlined, capitalized word shows emphatic stress, enunciated louder than surrounding speech.
↑↓	Indicate rising/falling intonation
< >	false start
o </>	incomplete word (complete *of*)
Items in brackets indicate non-transcribable vocalizations or other actions	(chuckle) / (slight intake of breath) / (breath intake) (throat clearing) / (subvocalizing)

Appendix 2: Questionnaire

Section 1 (Ad-hoc versus Institutionalized Arbitration)
To what extent do you think it is the case that corporations often prefer 'institutionalized' arbitration to 'Ad-hoc' arbitration?

Section 2 (Arbitration clauses)
Arbitration clauses are said to determine the form and legal basis of the whole arbitration process. What do you believe are the most critical aspects of such arbitration clauses?
Multinational corporations often develop a 'standard' corporate clause and insist that their contract and commercial personnel should not deviate from it. What kind of an impact do you think such a 'standard' corporate clause might have on the whole arbitration process?

Section 3 (Confidentiality in Arbitration Practice)
One of the main reasons for preferring arbitration to litigation in international commercial disputes is that arbitration tends to preserve confidentiality in that it encourages privacy in relation to business practices and trade secrets of the parties. To what extent is confidentiality an important consideration for the parties at dispute today?
To what extent does the relatively informal nature of arbitration proceedings, as against the more formal practices of litigation, make it a more attractive alternative for parties at dispute?
To what extent do you think it is the case that this informal nature of arbitration processes and proceedings is giving way to more formal ones often similar to those found in litigation?

Section 4 (Speed and duration- extension of time-limit)
One of the reasons why parties at dispute are said to prefer arbitration to litigation is that arbitration is deemed to be faster. Is this still a valid consideration? In your view, do parties at dispute voluntarily agree to prolong arbitration proceedings? If so, why do they do this? How is such an agreement to prolong the arbitration proceedings arrived at?

Section 5 (Costs)
International commercial arbitration is said to be at least as expensive as trans-national litigation for medium/smaller cases, while possibly representing better value for money in more complex cases. Do you think this is still the case?

Section 6 (Intervention from national laws and courts)

Is it the case that intervention through national laws or courts has had a serious effect on arbitration as a method of resolving disputes? If so, what kind of impact do you think court intervention has on the arbitration process?

Do you think parties at dispute prefer an appeal system within the framework of arbitration proceedings to the one within the system of national courts?

To what extent do such interventions through national laws and courts tend to compromise the integrity of arbitration processes and procedures?

Section 7 (Specialist background of Arbitrators)

The original aim of arbitration was to help resolve disputes *'amicably'*, by which was meant involving the active co-operation of the parties to the dispute. In what ways do you think the frequent appointment of lawyers as arbitrators has affected the *'amicability'* of the whole arbitration procedure?

Section 8 (Finality of arbitration awards)

Traditionally, one of the advantages of arbitration has been said to be its finality. In recent years, however, the number of applications challenging arbitration awards has been on the increase. In your opinion, does this trend contribute toward making arbitration more similar to litigation, thus compromising the integrity of arbitration process?

Section 9 (Cross-examination in Arbitration)

How important is the role of cross-examination in International Commercial Arbitration practice?

What is the role of the tribunal in controlling cross-examination?

In your view and in your context, is it the case that cross-examination in civil law court proceedings is a relatively less familiar phenomenon? If so, what are the reasons for this?

In your view is it the case that cross-examination of witnesses forms one of the most important aspects of international arbitration proceedings?

What sorts of challenges does cross-examination pose to arbitrators and legal counsels from different legal cultures, especially in terms of somewhat different expectations as to its role?
Do you believe that Civil Law lawyers are relatively less familiar with cross-examination techniques? If so, do you think that there is a need for specific training for this kind of skill?
How do you characterize the style of cross-examination used by civil law lawyers and arbitrators in international arbitration proceedings (e.g. hostile, loud, risky, insistent, long, friendly, flexible, use of 'speech-questions' , open questions etc.)?
Do you believe that it is a common practice for arbitration practitioners to prepare witnesses for cross-examination? If so, how is it done? Are there any cultural issues involved in direct versus cross-examination?

Section 10 (Language use in arbitration)
Are there any specific guidelines provided on language policy in arbitration in your context?
How is the language choice negotiated in a multilingual international arbitration setting?
Is English generally preferred even where it is not the first language of the parties?
To what extent does language choice influence the choice of arbitrator?
How common is the use of interpreters in international arbitration?

Section 11 (Advantages of International Commercial Arbitration)
Please rate the following aspects and considerations for preferring arbitration to litigation in international commercial contexts. (Identify the most important by #1 and then follow with (#2, #3 etc) in order of decreasing importance.

REASONS FOR PREFERRING ARBITRATION OVER LITIGATION
Flexibility and informality of processes and procedures, encouraging active participation of the parties in most areas of decision-making
Enforceability of arbitration awards
Confidentiality and privacy in arbitration proceedings
Participation in the selection of arbitrators
Relatively lower costs as compared with litigation

Enforceability of awards
Relative speed of completion of arbitration proceedings
Freedom in the choice of venue of arbitration (neutrality of venue, preferred legal system)
Costs of arbitration
Challenge to arbitration awards-Interference from national laws and courts
Appeal system within the arbitration framework

Section 12 (Areas of 'concern' in International Commercial Arbitration)

Please rate the following as areas of concern in international commercial arbitration, which, in your view, are likely to make it less attractive as an instrument of alternative dispute resolution:
(Please identify the most important by #1 and then follow with (#2, #3 etc) in order of decreasing importance)
Flexibility and informality of processes and procedures, encouraging active participation of the parties in most areas of decision-making
Enforceability of arbitration awards
Confidentiality and privacy in arbitration proceedings
Participation in the selection of arbitrators
Relatively lower costs as compared with litigation
Enforceability of awards
Relative speed of completion of arbitration proceedings
Freedom in the choice of venue of arbitration (neutrality of venue, preferred legal system)
Costs of arbitration
Challenge to arbitration awards
Interference from national laws and courts
Appeal system within the arbitration framework

Section 13 (The future of arbitration)

Do you believe that arbitration will continue to be the preferred method for resolving cross border commercial disputes?
In your view, to what extent, and in which particular ways, are other forms of dispute resolution (e.g. conciliation and mediation) likely to supplant arbitration procedures?

In the views of at least some arbitrators, arbitration practice seems to be being 'colonized' by the processes of litigation, in that it has become very similar to litigation. In your experience, what aspects of the contemporary arbitration process make it similar to litigation?

Focus on arbitration awards

Giuliana Garzone

Arbitration Awards in the East and the West: A Comparative Analysis with a Focus on Domain Name Dispute Resolution

1. Aim, scope and method

This chapter focuses on domain name arbitration awards, and compares awards issued by two Asian institutions with those issued by two Western providers in order to verify whether these two categories differ to any extent in terms of structure or textual and discursive traits. A further aim is to identify any distinctive peculiar features in domain name awards issued by Asian arbitrators. In pursuing these objectives, one has to keep in mind that the differences between awards issued in the East and in the West may be minor, given that many of the top arbitrators operating in Asian dispute resolution centres were educated in European universities and/or trained in European ADR institutions.

The basic methodological framework of this study lies in discourse analysis as well as in genre analysis (cf. e.g. Brown/Yule 1983; Swales 1990, 2004; Bhatia 1993, 2004; Schiffrin *et al.* 2001; Blommaert 2005). It also draws on specific literature on alternative dispute resolution in general, and on arbitration awards in particular. Arbitration discourse has been studied extensively in many of its realizations (arbitration rules, arbitration laws, arbitration institutions' website texts, online mediation texts, arbitration clauses, spoken texts, arbitration awards, etc.). Arbitration awards have mostly been the object of scattered studies focusing on specific traits, e.g. Degano (2010) on indicators of argumentation, Maci (2010) on syntactic complexity in Italian arbitration awards; Sala (2010) on discursive aspects, etc.), with the exception of an edited volume published relatively recently focusing on the discursive aspects of arbitration awards as a genre (Bhatia/ Garzone/ Degano 2012) including chapters on awards' generic structure, and on the syntactic and discursive aspects of English, Chinese, Italian, French and Spanish commercial arbitration awards and sports awards. These studies are the starting point for the research presented here, which also makes reference to some works produced in the legal field on domain name dispute resolution (Rana/Srivastava 2011; Jayakar 2012; Anand/ Kamath 2013) with a focus on Asian institutions.

For categorization purposes, Lexis Nexis distinguishes at least eight types of arbitration awards:

1. Commercial arbitration awards
2. Securities arbitration awards
3. International arbitration awards
4. Patent arbitration awards
5. Maritime arbitration awards
6. Construction awards
7. Domain Name Dispute awards
8. Labour & Employment arbitration awards.[1]

For obvious reasons, amongst these categories domain name dispute awards are relatively newcomers, as they deal with cases related to website names, i.e. cases of cybersquatting (i.e. registering, trafficking in, or using an Internet domain name that sounds similar to a widely known company or product, e.g. a trademark, with the intention of selling it or profiting from its use), domain name hijacking or domain theft (i.e. the process by which registration of a currently registered domain name is transferred without the permission of its original registrant: <http://definitions.uslegal.com>) and other disputes relating to trademark domain names. In the last few years they have been growing in importance as the sheer number of existing websites leaves ample scope for frauds and other forms of intentional illegal appropriation of domain names and determines a rise in the number of disputes and conflicts in this area.

1 Cf. <http://law.lexisnexis.com/infopro/zimmermans/disp.aspx?z=1180#AWA. Unless otherwise indicated, all websites were last visited on April 14th, 2015.

Before proceeding with the analysis of the structure of domain name arbitration awards, some general considerations about domain name dispute resolution are in order.

2. Internet domain names and domain name dispute resolution

Globally, in the management of Internet domain names the most important institution is the Internet Corporation for Assigned Names and Numbers (ICANN). ICANN is a not-for-profit public-benefit corporation based in the U.S. with participants from all over the world that is responsible for the coordination of unique identifiers related to the Internet Domain Name System, including policy development for the internationalization of that System. It has also established the Uniform Domain-Name Dispute-Resolution Policy (UDPR) to which domain name disputes are subject globally.

As regards 'generic Top-Level Domain Names' or 'gTLDs', i.e. domain names that do not refer to a single country (e.g. .com, .info, .net and .org), according to the new gTDL procedures, introduced in 2008,[2] dispute resolution proceedings will be administered by one of three Dispute Resolution Service Providers appointed by ICANN as a function of the kind of dispute to be resolved (International Centre for Dispute Resolution of AAA, Arbitration and Mediation Center of the World Intellectual Property Organization, the International Centre for Expertise of the International Chamber of Commerce).[3] In the case of Country Code Top-Level Domain Names (ccTLD), i.e. domains that are specific to single countries (e.g. .it for Italy, .fr for France, .us for the USA, etc.), disputes are initiated locally, and usually administered by a limited number of ICANN-approved dispute resolution service

2 Cf. <https://www.icann.org/news/announcement-4-2008-06-26-en?routing_type=path>.

3 Cf. Art 3, 'New gTLD Dispute Resolution Procedure' attachment to Module 3 (ICANN 2012).

providers, and notably the Asian Domain Name Dispute Resolution Centre, the WIPO Arbitration and Mediation Center, the National Arbitration Forum, the Czech Arbitration Center for Internet Disputes (specialized in .eu disputes) and the Arab Center for Domain Name Dispute Resolution (ACDR). However – as will be seen shortly – some countries rely on national dispute resolution providers that are not under ICANN's direct supervision, e.g. India.

The corpus investigated in this chapter, designed to make comparison possible between Western and Eastern institutions, includes awards issued within the framework of the following Western providers:

- The WIPO (World Intellectual Property Organisation) Arbitration and Mediation Center, based in Geneva with a further office in Singapore, which defines itself "the global forum for intellectual property services, policy, information and cooperation", one of the most important institutions globally, which also administers gTDL disputes, and has so far processed over 27,000 cases under the Uniform Domain Name Dispute Resolution Policy (UDRP);
- the National Arbitration Forum (Nat. Arb. Forum), based in Minneapolis, which since it was selected as an ICANN-appointed international dispute resolution provider for cTLD disputes in 1999 has handled over 20,000 disputes worldwide;

and the following Asian providers:

- the Asia Domain Name Dispute Resolution Centre (ADNDRC), a non-profit institution, jointly established by the China International Economic and Trade Arbitration Commission (CIETAC) and the Hong Kong International Arbitration Centre (HKIAC) in 2002, with offices in Beijing, Hong Kong, Seoul and Kuala Lumpur, a dispute resolution service provider accredited by ICANN;
- the National Internet Exchange of India (NIXI), a not-for-profit Organization under section 25 of the (India) Companies Act 1956, which was registered on 19th June, 2003. NIXI was set up for 'peering of ISPs', i.e. the arrangement of traffic exchange between Internet Service Providers, for the purpose of routing the domestic traffic within the country, instead of taking it abroad, thereby resulting in better quality of service (<http://www.nixi.in/>).

> NIXI purports to be managed and operated on a neutral basis, in line with the best practices for such initiatives globally. Since 2005, NIXI also manages the .IN Registry (<https://registry.in>).

Among these four institutions, NIXI is a case apart in that India, alleging as a reason the jurisdictional difficulties due to Internet's being a global medium, has decided to follow a different policy for .IN domain names. In 2005 it introduced the .IN Dispute Resolution Policy (.INDRP), which has been entrusted to NIXI. INDRP claims to be in line with the Indian Information Technology Act 2000 and with the internationally accepted Uniform Domain-Name Dispute-Resolution Policy. But, in actual fact, the INDRP remains unique and to some extent diverges from the latter policy.

As will be discussed in detail in Section 3, there are some differences in the Rules associated with the Policy which can be of some consequence, and there are some procedural divergences. The most important of such divergences is that under the UDRP a complainant may combine multiple domain names into one consolidated complaint, but this is not possible in India, where the fact of having separate procedures for multiple wrongfully registered names for the same entity may lead to inconsistent decisions being passed with respect to the same trademark (as was the case recently with Dell Inc.: cf. Anand/Kamath 2013). A further difference regards the composition of the arbitration tribunal, which under UDRP is called 'panel', consists of one or three arbitrators or 'panelists', and as a possible remedy can only order cancellation and transfer of the domain name, while under INDRP there is always a sole arbitrator, who is also empowered to award costs as s/he deems fit.

The details of the corpus are as follows:

	Asian Domain Name Dispute Resolution Centre (ADNDRC)	*National Internet Exchange of India (NIXI)*	*US National Arbitration Forum (Nat. Arb. Forum)*	*WIPO Arbitration & Mediation Centre*
Tokens	36,284	28,465	40,220	32,465
Types	3,873	3,492	2,619	4,020
STTR	30.98	32.99	35.33	33.71

Table 1. Corpus details.

As anticipated above, the two Asian institutions operate very differently, as the Asia Domain Name Dispute Resolution Centre administers proceedings according to ICANN Rules under the Uniform Domain Name Dispute Resolution Policy, which it integrates with its own supplemental rules, while NIXI operates independently under Indian law.

3. Generic structure of domain name dispute awards

In this section, the generic structure of domain name dispute resolution awards will be examined to highlight invariables and differences. For the generic structure of arbitration awards in general we rely on Bhatia/Lung (2012), which proposes a Discursive Hierarchical Pattern (DHP) which represents a generalization based on the analysis of a representative number of awards, and contains four moves, each move including a certain number of Steps (S). In Table 2 below, this structure, with moves codified by means of figures from 1 to 4, is compared with the structure identified in domain name awards. The left-hand column reproduces Bhatia and Lung's (2012: 25–26) scheme, while on the right the structure of domain name awards is represented:

Move structure of awards in general	**Move structure of domain name awards**
Heading (ArbDHP-Pre-1)	**Heading (ArbDHP-Pre-1)**
Move 1 – Recitals (Background information) (ArbDHP-1)	**Move 1 – Background information (ArbDHP-1)**
ArbDHP-1-S1: Introducing the parties	ArbDHP-1-S1: The Parties
ArbDHP-1-S2: Competence of the Tribunal	
ArbDHP-1-S2a: Arbitration agreements	
ArbDHP-1-S2b: Appointment of the Tribunal / arbitrator	
ArbDHP-1-S3: Pre-hearing proceedings and applicable law	

Move structure of awards in general	Move structure of domain name awards
ArbDHP-1-S4: General statements of a dispute	ArbDHP-1-S4: Domain Name, Registrar and Policy
Move 2 – Details of the disputes (ArbDHP-2)	**Move 2 – Details of the disputes (ArbDHP-2)**
ARbDHP-2-S1: Summary of agreed facts	ARbDHP-2-S1a: Factual Background ARbDHP-2-S1b: Procedural History
ARbDHP-2-S2:Submissions and Claims / Counterclaims by the parties	ARbDHP-2-S2: Parties' contentions
ArbDHP-2-S2a: Claimant's submission and claims	ArbDHP-2-S2a: Complainant
ArbDHP-2-S2b: Respondent's submission and defence / counterclaims	ArbDHP-2-S2b: Respondent
ArbDHP-2-S3: Relief sought by the parties	ArbDHP-2-S3: Relief sought by the parties
Move 3 – Reviews of contentions and claims (The tribunal's reasoning) (ArbDHP-3)	**Move 3 – Reviews of contentions and claims (ArbDHP-3)**
ArbDHP-3-S1: Analyses	ArbDHP-3-S1: Discussion and findings
ArbDHP-3-S1a: Factual analysis (evidence)	ArbDHP-3-S1a: Identical or confusingly similar (includes conclusion: ArbDHP-3-S2a: Identical or confusingly similar)
ArbDHP-3-S1b: Legal analysis (agreements)	ArbDHP-3-S1b: Rights and Legitimate Interests (includes conclusion: ArbDHP-3-S2b: Rights and Legitimate Interests)
ArbDHP-3-S1c: General principles of good faith (Optional)	ArbDHP-3-S1c: Bad Faith (includes conclusion: ArbDHP-3-S2c: Bad Faith)
ArbDHP-3-S2: Conclusions of factual analysis and conclusions of legal analysis	ArbDHP-3-S2a: Identical or confusingly similar ArbDHP-3-S2b: Rights and Legitimate Interests ArbDHP-3-S2c: Bad Faith (included in ArbDHP-3-S1a, ArbDHP-3-S1b and ArbDHP-3-S1c above)
Closure: The Award (ArbDHP-4)	**Closure: The Award (ArbDHP-4)**

Move structure of awards in general	Move structure of domain name awards
ArbDHP-4-S1: Final decision of the dispute facts and law	ArbDHP-4-S1: Decision
ArbDHP-4-S2: Dispute resolution (the award) & Calculation exercise	ArbDHP-4-S2: Decision on cost award
ArbDHP-4-S3: Operative directions	ArbDHP-4-S3: Operative Directions

Table 2. Structure of awards in general (Bhatia/Lung 2012: 25–26) vs structure of domain name awards.

As Table 2 shows, the structure of domain name awards is perfectly parallel to that of other kinds of awards, but is slightly reduced because it does not feature the steps relative to Tribunal's competence and arbitration agreement (ArbDHP-1-S2, ArbDHP-1-S2a, ArbDHP-1-S2b, ArbDHP-1-S3) which are not relevant in the case of domain name disputes. A distinctive element of domain name awards is that the analyses (ArbDHP-3-S1) are organized on the basis of the three main criteria relied on for the identification of domain name breaches, i.e. identity or confusing similarity, rights and legitimate interests, and bad faith. Furthermore, in domain name awards the analysis of each of these criteria generally also includes its own conclusions, while in most other kinds of awards, conclusions are given all together separately in a specific step (ArbDHP-3-S2) at the end of all the analyses and reasoning. For instance, this is an example of conclusions set forth at the end of the 'bad faith' point in a WIPO award and in a NIXI award respectively:

(1) The Panel concludes that the Respondent fails to demonstrate use in good faith under para.4b of the Policy at all. (WIPO, Jeanette Winterson v. Mark Hogarth, 2000).

(2) In conclusion, for the reasons discussed, the Arbitrator finds the disputed domain name has been registered and used in bad faith under paragraphs 4 and 6 of the [INDR] Policy. (NIXI, Societé des Produits Nestlé versus NESCAFE Limited, United Kingdom, 2009).

If then one examines comparatively the four sets of awards under discussion here, it appears that the four institutions issue decisions that are very similar in move structure, although there may be minor differences in the ranking of headings and sub-headings, as can be seen from Table 3.

INDIA		*ASIAN CENTRE*		*WIPO Arbitration & Mediation Center*		*NAF*	
Heading	1	Heading		Heading	1	Heading	!
The Parties	1.S1	The Parties and Contested Domain name	1.S1 + 1.S4	The Parties	1.S1	The Parties	1.S1
The Domain Name, Registrar and Policy	1.S4			The Domain Names and Registrar	1.S4	Registrar and Disputed Domain Name	1.S4
Factual background	2.S1a	Procedural history	2.S1b	Procedural history	2.S1b	Procedural history	2.S1b
Procedural history	2.S1b	Factual background	2.S1a	Factual background	2.S1a	Factual background	2.S1a
						Relief sought by the Parties	2-S3
PARTIES' CONTENTIONS	2.S2	PARTIES' CONTENTIONS Includes Complainant and Respondent as point A & B	2.S2 + 2.S2a + 2.S2b	PARTIES' CONTENTIONS Includes Complainant and Respondent as point A & B	2.S2 + 2.S2a + 2.S2b	PARTIES' CONTENTIONS Includes Complainant and Respondent as point A & B	2.S2 + 2.S2a + 2.S2b
Complainant	2.S2a						
Respondent	2.S2b						
DISCUSSION AND FINDINGS	3.S1	FINDINGS includes points A, B & C	3.S1	DISCUSSION AND FINDINGS includes points A, B & C	3.S1 + 3.S1a/b/c + 3.S2	FINDINGS (only bare facts)	3.S1

INDIA		*ASIAN CENTRE*		*WIPO Arbitration & Mediation Center*		*NAF*	
A. Identical or Confusingly Similar	3.S1a/b + 3.S2					DISCUSSION with points A, B & C	3.S1a/b/c + 3.S2
B. Rights and Legitimate Interests	3.S1a/b + 3.S2						
C. Bad Faith	3.S1a/b/c + 3.S2						
Decision	4.S1 + 4.S2	Decision (includes operative directions, if any)	4.S2	Decision (includes operative directions, if any)	4.S1 + 4.S2 + 4.S3	Decision (includes operative directions, if any)	4.S2 + 4.S3
Operative directions	**4.S3**						

Table 3. A Synopsis of Moves and Steps in corpus awards.

Within this picture of overall uniformity, NIXI awards tend to be more analytical, as they maintain a separate paragraph for each step, being the only ones that always have a distinct sub-section for each of the three 'elements' discussed. They also have a separate step and sub-heading for 'Operative Directions' in Move 4, after the Decision proper, given that NIXI, not operating within the framework of ICANN, is the only institution that can also award costs, in addition to ordering the transfer of the dispute domain name as a remedy.

Besides, it must be noted that occasionally there are also some minor variations inside each single corpus, with few awards – mostly the less recent ones – being rather concise and others featuring variations in the organization of sections and sub-sections, which may be seen as evidence that the relative uniformity of the majority of texts may be the result of a deliberate effort of standardisation still under way.

4. Discursive organization

After analysing the move structure of domain name arbitration awards, now attention will be addressed to the overall discursive organization of the four sets of awards, which again appears to be relatively uniform. In the initial part, i.e. the recitals (ArbDHP-Pre_1), and Moves 1 and 2 (ArbDHP-1 and ArbDHP-2) which include the details of the dispute, the procedural history and the facts of the case, as well as disputants' contentions, an important component – indeed distinctive of this sub-genre of awards – is the construction of the disputants' reputation, and in particular the Complainant's, because it is a crucial element for deciding if it is reasonable to presume that for any illegitimate reason, and in particular in order to obtain profit, someone has registered a domain name associated with him/her. This section focusing on the Complainant's reputation is usually included in the Factual Background section (ArbDHP-2-S1a), or – more rarely – in the subsections devoted to Complainant's and Respondent's allegations (ArbDHP-2-S2a and ArbDHP-2-S2b). Usually this 'reputation' piece includes a narration of the evolution of a disputant's status, e.g.

(3) The Complainant is known as “Alibaba”, or “阿里巴巴” in Chinese, and operates its business through a number of subsidiaries and affiliates (collectively, the ‘Group’). The Group was founded in 1999. It has since grown to become a global e-commerce operator with offices in about seventy cities across China, and in Hong Kong, Taiwan, Korea, India, Japan, Singapore, USA and Europe. In 2003 […]. (ADNRDRC, Alibaba Group Holding Limited vs 1. Domains By Proxy, LLC; and 2. Jinbo Liu, 2014)

(4) According to Interbrand’s table of the world’s most valuable brands, NESCAFE was ranked 24th (+4%) in 2007 and valued at USD 12,950 Billion. NESCAFE was the most valuable Swiss brand, and the winner of the coffee category in the United Kingdom and in Spain for the Reader’s Digest ‘European trusted brands’ in 2007. (NIXI, Societé des Produits Nestle SA Switzerland vs Nescafe Ltd, UK, 2009)

The Parties’ Contentions section (ArbDHP-2-S2) mainly consists of language reports in various forms. In NIXI awards the tendency is to repeat the reporting verb at the beginning of every paragraph, or even every sentence:

(5) Tracing the history of its NESCAFE mark, *the Complainant states* it was exported in France and Great Britain when United States of America entered World War II. The Complainant *states that* […]. (NIXI, Societé des Produits Nestle SA Switzerland vs Nescafe Ltd, UK, 2009)

(6) *The Complainant points out that* the Respondents registered the Disputed Domain Name on 21 March 2014, more than 6 years after the Complainant first started using its ‘TAOBAO MALL’ trade mark, […]. (ADNRDRC, Alibaba Group Holding Limited vs 1. Domains By Proxy, LLC; and 2. Jinbo Liu, 2014)

In some cases, a more streamlined summarized approach is preferred, for instance in ADNDRC awards:

(7) The Complainant’s contentions may be summarized as follows:
(i) The Complainant has used ‘wapop’ as the name for a performance organized by them since 2012 and the performance is widely recognized in Korea and Southeast Asia under that name. The Complainant also registered ‘wapop’ with the Korean Intellectual property Office for goods and services in numerous classes. [..] (ADNDRC, WAPOP Co.Ltd. Vs 21562719 Ont Ltd, 2014)

This occurs frequently also in WIPO awards, where the description of contentions takes only few lines per disputant (in the corpus, on average

7 lines), and even more in National Arbitration Forum awards, where summarised contentions were customary in a not too distant past, although today a more detailed exposition is customary.

(8) A. Complainant contends that the domain name <juliaroberts.com> is identical to and confusingly similar with the name 'Julia Roberts' and the common law trademark rights which she asserts in her name pursuant to the Policy paragraph 4(a)(i).
Complainant contends that Respondent has no rights or legitimate interest in the domain name <juliaroberts.com> pursuant to the Policy paragraph 4(a)(ii).
Complainant contends that Respondent registered and is using the domain name <juliaroberts.com> in bad faith in violation of the Policy paragraph 4(a)(iii). (WIPO, Julia Fiona Roberts v. Russell Boyd, 2000)

(9) A. Complainant
The <zaploan.com> domain name is identical to Complainant's ZAPLOAN mark.
Respondent has no rights or legitimate interests in the disputed domain name.
Respondent registered and used the disputed domain name in bad faith. (Nat. Arb. Forum, Americor Mortgage Inc., Troy, MI v. Robert D. Bowman, 2002)

As already pointed out in §3 above, a distinctive element of domain name dispute awards is that the sub-sections included in the 'Discussion and Findings' Step (ArbDHP-3-S1) are all taken up by the consideration of the three criteria laid out in the Policies (ArbDHP-3-S1a, ArbDHP-3-S1b, ArbDHP-3-S1c). Each of them is examined checking whether it applies to the case at hand and, as anticipated above, at the end of every sub-section a conclusion on the relevant specific point is put forth. Although reference could be made to UDRP (or INDRP in the case of NIXI), in the text the three criteria are always cited in full. This is the formula appearing in most WIPO awards, to introduce the specification of the three criteria:

(10) The Policy Para. 4a provides that the Complainant must prove **each** of the following:

- that the Respondent's domain name is identical or confusingly similar to a trademark or service mark in which the Complainant has rights; and
- the Respondent has no rights or legitimate interests in respect of the domain name; and
- the domain has been registered and is being used in bad faith. and [...].

(WIPO, Winterson v. Mark Hogarth, 2000)

And in Nat. Arb. Forum awards:

(11) Paragraph 4(a) of the Policy requires that the Complainant must prove each of the following three elements to obtain an order that a domain name should be cancelled or transferred: (1) the domain name registered by the Respondent is identical or confusingly similar to a trademark or service mark in which the Complainant has rights; and […]. (Nat. Arb. Forum, Americor Mortgage, Inc. v. Robert D. Bowman, 2002)

In Asian DNDRC awards:

(12) The Panel notes that the Policy provides, at paragraph 4(a), that each of three findings must be made in order for the Complainant to prevail: i. Respondent's domain name must be identical or confusingly similar to a trademark or service mark in which Complainant has rights; […]. (ADNDRC, WAPOP Co. ltd. v. 21562719 Ont Ltd, 2014)

The three introductory sentences are similar, but there are differences in the wording: WIPO formulates consideration of the three criteria as an unconditional obligation of the Complainant, Nat. Arb. Forum, as a necessary action to obtain the cancellation or transfer of the domain name under dispute, and the Asian Centre as a condition for the prevalence of the Complainant.

In actual fact in the case of these three institutions the quotation of the three criteria to be met is purely conventional or ritualistic. But in the case of the fourth institution, NIXI, which is the only one that does not operate within the framework of ICANN, it is really necessary because, although the criteria are essentially the same, in INDRP Rules after the first element the conjunction *or* is used instead of *and*, and this is potentially problematic.

(13) Any Person who considers that a registered domain name conflicts with his legitimate rights or interests may file a Complaint to the .IN Registry on the following premises:
  (i) the Registrant's domain name is identical or confusingly similar to a name, trademark or service mark in which the Complainant has rights; **or**
  (ii) the Registrant has no rights or legitimate interests in respect of the domain name; and
  (iii) the Registrant's domain name has been registered or is being used in bad faith. (<https://registry.in/>.)

If this text is compared with the wording in examples (10), (11) and (12) above, based on UDRP, it is clear that the only difference, i.e. the omission of the conjunction *and* at the end of the first point, and its replacement with *or*, is not without consequences for the sake of its interpretation. While in UDRP all three requisites must be satisfied, according to INDPR in order to succeed a complainant may simply satisfy the first element, or only the second and third element (conjoined with the phrase *and*) and not necessarily the first. So arbitrators often prefer to prevent problems by quoting the criteria in their awards in a corrected version. For instance, in case Maruti Suzuki India Limited vs Nitin Bhamri (2010), starting his discussion of findings Arbitrator Harini Narayanswamy quotes the criteria to be followed, using at the end of each point the conjunction *and*, with the effect of correcting the incoherence of the original INDRP statement:

(14) The .IN Policy, Paragraph 4 requires the Complainant, to establish the following three elements:
 (i) The domain name is identical or confusingly similar to a name, trademark or service mark in which the Complainant has rights, and
 (ii) The Respondent has no rights or legitimate interests in respect of the domain name; and
 (iii) The Respondent's domain name has been registered and is being used in bad faith. (NIXI, Maruti Suzuki India Limited vs Nitin Bhamri, 2010)

In other cases the criteria are not reformulated explicitly, but the arbitrator's reasoning obviously considers all three criteria, conceptually following the UDRP orientation. But, of course, taken as they are, these provisions may have disastrous consequences, favouring the complainant (cf. Rana/Srivastava 2011; Anand/Kamath 2013), although the impact that this textual variation has had so far on decisions has not yet been quantitatively assessed.

In the discussion that follows, as anticipated, each of the three elements is dealt with separately, in some cases in depth, and at the end of the discussion of each single point a conclusion is given. See the following example from an award issued by NIXI:

(15) The first criterion requires the Complainant to prove that the domain name registered by the Respondent is identical or confusingly similar to a mark in which it has rights. The Arbitrator finds the Complainant has provided evidence of its

ownership rights in the trademark BARCLAYCARD and its use in India. The Complainant has also demonstrated its prior adoption of the BARCLAYCARD mark for its services and has therefore established its rights in the mark.
It is well recognized that incorporating a trademark in its entirety, particularly if the mark is an internationally well-known mark, is sufficient to establish that the domain name is identical or confusingly similar to the Complainant's registered mark. See for instance *Ingersoll-Rand Co. Frank Gully d/b/a Advcomren*, WIPO Case No.D2000–0021. <ingersol-rand.net>, and *Boehringer Ingelheim Pharma GmbH &Co.KG v. Philana Dhimkana,* WIPO Case No.2006–1594, where it was held that, if a well known trademark was incorporated in its entirety, it is sufficient to establish that a domain name is identical or confusingly similar to the Complainant's registered mark. The Arbitrator finds the BARCLAYCARD trademark has been used in its entirety in the domain name. Incorporating the term BARCLAYCARD and adding the letter 's' to the trademark in the domain name does not distinguish the domain name from the mark. See *Deutsche Telkom AG v. Vision Computer S.L,* WIPO Case No. D2001–1240. For the reasons discussed, the Arbitrator finds that the disputed domain name is confusingly similar to the Complainant's mark BARCLAYCARD. (NIXI, Barclays Bank Plc v. Oniker Privacy services, 2009)

As can be seen, although – as is customary – in the paragraph preceding this excerpt the three elements to be considered have been set out, in the discussion of the first of them there is again a reformulation of the same ("The first criterion requires ..."), which is then followed by the arbitrator's findings and reasoning leading up to his conclusion. It is interesting that in his reasoning the arbitrator makes mainly reference to earlier WIPO cases, and only occasionally to NIXI decisions, thus implicitly recognizing that WIPO is the main reference institution whose decisions generate case law. The fact that this reference is introduced by means of the expression "It is well recognized ..." indicates that the reliance on this prior case is aimed at making reference to a generally established principle deriving from precedents (*stare decisis*).

A similar discursive structure can be found in the conclusion of the same point in an ADNDRC award:

(16) A. Identical or Confusingly Similar
The Panel accepts that the Complainant has rights in respect of the UNSTOPPABLE trade mark on the basis of its trade mark registrations in the United States of America and Canada.
It is well-established that when making an enquiry as to whether or not a trade mark is identical or confusingly similar to a domain name, the generic

> top-level domain extension, in this case '.com', may be disregarded (see Rohde & Schwarz GmbH & Co. KG v. Pertshire Marketing, Ltd, WIPO Case No. D2006–0762).
> The Panel accordingly finds that the Disputed Domain Name is identical to the Complainant's UNSTOPPABLE mark in which the Complainant has rights, and that paragraph 4(a)(i) of the Policy is satisfied. (ADNDRC, Fiskars Corporation v. The Unstoppable Sdn Bhd, 2014)

Although less complex, the structure of reasoning here is very similar to that discussed previously, with the first statement admitting the Complainant's alleged rights, followed by a reference to a case – actually, a WIPO case – introduced here with "it is well-established …", and a conclusion based on the precedent referred to and on reasoning. In actual fact, in the ADNDRC corpus reference to precedents seems to be less frequent than in NIXI awards.

In general, reference to precedents is quite common in the awards of the two Western institutions, and WIPO decisions are certainly the most widely relied on. In Nat. Arb. Forum awards reference can also be found to its own prior decisions and to those of other institutions (e.g. those of the British Columbia International Commercial Arbitration Centre).

This tendency to rely on prior cases reflects a trend that has emerged in certain areas of arbitration today, especially in sports arbitration and investment arbitration, but much less in commercial arbitration. As Kaufman-Kohler (2007) points out, this unevenness is mainly due to the fact that certain legal domains need consistency and predictability more than others, so they use precedent as an instrument to gather jurisprudence. Thus it can be hypothesised that on account of the relatively recent origin of Internet domain name disputes adherence to precedent is meant to establish a body of rules to be applied in this field. As Kaufman-Kohler (2007: 375) points out relying on Norberto Bobbio, "the less developed the body of rules is, the more important the role of the dispute resolver will be with respect to the creation of rules." This observation also implies that conferring a precedential value on decisions involves the attribution of a high degree of authoritativeness to arbitrator or panel/panelists.

In the next section the focus will shift to texts, looking for linguistic evidence of how arbitrators/panellists are constructed discursively, also making recourse to corpus linguistic tools.

5. Linguistic aspects

If one looks more closely at the (micro)linguistic aspects of the awards included in the corpus, it is immediately evident that there are some fundamental variations in the vocabulary used. In UDRP the persons in charge of managing the DR process are not denominated *arbitrators*, but rather *panelists*, as they are part of a *panel* of arbitrators. In the 'Definitions' in Art. 1 of the Rules for Uniform Dispute Resolution Policy (<https://www.icann.org/resources/pages/rules-be-2012-02-25-en>) they are thus defined:

(17) **Panel** means an administrative panel appointed by a Provider to decide a complaint concerning a domain-name registration.
Panelist means an individual appointed by a Provider to be a member of a Panel. (Art. 1)

This vocabulary is used consistently by ADNDRC, WIPO and Nat. Arb. Forum, but not by NIXI as its procedures are not based on UDRP. Rather, they are governed by Arbitration and Conciliation Act 1996 and by INDRP and the associated Rules of Procedure (<https://registry.in/INDRP%20Rules%20of%20Procedure>). In NIXI the word *arbitrator* is used, which is thus defined:

(18) **Arbitrator** refers to the experts who have expertise on computer and/or laws, possess a high sense of professional ethics and are capable of rendering independent and unbiased decisions in domain name disputes. (Art.1)

The word *arbitrator* is used only in the NIXI corpus, where it occurs 182 times, and so is the word *award*, which incidentally appears nearly exclusively in the headline of awards on the front page as 'Arbitration Award'. Instead, the title of awards issued by the other three institutions is presented as a *decision*, often as *administrative panel decision*. In the body text, NIXI itself prefers *decision* to *award*.

It can be inferred that Domain Name Dispute Centres have chosen to use vocabulary in their operations that is different from that used in other types of arbitration in order to confer a distinctive character on it. In this respect, the behaviour of the two Asian institutions is not uniform, with ADNDRC aligned with the two Western centres and NIXI being unique in its use of 'standard' arbitration vocabulary.

5.1 Illocutionary verbs and arbitrator's/panel's authoritativeness

A further interesting aspect to be explored is the environment in which the main arbitration words are used in the corpora being examined. In particular, we shall focus on 3rd person verb forms collocating with *arbitrator* or *panel/panelist* that contribute to defining the arbitrator's role and authority. For this purpose, the concordance of the word *arbitrator* for NIXI and *panel* for the other institutions has been obtained, including all illocutionary verbs (Searle 1975: 354–361; cf. Garzone 1996: 38–41) that express decisions (declaratives), and orders (directives), having a performative value, as well as other illocutionary verbs expressing evaluation and reasoning (essentially representatives) collocating with *arbitrator* or *panel* were extracted.

NIXI awards are those that show the smallest range of lexical variation with only ten different lexical types of illocutionary verbs. Notable is the predominance of the verb *finds*, with 72 hits, a verb which – as will be seen shortly – has a complex meaning in the legal sphere. Another verb having a similar meaning is *holds* (2 hits), while performatives with a directive meaning are *orders* (9 hits), and *directs* (2 hits). Other illocutionary verbs collocating frequently with *arbitrator* with an essentially representative meaning are *notes* (10 hits), *proceeds* (8 hits), *is satisfied* (4 hits), while *deems* occurs twice, and *is convinced* and *views* only once.

At the opposite end of the spectrum, ADNDRC awards are the most lexically varied for this kind of verbs, with 25 different types. Also here *finds*, although less recurrent, is the most frequent verb, with 56 hits, followed by its (near) synonym *holds* (10 hits) and *decides* (4 hits), and the negative *rejects* (5 hits). Directive verbs *orders* and *rules* appear twice each. The verb form *accepts* is also noticeably frequent, with 18 hits, as it appears to be a stylistic peculiarity of ADNDRC awards that the Panel in discussing the Complainant's and Respondent's submissions with regard to each of the three elements, declares point by point if it considers their statements to be acceptable, as in the following example:

(19) Secondly, the Panel *accepts* the Complainant's submission that the disputed domain name <tmall.company> incorporates the Complainant's 'TMALL' in its entirety; [...]. (ADNDRC, Alibaba v. (1) Domain By Proxy, LLC; (2) Jinbo Liu, 2014)

Other illocutionary verbs found in ADNDRC awards include four occurrences of *notes*, three of *deems* and *thinks* respectively, two hits each for *concludes* and *considers*, and one occurrence of *infers*, *pays more attention to*, *recognizes*, *wants to point out*, and *would like to say*. In terms of lexical variety, the Nat. Arb. Forum and the WIPO sub-corpora are in an intermediate position with respectively 15 and 16 lexical types of illocutionary verbs.

In the way of declaratives, in addition to 28 hits of *finds*, which also here – as in all the other sub-corpora – is by far the most frequent verb form, the Nat. Arb. Forum sub-corpus also features nine instances of *concludes*, plus two of *may conclude*. Other illocutionary verbs occurring in Nat. Arb. Forum decisions are *proceeds* (8 hits), *agrees*, *considers*, *relies*, *views*, and *is of the view that*, with two hits each, and one occurrence of *observes*, *deems*, *exercises (its discretion)*, *retains*, and *shares the opinion that*.

Similary, the WIPO sub-corpus – which is 10% bigger than the others, which are very similar in size – has *finds* as top of the list with 42 hits, together with *concludes* (13 hits), *decides* and *rules* (1 hit). The other illocutionary verbs used are *recognizes* (6 hits), *notes* (6 hits), *refers* (5 hits), *admits* and *is satisfied* (3 hits), *agrees* (2 hits), and *considers*, *recalls*, *requires*, *is convinced*, *wishes (to address)* occurring only once, with the notable absence of verbs that appear in all the other sub-corpora, e.g. *deems* and *holds*.

Considering these data, it is evident that again it is the NIXI corpus that stands out for being much less varied in its lexical choices.

Particularly noteworthy is the very high frequency of *finds*, which is more or less twice as high as that recorded in the WIPO corpus and nearly three times as high as in the Nat. Arb. Forum corpus. Before going on to discuss its use in the four sub-corpora, a few words about its legal meaning are in order, *find* being one of those terms that Mellinkoff (1963: 11) defines "common words with an uncommon meaning". According to *Black's Law*, in the legal domain *find* means "to determine a fact in dispute by verdict or decision" (Garner 2004: *ad vocem*). *Webster's* (1981) proposes a more delicate definition for the use of *find* in a legal context, seeing two possible albeit conceptually similar meanings: "a. to determine after judicial enquiry; b. to pronounce as an official act (an indictment, verdict or judgment)". It is in the latter meaning that this verb is used in awards issued by all four institutions at the end of the discussion of each of the three crucial elements – resemblance, existence of rights or interests, and bad faith – for the determination of the final decision:

(20) For the reasons discussed, the Arbitrator *finds* that the disputed domain name <marutisuzukieeco.co.in> is confusingly similar to the Complainant's trademark. (NIXI, Maruti Suzuki India Limited v. Nitin Bhamri 2010)

(21) The Panel therefore *finds* that the Complainant has proved that the Respondents have no right or legitimate interest in respect of the Disputed Domain Name for the purposes of paragraph 4(a)(ii) of the Policy. (ADNDRC, Alibaba Group Holding Limited vs 1. Domains By Proxy, LLC; and 2. Jinbo Liu, 2014)

(22) For all of these reasons, the Panel *finds* that the Complainant has failed to meet its burden, on a balance of probabilities, that Respondent has used the disputed domain names <royalcaribbeancruiseline.com>, <royalcaribbean cruiesline.com> and <royalcaribbeancruieslines.com> in bad faith. (Nat. Arb. Forum, Royal Caribbean Cruises Ltd. v. Michael Urbanczyk, 2008)

(23) Therefore, the Panel *finds* that Respondent has no rights or legitimate interest in the domain name <juliaroberts.com> and that the requirement of the Policy paragraph 4(a)(ii) is satisfied. (WIPO, Julia Fiona Roberts v. Russell Boyd, 2000)

It must be noted that in ADNRDRC and Nat. Arb. Forum awards recourse to *finds* is not systematic as this verb does not appear at all in two of the ADNDRC files and in other two it appears only in the recurrent formula: "The sole Panelist finds that the Panel is properly constituted", while in the Nat. Arb. Forum sub-corpus it recurs only in six files out of ten. In WIPO the number of occurrences is lower but *finds* appears in all files with a reasonably even distribution.

In its other meaning ("to determine after judicial enquiry") *finds* is used to express the arbitrator's views and factual statements that are to be relied on as ascertained facts to determine the final decision, and therefore also take on a performative meaning, because they become true for the sake of the final decision for the only fact of being uttered.

(24) The Panel finds that the 2nd Respondent is the registrant of the Disputed Domain Name that was initially registered by the 1st Respondent as a proxy service provider for the 2nd Respondent. (ADNRDRC, Alibaba Group Holding Limited vs 1. Domains By Proxy, LLC; and 2. Jinbo Liu, 2014)

(25) Furthermore, the Panel finds that the addition of the top-level domain '.com' is irrelevant in determining whether the <royalcaribbeancruiseline.com>, <royal caribbeancruiesline.com> and <royalcaribbeancruieslines.com> domain names are confusingly similar to Complainant's marks. (Nat. Arb. Forum, Royal Caribbean Cruises Ltd. v. Michael Urbanczyk, 2008)

(26) The Panel finds that Respondent is using the disputed domain name to intentionally attract, for commercial gain, Internet users to the website, by creating a likelihood of confusion with the Complainant's mark as to the source, sponsorship, affiliation or endorsement of the website. (WIPO, BookIt.com, Inc. v. PrivacyProtect.org / ICS INC., 2013)

However, this use is relatively rare in all the sub-corpora except for NIXI, where it is very frequent. It is used for instance to describe the determination of the facts of the case by the arbitrator, as in the following example:

(27) The Arbitrator *finds* there is no evidence on record to show that the Respondent has any trademark or other rights in the disputed domain name. (NIXI, Société Des Produits Nestle SA, SWITZERLAND v. NESCAFE Limited,United Kingdom, 2009)

and in the evaluation of the effectiveness of the parties' submissions:

(28) The Arbitrator *finds* the Complainant's argument tenable that the Respondent ought to have been aware of the Complainant's rights in ORKUT trademark. (NIXI, Google Inc. v. R.Jain, 2008)

(29) The Arbitrator *finds* the disputed domain name incorporates the Complainant's trademarks MARUTI SUZUKI and EE CO in its entirety. (NIXI, Maruti Suzuki India Limited vs Nitin Bhamri, 2010)

These examples contribute to illustrating the extensive use of the verb form *finds* in the NIXI sub-corpus. The declarative value of *finds* in the final statements at the end of the discussion of the three elements embodies the arbitrator's decision and accounts for the fact that in NIXI awards in the final section titled 'Decision' there is generally no statement of the findings, but only the order to transfer the disputed domain name or the rejection of the request.

(30) Decision
For all the reasons discussed above the Arbitrator *orders* that the Domain Name <orkut.in> be transferred to the Complainant. (NIXI, Google Inc. v. R. Jain, 2008)

Of course, as Searle (1975: 359) points out, in order to be felicitous (i.e. 'valid') declarations with *finds*, and other verbs having a performative value, need to involve an extra-linguistic institution and a system of constitutive rules that may confer on the arbitrator the power to produce valid utterances. This partly applies also to the other use of *finds* identified in the award corpus, as in examples (28) and (29) which in terms of illocutionary force is essentially representative, but it is a special kind of representative subject to felicity conditions like declarations, as Searle (1975: 360) explains: "In certain institutional situations we not only ascertain the facts, but we need an authority as to what the facts are after the fact-finding procedure has gone through". These illocutionary acts have the force of declarations, and Searle (1975: 361) proposes to call them 'representative declarations'.

All these considerations indicate that the ultimate effect of the high frequency of the verb form *finds* collocating with *the arbitrator* in the NIXI corpus is that of conferring great authoritativeness on the arbitrator. An effect that may partially apply also to the awards issued by the other three institutions, but certainly to a much lesser degree.

The absence of a declarative in the final decision, which features only a directive, i.e. the order given with regard to the disputed domain name, which we have seen to be typical of NIXI awards, can seldom be found in the rest of the corpus. In ADNDRC awards the final decision is not expressed constantly with the same wording, rather its formulation varies, with recourse to different verb forms (*holds*, *concludes*) or to an impersonal form, followed by the order ensuing from the decision:

(31) In light of all the foregoing findings and in accordance with Paragraphs 4(a), 8(a) of the Policy and 5(e) of the Rules, the Panel *holds*: That the disputed domain name […]
As such, the Panel rules that the disputed domain name <qqclass.com> shall be transferred to the Complainant Tencent Technology (Shenzhen) Co. Ltd. (ADNDRC, Tencent Technology (Shenzhen) Co. Ltd. v. Weizhen Wan, 2014)

(32) Having established all three elements required under the Policy, the Panel *concludes* that relief should be granted. Accordingly, it is ordered that the disputed domain name, <wa-vietnam.com> be TRANSFERRED to the Complainant. (ADNRDRC, Cong Ty Tnhh Welding Alloys Viet Nam v. Viet Cuong Nguyen, 2014)

(33) For the foregoing reasons, the Complaint is denied. (ADNDRC, Fiskars Corporation v. The Unstoppable Sdn Bhd, 2014)

In contrast, in Nat. Arb. Forum decisions, there is a recurrent standard formulation featuring the verb form *concludes*, as follows:

(34) Having established all three elements required under the ICANN Policy, the Panel concludes that the requested relief shall be hereby granted. Accordingly, it is Ordered that the domain name <zaploan.com> be transferred from Respondent to Complainant. (Nar. Arb. Forum, Americor Mortgage, Inc. v. Robert D. Bowman, 2002)

Also variations are admitted, e.g. *it is the decision of*, as in the following example:

(35) *It is the decision of* the undersigned that the disputed Domain Names shall not be transferred to the Claimant. (Nat. Arb. Forum, Western Hay Company Valdosta GA v. Carl Forester DeFuniak Springs FL, 2000)

In the Decision section of WIPO awards the verb *to find* is hardly ever used, and the wording of the final decision is subject to variation, making recourse to the verb forms *decides* or *concludes*, or in some cases even using an impersonal form thanks to the use of the passive voice e.g.

(36) For all the forgoing reasons, the Panel *decides* that the Complainant has proved each of the three elements of para. 4 of the Policy. Accordingly, the Panel requires that the registrations of the domain names Jeanettewinterson.com; jeanettewinterson.org; and jeanettewinterson.net be transferred to the Complainant. (WIPO, Jeanette Winterson v. Mark Hogarth, 2000)

(37) The Panel *concludes* (a) that the domain name <juliaroberts.com> is identical to Complainant's common law trademark in her name 'Julia Roberts', (b) that Respondent has no rights or legitimate interest in the domain name and (c) that Respondent registered and used the domain name in bad faith. Therefore, pursuant to paragraphs 4(i) of the Policy and 15 of the Rules, the Panel orders that the domain name <juliaroberts.com> be transferred to Complainant Julia Fiona Roberts. (WIPO, Julia Fiona Roberts v. Russell Boyd, 2000)

(38) For the foregoing reasons, the Complaint is denied. (WIPO, Nintendo of America Inc. v. Domain Privacy Group / Domain Admin 2013)

As can be seen, in the Decision section of the award the three ICANN institutions are aligned in formulating the final verdict in one sentence, followed by another sentence that issues the final order resulting from the decision made. In doing so, as in other parts of the award, they tend to make recourse to a more varied vocabulary than that found in NIXI awards.

6. Conclusions

In this work, domain name resolution awards issued within the framework of four institutions, two based in Asian countries and two based in the West, have been analysed and examined comparatively, looking at the general rules governing their procedures, describing and discussing critically their generic structure, discursive organisation and lexical peculiarities. The analysis has identified an unexpected degree of uniformity in the drafting and organization of texts in macro-structural terms, probably due on the one hand to the pivotal role of ICANN, and on the other to the background of arbitrators/panelists, most of whom – we can presume – have attended law schools adopting a similar approach, mainly in English-speaking countries, and have been trained in the same institutions. Of course, there are slight differences and peculiarities among awards issued by the various arbitration centres, but it was not possible to identify any such peculiarities that may be seen as distinctive of Asian institutions vs Western institutions. In actual fact, the institution that stands apart and shows some distinctive traits that distinguish it from the other three is NIXI. The generic structure of the awards it issues is the most complete and analytically structured, and its lexical choices rely on the standard terms for arbitration, while all the other institutions prefer domain-dispute-resolution-specific words. But, above all, NIXI awards are characterised by a strongly marked discursive emphasis on the Arbitrator's authoritativeness and power, which is constructed mainly through the consistent use of the verb form *finds* collocating with *arbitrator*.

The awards issued by the other arbitration centre based in Asia, ADNDRC, are in line with the model set by the WIPO Arbitration & Mediation Centre, which is the oldest and most well-established ICANN arbitration centre. Overall, awards issued by ADNDRC, Nat. Arb. Forum and WIPO lay less emphasis on panelists' power and are, to some extent, slightly more streamlined in structure, with wider scope for lexical variation.

In light of these findings, it would not be correct to argue that there is an 'Asian style' in Domain Name Arbitration Awards, as the divide seems to be between NIXI on the one hand and ADNDRC, WIPO and Nat. Arb. Forum on the other.

References

Anand, Pravin / Kamath, Raunaq 2013. Domain Name Dispute Resolution: An Indian perspective. *WIPR World Intellectual Property Review*, 01/04/2013. <http://www.worldipreview.com/article/domain-name-dispute-resolution-an-indian-perspective>.

Bhatia, Vijay K. 1993. *Analysing Genre: Language in Professional Settings*. London: Longman.

Bhatia, Vijay K. 2004. *Worlds of Written Discourse. London*: Continuum.

Bhatia, Vijay K. / Lung, Jane 2012. Analysing International Commercial Arbitration Awards as Genre. In Bhatia/Garzone/Degano (eds), 23–46.

Bhatia, Vijay K. / Candlin, Christopher N. / Gotti, Maurizio (eds) 2010. *The Discourses of Dispute Resolution*. Bern: Peter Lang.

Bhatia, Vijay K. / Garzone, Giuliana / Degano, Chiara (eds) 2012. *Arbitration Awards: Generic Features and Textual Realisations*. Newcastle-upon Tyne: Cambridge Scholars.

Blommaert, Jan 2005. *Discourse*. Cambridge: Cambridge University Press.

Brown, Gillian / Yule, George 1983. *Discourse Analysis*. Cambridge: Cambridge University Press.

Degano, Chiara 2010. Indicators of Argumentation in Arbitration Awards: a Diachronic Perspective. In Bhatia/Candlin/Gotti (eds), 189–205.

Garner, Bryan A. 2004. *Black's Law Dictionary*. St. Paul, Minn: Thomson West.

Garzone, Giuliana 1996. *Performatività e linguaggio giuridico. Una proposta di classificazione. Con osservazioni contrastive inglese-italiano*. Milano: Centro Linguistico Università Bocconi.

ICANN 2012. *New gTLD Applicant Guidebook, Version 2012-06-04*. <http://newgtlds.icann.org/en/applicants/agb>.

Jayakar, Krishna 2012. India's Domain Name Dispute Resolution Process: An Empirical Investigation. *SSRN Electronic Journal* 03/2012. DOI: 10.2139/ssrn.2032096.

Kaufmann-Kohler, Gabrielle 2007. Arbitral Precedent: Dream, Necessity or Excuse? *Arbitration International* 23/3, 357–378.

Maci, Stefania 2010. The Modus Operandi of Litigation in Arbitration. In Bhatia/Candlin/Gotti (eds), 69–83.

Mellinkoff, David 1963. *The Language of the Law*. Boston: Little Brown & Co.

Rana, Lucy / Srivastava, Rishu 2011. Balancing the Odds: An Evaluation of the .IN Domain Name Dispute Resolution Policy, *WIPR World Intellectual Property Review* 01/12/2011. <http://www.worldipreview.com/article/balancing-the-odds-an-evaluation-of-the-in-domain-name-dispute-resolution-policy>.

Sala, Michele 2010. Arguing the Case: Discoursal Aspects of Italian Commercial Arbitration. In Bhatia/Candlin/Gotti (eds), 165–188.

Schiffrin, Deborah / Tannen, Deborah / Hamilton, Heidi E. (eds) 2001. *Handbook of Discourse Analysis*. Oxford: Blackwell.

Searle, John R. 1975. A Taxonomy of Illocutionary Acts. In Gunderson, K (ed.) *Minnesota Studies in the Philosophy of Science.* Vol. VII: *Language, Mind and Knowledge*. Minneapolis: University of Minnesota Press, 340–369.

Swales, John M. 1990. *Genre Analysis: English in Academic and Research Settings.* New York: Cambridge University Press.

Swales, John M. 2004. *Research Genres: Explorations and Applications*. Cambridge: Cambridge University Press.

Webster's Third New International Dictionary of the English Language 1981. Edited by Philip Babcock Gove. Springfield, Mass.: Merriam-Webster Inc.

Michele Sala

Deonticity and Authoritativeness in Hong Kong International Arbitration Awards

1. Introduction

This chapter investigates the linguistic, rhetorical and pragmatic features of arbitral awards drafted in English by the Hong Kong International Arbitration Centre (HKIAC), with a specific focus on those resources which are meant to enhance deonticity and authoritativeness, and, ultimately, to make arbitration discourse readable as a normative type of communication (Nariman 2000, Bhatia *et al.* 2003). The reason behind this choice is that the international character of HKIAC requires drafters to produce texts which will be recognized as authoritative by both Civil Law and Common Law discursive standards. Our aim is to discover whether and through what linguistic resources experts try (and manage) to limit as much as possible the risk of challenge. As has often been recognized (Park/Paulsson 1983; Bhatia *et al.* 2003; Park 2006; Ping 2011), one of the most problematic aspects of arbitration as an alternative dispute resolution procedure is the possible challengeability of its pronouncements, and this applies also to the case of arbitration in Hong Kong (Haley 2012). As a matter of fact, on the official webpage of the HKIAC, among the 'Arbitration Rules and Guidelines' we read that, on the one hand, "awards […] shall be final and binding on the parties [and] the parties undertake to carry out any award without delay"[1] and, on the other, we read that arbitrators and awards may be challenged

1 <http://www.hkiac.org/en/arbitration/arbitration-rules-guidelines/hkiac-administered-arbitration-rules-2008/19-arbitration/arbitration-rules/25-hong-kong-international-arbitration-centre-administered-arbitration-rules-2#29>.

> if circumstances exist that give rise to justifiable doubts as to the arbitrator's impartiality or independence, or if the arbitrator does not possess qualifications agreed by the parties, or if the arbitrator becomes *de jure* or *de facto* unable to perform his or her functions or for other reasons fails to act without undue delay.[2]

As we can see, the authority of the arbitrator seems to be a major issue with respect to the validity of the award. On this basis, it becomes relevant to identify the ways of codifying meanings that are considered to be crucial by members of the Hong Kong arbitration board in order to effectively shape legal concepts, report facts, represent actors, roles, and actions, so as to corroborate the arbitrator's authority and ultimately reinforce the performative and prescriptive nature of the final decision. Although the language found in these texts is highly formulaic (this being typical of legal discourse in general, cf. Tiersma 1999, Gibbons 2003, Gotti 2012) and characterized by the occurrence of the same or similar expressions across texts – and even though this phenomenon may be due to the fact that in specialized communication concepts are easily formulated through pre-fabricated multi-words units (Erman/Warren 2000) and recurrent lexical bundles (Biber *et al.* 1999) without writers being fully aware of this – our assumption is that any linguistic choice, whether fully conventional or slightly 'deviant', whether deliberate or subconscious, has a specific pragmatic purpose in terms of the impact the award is going to elicit.

Based on a corpus of 78 arbitral awards (available on the HKIAC site at <www.hklii.hk/eng/>, last accessed on 7 January 2015) this chapter seeks to investigate the arbitrators' linguistic and rhetorical choices found in the final section of such texts, the Decision section – where the actual arbitral pronouncement is expressed – with a specific focus on the metadiscursive resources employed to boost authoritativeness and to enhance the legal validity of the decision. For this purpose, specific emphasis will be placed on attributive resources, i.e. the terms which are employed to represent the arbitrator (which may vary in terms of personalization and preciseness/vagueness) on the one hand, and on

2 <http://www.hkiac.org/en/arbitration/arbitration-rules-guidelines/hkiac-administered-arbitration-rules-2013/practice-note-on-the-challenge-of-an-arbitrator>. See also Haley (2012: 21–24).

deonticity markers, i.e. the verbs and verbal construction used to codify the arbitral decision, on the other.

2. Material

As mentioned above, the present analysis investigates awards available on the HKIAC website, where it is possible to browse through 105 Awards (indicated as 'Decisions') only 78 of which are written in English, these being the focus of the present analysis. According to the information found on the homepage, the database is said to contain a selection of the HKIAC Panel Decisions from 2001, thus covering a 13-year time span. Possibly for copyright and privacy reasons, a disclaimer warns the reader that all the materials in the database are reproduced by permission "but do not purport to be the official or authorised versions" (for which "users should refer to their respective official publications").[3] Nonetheless, it is specified that 'every effort' has been made to ensure the accuracy of the uploaded texts with the original, authentic and authorized versions. This final specification alone does confer 'authoritativeness' and representativeness to the materials with respect to their official and published versions. However, for the sake of completeness, all the texts have been read through and were found to bear the date of their pronouncement, the case number and the signature of the Panelist(s), which are distinctive features of the definitive version, whereas some others are actually scanned copies of the authentic texts. This step was required to rule out any risk of dealing with mere drafts or working versions of the awards, thus liable of major revisions at the linguistic and textual level, and make sure that we are analysing either the original material or their faithful replica.

More specifically, all the awards available on the website are instances of '.hk Domain Name Dispute Resolution', that is, they concern cases of contested web-domain names. The Panel is thus required to evaluate the Complainant's request against norms contained in

3 <http://www.hklii.hk/eng/hk/other/hkiac/>.

several paragraphs of the HKDNR Policy (Honk Kong Domain Name Dispute Resolution Policy) on the matter. The Panel can decide that a given domain name be transferred to the Complainant when three conditions are verified: 1) the Disputed Domain is confusingly similar to a mark in which the Complainant has rights; 2) the Respondent has no right or legitimate interest in respect of the Disputed Domain; 3) the Respondent has registered and has used the Disputed Domain in bad faith.

For this reason the structure of all awards is very similar, and is typically distinguished in six parts: the first is meant to introduce the parties, the Panel, and the disputed names; the second describes the procedural history of the case (i.e. how the case has been organized, when relevant material has been delivered to the Panel, when the complaint was filed, the amount that has been paid as a fee in connection with the case, etc.); the third and the fourth parts present respectively the factual background and the parties' contentions; the fifth section (generally labelled 'Findings'), usually the most articulated, presents the findings, evaluates the contentions with respect to the three Policy requirements mentioned above and provides the motivations leading to the final pronouncement; the sixth, usually the shortest (variably labelled as 'Conclusion', 'Decision' and – although rarely – 'Award'), contains the actual arbitral decision. Our analysis focuses on this final section, and is aimed at seeing how the arbitration decision is worded, that is, what linguistic and rhetorical choices are considered by the Panel to be the most appropriate to express their judgment on the case and for it to be perceived as binding. In order to avoid terminological confusion, the term 'Decision' will be henceforth used to refer exclusively to this section of the text, whereas the term 'award' will be used to identify the entire text containing the six parts described above.

As already mentioned, all the awards investigated here, and consequently their respective decision sections, do bear a high level of similarity. Far from being a problem or detrimental for this analysis, this peculiarity in fact enhances the focus on language. As all the awards are produced by the same Centre, and are written by a restricted group of Panelists (fewer than 20 were counted), dealing with the same type of dispute and using a similar template to textualize their pronouncements, they allow us to have a deeper insight into the specificity of the language: in these texts, variation – when it is found – cannot merely depend on contextual factors or the propositional content (which corresponds to either the acceptance or dismissal of the Complainant's request over a registered name), but is instead likely to have to do with the way the decision is (meant) to be received, thus being a matter of pragmatic effectiveness and deontic impact. For this reason here we will investigate how the effectiveness of the text is achieved by focussing, on the one hand, on authority-boosting strategies, that is the terminology used by arbitrators to represent themselves within the text as deliberating agents and, on the other hand, on deonticity-enhancers, that is the performative verbs and verbal constructions used to codify the arbitral decision.

3. Results and discussion

3.1 Authoritativeness: Attribution

To measure the level of authoritativeness which is implied in the Decision section, we will investigate here whether and how the deliberating agent, i.e. the arbitrator responsible of the arbitral decision, is lexicalized in the text. It is worthwhile to point out that in the heading of the award, i.e., at the very beginning of the whole award, the identity of the Panel member(s) – and most notably if it is a case of Sole Panelist (76 instances out of 78) – is clearly stated, together with other relevant details such as the identity of the Complainant and Respondent, the contested domain name and the case number. Therefore lexicalizing the agent of the decision may be redundant or unnecessary, and textualizations like the following, where no agency is indicated, would be quite expected:

(1) Therefore, this complaint fails and is hereby dismissed. (Award 11)

(2) In accordance with Paragraph 4(i) of the Policy and Paragraph 15 of the Rules, the Disputed Domain Name […] is ordered to be transferred to the Complainant. (Award 92)

However, the majority of the texts in our corpus do indeed lexicalize the persona of the arbitrator(s), and they do so in three different ways: through first person markers (*I, my, me, mine*), through the term *Panelist*, or through the general term *Panel*, as the examples below show:

(3) *My* decision, therefore, is that the domain name […] now registered in the name of the Respondent SHALL BE CANCELLED. (Award 1)

(4) In view of the above findings, the *Panelist* concludes that the relief requested by the Complainant shall be granted and hereby orders that the Disputed Domain Name registration […] shall be transferred to the Complainant. (Award 55)

(5) Given the worldwide reputation and use of the Trade Marks by the Complainant, the *Panel* exercises its discretion to transfer the Disputed Domain to the Complainant or its designated representative in Hong Kong so as to avoid a third party registering the Disputed Domain for improper purposes. (Award 76)

As we can see in the extracts above, cases of singular personalization and the use of the term *Panelist* both presuppose identity between the figure of the arbitrator and its linguistic representation, especially in terms of number (either in general terms or by framing the agent within a legal taxonomy, respectively), whereas the term *Panel* is vaguer and is used as a collective noun dissimulating the persona of the single arbitrator behind the idea of a collective unit, sharing views and responsibility, thus rhetorically dissociating the final pronouncement – which is meant to be objective – from a specific agent, who may instead be perceived as having a subjective interpretation of the case. This is likely to grant and corroborate the impression of impartiality.

The occurrence of these markers can be found in Table 1, expressed in absolute figures. Since such terms are not mutually exclusive, more than one agency marker (i.e. the terms *Panelist* and the first person pronoun) can be used within the same texts, and the different occurrences will be counted in the respective columns in the tables below. This explains the fact that the total occurrences of the various items may outnumber the total of the Decision texts analysed here.

personal	*Panelist*	*Panel*	zero
12	9	99	27

Table 1. Attributive resources in the Decision section.

A relevant aspect of the data in the table is that, even though the majority of the awards in our corpus are drafted by a Sole Panelist, he/she tends to lexicalize his/her persona through the term *Panel* rather than as a single agent. Quite interesting is also the fact that zero attribution is largely preferred over singular markers (first person and *Panelist*). Both these trends seem to reflect a concern for objectiveness, which is more easily attained by dissociating the pronouncement from a single, hence possibly subjective, agent.

3.2 Deonticity: Performative verbs

When observing the verbs associated with the deliberating agent and used to describe the actions he/she performs in these sections of the award, it was possible to find a recurrent template after which Decisions are modelled, and this consists of two distinctive moves: a preparatory move and a conclusive one. The preparatory move has the function of both synthesizing the case, framing it with respect to the requirement of the Policy, and substantiating and circumstantiating the arbitral decision, which is then codified in the conclusive move, consisting in either the acceptance or dismissal of the Complainant's request. The conclusive move is the only necessary move for the award to be valid, but we have found that the preparatory move is very frequently combined with it (91% of the cases). This piece of evidence is quite significant. As a matter of fact, although the preparatory move can be considered as redundant, since it merely replicates, though in a condensed way, what was already presented in detail in the 'Findings' section, it has the function of conferring semantic autonomy to the whole 'Decision' section, which is thus self-standing and self-sufficient, containing all elements which are necessary and sufficient to understand the arbitral decision and what motivated it.

The following paragraphs will investigate how meaning is organized in the two moves for them to be effective. More specifically, the focus will be on the verbs and phrases used to introduce the typical act performed by the two moves respectively, that is, the assessment of the case and the wording of the arbitral pronouncement.

3.2.1 Preparatory move

The function of this move is to present the interpretation of the case on the part of the arbitrator. Although it encodes a cognitive act and, as such, is necessarily subjective, it needs to be perceived as impartial as possible, which is the ultimate goal of Arbitration and of Litigation in general (Bennett 2012, Solan 2012). For this reason, in order to discover how these two conflicting poles – i.e. interpretive subjectivity and objective reality – are harmonized and balanced, we will analyse here the assessing verbs which are used to express the arbitrator's point of view, and the type of assessment used to represent reality.

3.2.1.1 The assessing verbs

The Panelist's assessment, i.e. his/her interpretation of the dispute and how it is to be dealt with, is mainly represented by four verbs or related expressions, namely, *conclude*, *decide* (or *determine*), *find* (and forms like 'our findings are…') and *hold*, each of which bearing specific implications or nuances of meaning as to the action performed and the object of the assessment, as we can see in the examples below.

(6) For the reason set out above, the Panel *finds* that the disputed domain name registered by Respondent is confusingly similar to the First Complainant's registered trademarks […]. (Award 73)

(7) The Panellist accordingly *decides* that the Complainant does have the locus standi to bring this complaint as required by paragraph 4(a)(i) of the Policy. (Award 33)

(8) The Panel *concludes* that the Complainant has failed to prove that the disputed domain name was registered in bad faith and, for this reason, dismisses this Complaint. (Award 93)

(9) In the light of all the foregoing and in accordance with Paragraph 4(a) of the Dispute Resolution Policy, the Panel *holds* that the Disputed Domain Name [...] contains a mark which is identical to the Trade Mark. (Award 83)

The verb *find* is mainly a representative/constative verb, presupposing an existing state of affairs that is eventually revealed or becomes evident. Such a verb implies a passive role on the part of the Panel, which is limited to the observation of the reality and the acknowledgment of its characteristics. In a word, the drafter observes what is there to be observed. The verb *decide* (and its synonymical form *determine*) has a declarative and performative function, presupposing a deliberate and conscious action on the part of the agent with respect to a given reality. For this reason it presupposes the active role of the arbitrator in establishing how events are to be interpreted and also entails a certain degree of arbitrariness behind this action. To better understand this point, let us consider by contrast the verb *conclude*, which also has a declarative and performative function: this verb also implies the active role of the arbitrator but presupposes an act which is very much circumstantiated and limited in scope, since it presupposes given premises on the basis of which a given evaluation can be expressed, thus ruling out arbitrariness. A limited number of occurrences of the verb *hold* are also found, which contains an element of cognition. As we can see in (9), such a verb emphasizes the assessment of reality as an act of interpretation, thus bearing also a possible – if remote – element of tentativeness. This could be dangerous and detrimental for this type of text, hence its contained use in the corpus. On the basis of these considerations it would be possible to establish a hierarchy between verbs which imply a lower vs. a higher degree of judgement and evaluation, thus possibly of arbitrariness, ranging from the least marked, with the verbs *find* and *hold* (by which the drafter's interpretation coincides with what has been observed), then the verb *conclude* (where the interpretation is derived from observation), to the most marked, with the verb *decide* (by which the drafter's interpretation is more relevant than the observed reality). Finally, for the sake of completeness, we have also encountered some cases where the action of assessing was left implicit, as in the examples below:

(10) In the light of the foregoing paragraphs, the elements of paragraph 4(a) of the Policy are present in this case. (Award 97)

(11) The Complainant has proved the case. (Award 103)

By the use of such expressions the emphasis is placed on the state of affairs rather than on its interpretation and its interpreting agents. Before discussing frequencies of such verbal constructions, it is interesting at this point to examine how drafters portray the facts causing them to take given decisions.

3.2.1.2 The assessed reality

The assessment verbs seen above introduce the reasons on the basis of which the arbitrators justify their decision. In the corpus analysed such reasons can be represented in three different ways, that is, either as motivations, or in terms of focus, or in terms of grantability.

- *Motivation:* The reasons substantiating the arbitral decision can be expressed as a list of causes or claims – either describing the (dis)respect of the conditions in the Policy (12) or through narrative bits (13) – which at the same time serve the purpose of synthesizing the case and favouring a given interpretation of the facts:

(12) From what has been set out above, I conclude that the disputed domain name [...] *is identical to the mark used by the Complainant in the course of its business, that the Respondent has no rights or legitimate interests in respect of the domain name and that that domain name has been registered and used in bad faith.* (Award 4)

(13) *Notwithstanding the relative weakness of the rights that can be claimed in Hong Kong in the name [...], the Complainant would seem to overcome the first hurdle set down by 4a(i) of the Policy. This being so, no justification has been propounded by the Respondent as to why he has a valid claim to the domain name* [...]. For the reasons stated in paragraph 5.5(3) herein I hold the Respondent has acted in bad faith. (Award 50)

- *Focus:* The assessment of the case can be expressed, more implicitly, in terms of focus, that is by referring to the Complainant's success or failure in proving their point or substantiating their requests (through expressions such as *x has/has not succeeded in proving y, y is proved by the Complainant, x has established its case, x has failed to prove y,* etc.), as the examples below show:

(14) […] the Complainant *has failed to prove* that the registration and use by the Respondent has been in bad faith. (Award 9)

(15) […] the Panel concludes that the Complainant *has established* its case. (Award 17)

- *Grantability:* The reasons for accepting or refuting the Complainant's request can be left totally implicit and their relevance can only be inferred by means of the drafter's evaluation of the complaint, i.e. by the measures the arbitrator considers to be appropriate with respect to the facts and to be carried out accordingly (this being generally lexicalized through the expression *the relief should be granted*, or synonymic forms), as in the following texts:

(16) […] the Panel concludes that relief should be granted. (Award 38)

(17) The Complaint is therefore allowed. (Award 76)

The ways of assessing reality can also be organized ranging from the least to the most evaluative (hence bearing an element of arbitrariness), namely, from assessment as motivations (by which the reality is described rather than judged or evaluated), to assessment as focus (where the end result is represented, but the steps leading to it are left implicit, thus reality is somehow filtered through an evaluative lens), to assessment in terms of grantability (where the assessment of reality is substituted by the drafter's interpretation of it).

The findings regarding the assessing verbs seen in the previous paragraphs and the assessment of reality investigated here are listed in Table 2, expressed in absolute figures (the data in the table reflect the fact that more than one assessing verb and more that one way of assessing reality can be used in the same text; the symbols (+E), (E), (-E) indicate the varying degree of evaluation and arbitrariness implied by the resources, ranging respectively from strongly evaluative, to mildly evaluative to non-evaluative.

Assessing verb		Assessed reality		
		Motivations (-E)	Focus (E)	Grantability (+E)
conclude (E)	19	4	6	10
decide/determine (+E)	17	14	1	–
find (-E)	12	3	10	–
hold	4	2	–	–
not mentioned	9	5	7	–

Table 2. Assessing verbs and resources to represent reality in the preparatory move.

In this move, when assessing the details of the case, drafters have to express their interpretation of it, a rhetorical operation which presupposes and combines both the possible (and dangerous) subjectivity of the deliberating agent and the objectivity of facts. What is striking here when observing the frequencies and distributions in the table is not the predominance of given verbal forms or types of assessment over others, since the variation in their use is not significant (especially if we consider the fact that occurrences of *find* and *hold* could be counted together, hence totalling 16 occurrences, since *find* is often used in the texts also as a synonym of *think*/*believe*, thus with a meaning comparable to *hold*), but rather the fact that certain verbs tend to be associated with a specific type of assessment. At this stage it is sufficient to point out that verbs conveying a strong element of judgement (+E, E) are usually combined with a representation of reality which mitigates or minimizes evaluation (-E, E), and vice versa.

3.2.2 Conclusive move

As to the conclusive move, here too the focus has been placed on the way the arbitral decision is formulated. Unlike the preparatory move which, as we have seen, displays a certain level of variation across the corpus, the conclusive moves are all very similar, since their purpose is to lexicalize the arbitrator's judgement in the most effective, concise and unambiguous way. The standard formulation (18, 19) consists of three main semantic units – i.e. (i) the agent (*Panel, Panelist,* or personal pronouns), (ii) active and performative verbs, (iii) a passive construction to indicate the action to be carried out (which corresponds to the alternative *be transferred* vs. *be dismissed/denied*), possibly expressed through modalizers (i.e. *shall* or *should*) – whereas exceptions to this patterns are very few (20, 21). The deontic character is conferred to this move by the verbs through which the arbitral decision is formulated, which are all performative forms – directive or declarative, (namely *order* in 36 cases, *decide* in 13, *require* in 9, *direct* in 7, *dismiss* in 3, and few other corresponding forms).

(18) […] this *Panel* (i) accordingly *directs* (ii) that the complaint shall *be dismissed* (iii). (Award 15)

(19) The *Panel* (i) *orders* (ii) that the disputed domain name […] *be transferred* (iii) to the Complainant. (Award 59)

(20) *I* (i) therefore *dismiss* (ii) this complaint. (Award 5)

(21) The Complaint *is dismissed* (iii). (Award 31)

The standard formulation of this move is very brief and concise, and limited to the representation of the three semantic units mentioned above. Cases of variation are very limited and they regard either instances where a summary of the Complainant's requests is lexicalized before being ratified (22) or where a short coda is added with specifications concerning the transferring / non-transferring of the disputed name (23), as we can see below:

(22) *The Complainant asks that the Disputed Domain Names be transferred to the Complainant.* The Panel orders that the Disputed Domain Names to be transferred to the Complainant. (Award 19)

(23) The Panel decides that the domain name […] be transferred to the Complainant or its solicitors in Hong Kong Messrs. […], *so as to avoid a third party registering the Disputed Domain Name for improper reasons.* (Award 83)

The effectiveness of this move highly depends on how the pronouncement is worded and, more specifically, on the level of authoritativeness expressed by the deliberating agent and the compelling formulation of the action to be carried out.

Authoritativeness is emphasized by the way attribution is handled, i.e. by the lexicalization of the arbitrator's persona. The majority of the cases, as discussed in 3.1, explicitly represent the agent – in this specific move respectively as *Panel* (53 occurrences), *Panelist* (4 occ.) or through personal pronouns (7 occ.) – as examples (18, 19, 22, 23) above show. In such cases the authoritativeness of the arbitrator – hence the binding quality of the arbitral decision – is automatically presupposed by the performative verb employed: the verb *order* or *reject* presuppose an agent who is in a position to perform both actions, on the basis of the power conferred upon him/her by the parties and 'the law'. However, there are also cases (16 in total) where the deliberating agent is not mentioned and is replaced by impersonal or passive forms, as we have seen in (21). Through this rhetorical resource the focus is transferred from the agent to his/her decision and the action it prescribes. Finally, for the sake of completeness, the existence of a limited number of idiosyncratic formulations (three in total) is to be acknowledged and is represented by uncharacteristically hedged formulations like the following:

(24) *I see no other reason not to comply* with the Complainant's requested remedy. (Award 33)

(25) [...] the Panel *believes that it is appropriate* to transfer the domain name [...] to Complainant and so orders. (Award 34)

These cases are understandably limited in that they minimize the role of the arbitrator, possibly jeopardizing the overall authoritativeness which is required for the deontic impact of such texts.

The frequency and distribution of deontic markers are listed in Table 3. The bold figures – together with the already noticed high frequency of the term *Panel* as attribution marker – seem to confirm, in quantitative terms, the three-unit structure defined above as the most recurring (hence possibly the most effective) way of codifying the arbitral decision.

DEONTICITY	Directive verbs		Modalizers		Passive construction	other
	active	*passive*	*shall*	*should*		
	64	13	9	12	**62**	1

Table 3. Deonticity in the conclusive move of the Decisions.

The evidence collected in 3.2 indicates a recognizable trend in the structuring of the Decision sections of HKIAC awards, which, as we have seen, can be broken down into two pragmatically different but complementary moves: the preparatory move and the conclusive one. Differences in pragmatics, quite expectedly, bring about differences also at the rhetorical level. As a matter of fact, the conclusive move, the only necessary one, with a marked declarative function, is very much standardized, short and leaving very little space for variation, whereas the preparatory move, which is intended to substantiate what is to be found in the conclusive one (thus having a distinctive informative and persuasive purpose), displays a higher level of variation, looser templates and a wider range of resources to carry out that purpose, possibly in relation to the specificity and empirical evidence concerning the case at hand. The only element which remains noticeable in the two moves is the frequent lexicalization of the deliberating agent through the collective term *Panel* rather than singulative expressions such as *Panelist* or first person pronouns. As seen above, rhetorically concealing the drafter's persona behind a collective entity, or alternatively through zero attribution (which is the second ranking strategy in terms of frequency), enhances the impression of impartiality, thus boosting the authoritativeness of the pronouncement.

In the preparatory move, when formulating the claim introducing the arbitral decision, drafters (although possibly subconsciously) seem to use verbs and phrases according to fixed collocations, i.e. *conclude* + 'grantability', *decide* + 'motivations', *find* + 'focus'. This may certainly be due to a mere replication of standard ways of codifying the content, but there may be other explanations to such collocates. As a matter of fact, a close observation of the occurrences (Table 2) reveals that they all seem to include both an element of evaluation and judgement (and that is precisely what the arbitrator is required to do) meant to corroborate the deontic quality of the text, and an element of objective observation, which should instead guarantee for the rightfulness and impartiality of the text. More specifically, *conclude*, which is a verb of volition and of discourse/argumentation – indicating the action carried out as a consequence of a given premise – is associated with 'grantability', i.e. an eminently evaluative assessment of reality, used here to explicitly anticipate the orientation of the final move (i.e. if *the relief is to be granted*, the Complainant's request will necessarily be accepted). In this way, the face-threatening potential and subjective implications related to this assessment are redressed by the verb *conclude,* which presupposes empirical conditions behind given conclusions. *Decide* (and its synonym *determine*), instead, presupposes an action which is less circumstantial and more context-free, and implies a high degree of arbitrariness, which is dangerous for these texts, since Decisions need to be (perceived) as well-founded and substantiated rather than arbitrary. For this reason *decide* is combined with 'motivations' and is here used almost exclusively to establish and declare the correspondence between facts and the conditions in the Policy (through formulations of the type *the Panel decides that the conditions in the Policy are (not) respected*). In this sense the verb is used as much with a referential function as for its declarative connotation. Finally, *find* is mainly a constative verb, and even when it is used as a verb of interpretation (with the meaning of *think* or *believe*) it still carries an element of representation, as if it were describing a state of affairs (objectively) observed rather than (subjectively) interpreted. For this reason it is easily combined with 'focus' resources and used to introduce elements of evaluation and judgement (i.e. success or failure in establishing a case) without sounding arbitrary.

Once the risk of impartiality is minimized by the preparatory move through the use of the collective (or zero) agent, and once the balance between the drafter's interpretation of the case and its empirical phenomenology has been rhetorically established, drafters move on to codify their decisions, in the conclusive move, through very standardized and fixed expressions, whose perlocutionary value is supposed to be clear in that they are easily recognizable, easy understandable, hence easily acceptable by the parties.

4. Concluding remarks

The validity of awards depends on the arbitrators' authority. If they want their pronouncement to be recognized as binding, they need to be perceived as authoritative and, at the same time, their decisions cannot be considered arbitrary, biased, or partial, in order to avoid any challenge to their awards. The conventional formulations available to HKIAC arbitrators, i.e. the expressions to which they usually resort when codifying decisions, manage to harmonize these two conflicting conditions, possibly even without the drafters being fully aware of their pragmatic potential.

By observing the data in Table 1 we have seen the general tendency for these Decision sections to resort to the term *Panel* rather than *Panelist* or a personal pronoun to refer to the deliberating agent. This is quite significant since – with the exception of 2 out of 78 texts – the person responsible for these Decisions is a 'Sole Panelist', very often indicated as such in the opening lines of the award itself. The choice of a collective noun to linguistically represent the persona of the arbitrator can easily be explained by the need to boost authoritativeness and minimize the impression of subjectivity and arbitrariness: as a matter of fact, by rhetorically relating the responsibility of the arbitral award to (someone speaking on behalf of) a team of experts, the character of collegiality is pragmatically conferred to the pronouncement, thus corroborating its validity and emphasizing its deontic impact. The same purpose is achieved by exploiting passive and impersonal forms, thus depersonalizing the wording of the arbitral decision.

Secondly, when considering the distribution of deonticity boosting resources in the preparatory and conclusive move, some important pieces of evidence come to the surface. In the preparatory move, when introducing the reasons for the final decision and preparing the ground for the decision to be appropriately perceived, drafters resort to expressions by which they manage, at the same time, to impose their decision and redress the threat represented by such imposition. As a matter of fact, when HKIAC arbitrators use phrases like *Panel decides, deliberates, dismisses, rejects*, etc, they are indeed stating their authority: the rhetorical presupposition is that the arbitrator has the authority to decide, either accepting or dismissing requests. This act of self-attribution of authority is face-threatening, but the formulations used by HKIAC arbitrators manage to rhetorically mitigate this threat by grounding their decisions and rejection into objective, empirical, observable evidence (for instance through assessing reality as 'motivations' or narrative bits, i.e. by making the reasons explicit, thus justifying a given interpretation). On the other hand, when HKIAC arbitrators assess the reality through non-evaluative verbs or formulations which do not presuppose any specific authority on the part of the assessing agent (i.e. through the verb *find*), this 'neutral' action is counterbalanced by representing reality as the result of an explicit act of evaluation (i.e. through assessment in terms of 'grantability' or 'focus'), an action which presupposes the judgment of the arbitrator and his/her authority, thus enhancing the deontic quality of the claim.

References

Bennett, Robert 2012. Constitutional Interpretation. In Tiersma/Solan (eds), 114–127.

Bhatia, Vijay / Candlin, Christopher / Gotti, Maurizio (eds) 2003. *Legal Discourse in Multilingual and Multicultural Contexts: Arbitration Texts in Europe.* Bern: Peter Lang.

Biber, Douglas / Johansson, Stig / Leech, Geoffrey / Conrad, Susan / Finegan, Edward 1999. *Longman Grammar of Spoken and Written English*. London: Longman.

Erman, Britt / Warren, Beatrice 2000. The Idiom Principle and the Open Choice Principle. *Text* 20/1, 29–62.

Gibbons, John 2003. *Forensic Linguistics. An Introduction to Language in the Justice System*. Oxford: Blackwell.

Gotti, Maurizio 2012. Text and Genre. In Tiersma/Solan (eds), 52–66.

Haley, Glen 2012. *Arbitration Guide*. Hong Kong: IBA Arbitration Committee.

Nariman, Fali S. 2000. The Spirit of Arbitration: The Tenth Annual Goff Lecture. *Arbitration International* 16/3, 261–278.

Park, William 2006. *Arbitration of International Business Disputes: Studies in Law and Practice*. Oxford: Oxford University Press.

Park, William / Paulsson, Jan 1983. Binding Force of International Arbitral Awards. *Virginia Journal of International Law* 23, 254–285.

Ping, Han 2011. Challenging Arbitral Awards. A Comparative Study of Chinese Law, British Law and UNCITRAL Model Law. *Frontiers of Law in China* 6/3, 418–446.

Solan, Lawrence 2012. Linguistic Issues in Statutory Interpretation. In Tiersma/Solan (eds), 87–99.

Tiersma, Peter 1999. Legal Language. Chicago: University of Chicago Press.

Tiersma, Peter / Solan, Lawrence (eds) 2012. *The Oxford Handbook of Language and Law*. Oxford: Oxford University Press.

Stefania M. Maci

'It is amply clear that there is no convincing evidence to infer that': Evidentiality in Indian Arbitral Awards*

1. Introduction

This study is an attempt to explore the degree of evidentiality used in arbitral awards from a linguistic perspective, with particular regard to the Indian context. This calls for a clear-cut definition of both *arbitration* and *evidentiality*. *Arbitration* is an alternative form of dispute resolution (ADR), where 'alternative' refers to the extra-judicial way of resolving disputes,[1] which is private (that is, confidential) and, as such, alternative to the public judicial process held in a court of law (Maci 2012). From a legal standpoint, *evidence* "includes the technical tools through which facts submitted by the parties to a judicial proceeding of any kind […] may become the proper basis for any judicial decision" (Ziccardi 2012: 63). This, however, has little to do with the linguistic concept of *evidentiality*. Aikhenvald (2004: 1) defines *evidentiality* as a conceptual category which "states the existence of a source of evidence for some information; that includes stating that there is some evidence, and also specifying what type of evidence there is".

Although in arbitration the parties agree that an independent arbitrator pronounces the final decision after considering the evidence submitted, the way in which language intersects with the law is of primary relevance here. The purpose of this chapter is to investigate the

* The research on which this chapter is based is part of the research project Progetto Italy® (Italian TALented Young ®esearchers) – Asian Arbitration Law (2014–2015).

1 See <http://www.camera-arbitrale.it/it/Arbitrato/index.php?id=5> [6/9/2014].

extent to which knowledge – of vital importance for the arbitrator when granting the award – is linguistically expressed by the parties involved in the arbitral procedure in terms of evidence intended as a 'source of information'.

2. Background: arbitration in India[2]

The first attempt at codifying arbitration rules in India was made under British jurisdiction back in the 18th century. When in 1859 the Code of Civil Procedure was established for India, arbitral provisions were first introduced, though they simply mirrored the British ones. It was only in 1940 that the first Arbitration Act was introduced in India. It was then further improved to a large degree at the beginning of 1996, when the Arbitration and Conciliation Act 1996 came into force (Motiwala *et al.* 2014). Arbitration proceedings have become necessary in India because the ordinary court system seems overburdened by backlogs and delays. In addition, while enhancing speed and efficiency in alternative dispute resolution, arbitration saves court fees, which in India are regulated by the State.

The 1996 Act is largely based on the UNCITRAL Model Law (1985) and the UNCITRAL Arbitration Rules (1976). It applies to any arbitrations in India and is divided into two parts: Part 1, which provides a framework for arbitration between Indian or foreign parties and Part 2, which is meant for foreign awards. The arbitration organisations commonly used to resolve large commercial disputes are: The Indian Council of Arbitration (ICA), whose headquarters are in New Delhi; the International Chamber of Commerce (ICC); and the Singapore International Arbitration Centre (SIAC).

2 <http://uk.practicallaw.com/9-502-0625> [22/8/2014].

3. Literature review: arbitration and evidentiality

3.1 Arbitration

From the legal perspective, extensive research has been carried out on arbitration, focusing on several issues dealt with in the many specialised journals on arbitration established in the last few decades, issues such as the role of international commercial arbitration (Brower 2008); the drafting and enforcement of arbitration awards (Zaiwalla 2003; Marriott 2004; Debattista 2005; Webster 2006); the appointment and number of arbitrators (Miles 2003; Kurkela *et al.* 2007) and their international function (Aksen 2007); the challenge of arbitrators and awards (Nicholas/Partasides 2007); and issues about confidentiality and transparency (Dessemontet 2001; Malatesta/Sali 2013). Recently, attention has also been paid to arbitration in developing countries, particularly in Asia (Ali 2010; Shah/Gandhi 2011). As far as India is concerned, arbitration has been investigated by offering interpretations of the Arbitration Act 1996 (Parthasarathy/Visalakshi 2007), and by taking into consideration the legal contradictions existing in Indian arbitral procedures (Agarwal 2008; Rendeiro 2011), whether amendments are possible (Rai 2012) and what right to appeal exists in India (Biswas 2012).

Within the applied linguistics field, recent investigation concerning arbitration has been carried out focusing not only on language use in everyday professional discourse (Bhatia *et al.* 2014), but also on the genre of arbitration awards, as well as on genre contamination between arbitration and litigation (Bhatia *et al.* 2010, 2012). As international arbitration involves both Civil and Common Law systems, the way in which different legal jurisdictions and cultures may linguistically affect arbitration has been evaluated by Hafner (2011). Attention has also been paid to in-group professional identities, the use of norms and their influence on professional communication (Bhatia/Evangelisti Allori 2011).

3.2 Evidentiality

Boas (1911) was possibly the first linguist who indirectly introduced the concept of evidentiality by referring to the suffix denoting the source of information in native American Kwakiuti. The term 'evidentiality' was introduced by Roman Jakobson (1957) as a label for a verbal category indicating the source of information on which the speaker's/writer's statement is based. It was, however, in the mid-1980s that a great interest in evidentiality began, with the work by Chafe and Nichols (1986), continued by Willet (1988) and later involving DeLancey (1997), Aikhenvald and Dixon (2003) and Aikhenvald (2004). Nowadays evidentiality is defined in various ways. The different theories can be grouped into two main approaches: a narrow and a broad definition of evidentiality.

In a narrow definition of evidentiality, "evidentials express the kinds of evidence a person has for making factual claims" (Anderson 1986: 273) and includes those linguistic markers indicating the source of information, i.e. whether information has been acquired as seen, heard, inferred or told (Aikhenvald 2003). Although this approach acknowledges that in about one quarter of the world's languages, marking the information source is obligatory and that these languages have a grammatical category of evidentiality – while other languages have evidential extensions of non-evidential categories (Aikkhenvald 2007) – such a narrow approach only considers as evidentials certain grammaticalized expressions, in particular morphemes (Mushin 2001; Aikhenvald 2004). This results in an almost total exclusion of English from such research (Bednarek 2006).[3]

The broad definition of evidentiality is based on the assumption that "[l]anguages typically provide a repertoire of devices for conveying [...] various attitudes toward knowledge" (Chafe 1986: 262), including the source and reliability of people's knowledge. As such, the term 'evidential' "covers much more than the marking of evidence per se"

3 This also explains why evidentiality was not studied in languages which do not have grammaticalized expressions of evidential markers until the 1980s. Indeed, the very fact that there are languages that express evidentiality in non-grammaticalized terms made linguists think that, for those languages, evidentiality did not exist (Bednarek 2006).

(Chafe/Nichols 1986: vii). In this approach, evidence is just one, but not the only one, of the epistemological considerations that are linguistically encoded in the concept of evidentiality (Chafe 1986). In this sense, evidentiality is concerned with matters of truth, certainty, doubt, reliability, authority, inference, stance and evidence (Chafe/Nichols 1986; Mushin 2001).

Any scholar focusing on the concept of evidentiality must decide whether to adopt the narrow or the broad view of evidentiality (Mushin 2001). If we take into consideration the narrow definition of evidentiality, we consider just one part of the greater study of epistemological positioning: that aspect of language which marks the speaker's/writer's source of information. If we analyse evidentiality in its broader definition, it implies much more: we will thus look at the basis of the speaker's/writer's knowledge as well as his/her attitude. Precisely because in an arbitral award a great deal depends on the reasoning of the arbitral panel based on the knowledge deriving from the (physical) evidence the arbitrators have at their disposal, the type of evidentiality analysed here will follow the broader definition drawn from Chafe (1986).

3.2.1 Theoretical framework

Chafe's definition of evidentiality involves several concepts. The first concept relates to the notion of the *mode of knowing*, i.e. the way in which knowledge is acquired. There are four distinctive modes of knowing: *belief*, *induction*, *hearsay* and *deduction*. Each mode of knowing depends on different *sources of knowledge*: belief, or opinion, and induction are concerned with *evidence*: the former with its absence, the latter with its presence; hearsay depends on *language* and deduction on *hypothesis* (Chafe 1986).

In Chafe's (1986) opinion, knowledge deriving from belief can be expressed by mental or cognitive verbs such as *think, believe, guess, suppose* and so on; when knowledge comes from induction, the most common marker is the modal verb *must*, together with such lexical items as *obvious, clear, evidently* and *seem*. He further claims that evidence can also denote a sensory source of knowledge. In this case, the evidential markers most commonly employed are *look, see, hear, feel, sounds* and *look like*. If knowledge is acquired through language, its source is based on hearsay, normally realized with such verbs as *say, tell, suggest, seem* and *suppose*, when metaphorically used with a rumour-like meaning and, in academic discourse, by citation and quotations. Deduction is the source of knowledge based on hypothesis, and normally expressed by such markers as *should* and *presumably*, and to a lesser degree, by *can, could*, and *would*.

Knowledge is information conveyed by the speaker/writer through evidential markers, and which proceeds along a continuum of *reliability* ranging from the most reliable to the least reliable knowledge. The (un)reliable knowledge that we acquire from different sources and with different modes is normally checked against what we already know, and which in our own mind forms the categories and frameworks found in the world we know. When there is no match, we have low *codability* verbally expressed by means of *hedges*; when a match occurs, it is in line with our *expectations*. According to Chafe (1986) reliability is expressed by means of epistemic expressions (adverbs, adjectives, modals etc.) indicating certainty, close or remote possibility, as well as epistemic modals. Hedges are present whenever we try to match the categories and framework of the world we already know with what we are learning. This tentative match is normally expressed with nouns, verbs, adjectives or predications such as *sort of*, or *about*. If, on the other hand, the match is possible, we have expectations, lexically realised with such expressions as *of course, in fact*, or *actually*, generally with connectives or adversatives, "which relate in various ways to expectations" (Chafe 1986: 271).

Clearly, in discourse, knowledge (un)reliability and a match against previously acquired experience overlap with the knowledge source and mode. On the contrary, the knowledge source and knowledge mode are inestricably dependent upon each other.

4. Research question

Considering that, to the best of my knowledge, no applied linguistics analysis has ever been carried on evidentiality and arbitral awards with particular regard to the Indian context, and given the extreme standardization of arbitral awards in their written form (Maci 2009, 2010, 2011, 2012), my preliminary investigation will focus on those linguistic forms regarded as evidential markers which show a degree of knowing in Indian arbitral awards. In particular, drawing from Chafe (1986), I will examine how degrees of knowledge are expressed in terms of belief, induction, hearsay and deduction. My research question (henceforth RQ) will therefore be the following:

RQ: What are the evidential markers whose source is defined in terms of belief, induction, hearsay and deduction used to show the various degrees of knowing?

The RQ draws on corpus linguistics analysis. Broadly speaking, corpus linguistics is "the study of language based on examples of real life language use" (McEnery/Wilson 2001: 1). It is an empirical approach since the enquiry starts from authentic data and aims at analysing and describing language use as realised in texts (Tognini-Bonelli 2001). Given the fact that no consistent linguistic investigation of Indian arbitral awards exists, in order to describe how evidentiality is realized in such a standardized genre, it seems necessary to investigate attested language use rather than just any theoretical implication. Consequently, the study carried out to answer the RQ may qualify for a corpus-based approach, in that it relies on both quantitative and qualitative techniques (Mair 1991; Biber/Conrad 2009).

5. Methodological approach

The analysis inherent to the RQ has been carried out with WordSmith Tools 6 (Scott 2012). Fifty-nine arbitral awards issued between 2012 and 2014, written in English, and dealing with domestic matters have been downloaded from the website of the Indian National Stock Exchange (NSE: <http://www.nseindia.com/invest/dynaContent/arbitration awards. jsp?requestPage=main&qryFlag=yes>). The site collects "all the disputes against the Trading Members/Sub-brokers/Authorised Persons with regard to trades and transactions done on the Exchange" or "Trading Members who have claim, dispute or difference against investors/ Sub-brokers/Authorised Persons/Clearing Members and visa versa [sic], with regard to the trades and transactions done on the Exchange or anything incidental thereto" (<http://www.nseindia.com/invest/resources/ download/asst_Arbitration_FAQs.pdf>, 22/08/ 2014). All downloaded awards are in .jpg format. They have been converted into Word format with Abbey Transformer, an OCR software and then saved in .txt so as to allow an analysis with WordSmith Tools.

Although I used an already established theoretical framework, following the broader definition of evidentiality provided by Chafe (1986) and drawing from Chafe's categories used to classify data, the approach I adopted is also text-driven, and thus similar to Tognini-Bonelli's (2001) concept of corpus-driven linguistics.[4] Indeed, the study has been preceded by a manual analysis of a small-scale text sub-corpus rather than by an approach based on automated large-scale corpus analyses. In other words, five awards were randomly selected and read in order to detect potential evidential markers, without categorizing them on an a priori basis. The markers were first identified according to the source of knowing. In other words, the first step was that of detecting whether there was evidence or lack of evidence, or whether the author of the text was using language as the source of knowing or making a

4 According to Tognini-Bonelli (2001), corpus-based linguistics is linguistics that uses a corpus to explain a theory, whereas corpus-driven linguistics is linguistics that formulates a theory on the basis of a corpus.

hypothesis. For instance, in (1) the text represents an evidential marker whose source clearly shows a lack of evidence (my emphasis):

(1) I think, there is no point in taking a distinctly evasive plea that the authorized person [...]. (arb_F&O_K_0030_2013)

Indeed, the cognitive verb *think* expresses a judgment or evaluation by the author on the basis of his/her reasoning. On the other hand, in (2) the source of knowing is specified by the verb *indicates* which refers to the evidence offered by the "latest report of [the] Inspector of Police":

(2) The latest report of [the] Inspector of Police, Cyber Crime P.S, Hyderabad on 29/01/2013 indicates that the investigation is in progress. (arb_CM_K_0043_2012)

In other cases, the source of knowing was offered by language, as in excerpt (3):

(3) The applicant admitted having provided the e-mail ID. (arb_F&O_K_0011_2013)

In others, the source of knowing could be a hypothesis, as shown in (4), where *should* indicates the deduction which can be made given the fact that the annexure is a public document and therefore must be regarded as genuine:

(4) This annexure being a public document should be deemed as genuine unless proved otherwise. (arb_CM_K_0004_2013)

The lexical evidential markers thus found were then grouped according to the mode of knowing defined by Chafe (1986) as the *belief*, *induction*, *hearsay* and *deduction* categories, which (1), (2), (3) and (4) respectively belong to. Each evidential marker was then analysed using WordSmith Tools 6 and all the resulting concordancing lists were checked manually in order to understand whether or not the item could be included as evidential. The category containing the verb form *may*, found in the sub-corpus of the five randomly selected awards, also contained the noun *May*, indicating the month, which clearly I had to delete from my computation because irrelevant for my analysis.

The quantitative analysis was then followed by a qualitative one (Miles/Huberman 1994; Coffey/Atkinson 1996), which has allowed the interpretation of the findings of my study.

6. Results and discussion

As shown in my previous research (Maci 2011), the genre of arbitral awards is made up of four moves:
(i) identification of the proceedings;
(ii) establishing the facts of the case;
(iii) deriving the *ratio decidendi*;
(iv) pronouncing the award.
The collected Indian arbitral awards comprising my corpus follow the same genre pattern. The analysis of the five randomly-selected Indian awards allowed me to detect 143 potential evidential markers, shown in Table 1 below:

Evidential markers				
acceptable	accordingly	acknowledged	acted	admits
admitted	advised	aforementioned	agreement	allegations
alleged	alleging	ambiguity	answer	answered
appeared	applicant	argued	argument	arguments
assured	averred	believe	bills	book
can	cannot	certificate	cheque	claim
claiming	clarified	clearly	communicates	communication
complaint	conclude	confirmation	confirmations	confirmed
consent	contact	contended	could	denied
deny	denying	documents	dubious	due
duly	e-log	email	email address	email-id
emails	evasive	evidences	explain	false
find	fully	heard	hearing	ID
indicated	inference	information	informed	inscription

Evidential markers				
insistent	instructions	irrelevant	it is clear	know
knowing	known	letter	lodged	logic
maintain	may	mentioned	mentioned	messages
mobile phone number	must	notes	notice	objections
observed	oral depositions	orally	ought to	papers
perused	petition	pointed out	prayed	promptly
proof	questionable	questioned	receipts	record
reference	registered e-mail	regular	regularly	reiterated
relevant	replied	reply	reportedly	reports
respondent	response	said	shall	shocked
should	signed	SMS	specifically	specify
stated	statement	states	stating	still
submitted	substantiate	suggestion	surprised	talk
telephonic instructions	told	transparent	true	undersigned
well	will	willing	would	written complaint
written statement	written statements	written submissions		

Table 1. List of potential evidential markers in the sub-corpus.

Each evidential marker was then analysed using WordSmith Tools 6 for concordancing, and each concordance was then checked manually to see whether the item was a real evidential or not. Verbs were also checked in their conjugated form even if that item was not present in the sub-corpus. For instance, if the item *believe* was present in the sub-corpus, the conjugated forms *believes* and *believed* were also 'hunted'. Once all the concordancing had been checked, the items were classified according to Chafe's (1986) interpretation. This led to the generation of 9,364 evidential markers grouped into the *hearsay, belief, induction* and *deduction* categories.

A closer analysis of my data allowed me to identify three subcategories that were not relevant for my study. Firstly, a large group of evidentials was actually formed by real tribunal proof and evidence, as examples (5) and (6) show:

(5) […] no other papers were given by him or sent by the respondent Company to her. (arb_F&O_K_0030_2013)

(6) […] based on the written statements and copies of relevant documents furnished by them and their oral depositions. (arb_CM_H_0005_2013)

Secondly, other evidentials were actually formed by domain-specific words. For instance, the term *hearing* in excerpt (7) indicates the 'tribunal listening to evidence' rather than the act of hearing somebody speaking, while *submitted* in (8) means '[of a disputed matter] referred to arbitration':

(7) The first sitting/hearing took place on December 4, 2012 when the applicant appeared in person. (arb_CM_K_0045_2012)

(8) However, Applicant had never submitted any complaint. (arb_CM_K_0025_2013)

Lastly, some words were evidential markers but used in a metadiscursive way, in the sense that they were meant to guide the reader within the text in order to find the information referred to. There were only five cases, i.e. the items *aforementioned* (2 hits), *said* (245 hits), *stated* (41 hits), *undersigned* (6 hits) and *explained* (5 hits), all of which are used in an adjectival role, as shown in the examples below:

(9) The Respondent in its defense has raised the aforementioned NSE circular. (arb_CM_C_0018_2013)

(10) But during the course of hearing he clarified that the said date was mentioned in Form No. 1 […]. (arb_CM_K_0013_2013)

(11) […] the undersigned sole Arbitrator had passed an award in the above referred Arbitration Matter. (arb_CM_M_0056_2012)

Of the remaining evidentials, only those which occurred more frequently than five times were taken into consideration. The reason lies in the fact that it has been observed that an item occurring five times or more is more likely to appear in multiple texts in the corpus, which may also convey less skewed results.

6.1 Hearsay evidentials

As stated by Chafe (1986), evidentials mark a hearsay source of evidence when the mode of knowing is language. In my corpus the majority of evidentials indicates that knowledge is expressed through 'language' and therefore indicates a hearsay source. This is clearly the rule, since the arbitral procedure requires that the arbitral panel collect any possible information so as to have a clear view of what happened in order to apply norms to the parties' behaviours and reach an objective and impartial award. Such information is gathered through hearings, which are then reformulated by the arbitrators or presented as written evidence indicated by the legal world as *disclosure* or *discovery*. Indeed, 90% of the award is based on disclosure, found in the second move of the generic pattern of the arbitral award ('establishing the facts of the case'), which is therefore characterised by an ample use of reported speech verbs and nouns related to discourse or speech, as we can see in Table 2 below:

Hearsay evidentials					
				Award word count	*140,357*
Item	*hits*	*TTR*	*Item*	*hits*	*TTR*
stated	190	1.35	explained	17	0.12
denied	95	0.67	called	14	0.09
claimed	90	0.64	clarified	14	0.09
consent [noun]	83	0.59	deny	14	0.09
informed	78	0.55	maintain	14	0.09
alleged [verb]	75	0.53	explain	13	0.09
confirmation [referred to 'trade' or 'log']	64	0.45	questioned	13	0.09
mentioned	61	0.43	replied	13	0.09
pointed out	59	0.42	reportedly	13	0.09

Hearsay evidentials					
			Award word count		*140,357*
Item	*hits*	*TTR*	*Item*	*hits*	*TTR*
alleged [past participle in an adjectival role]	55	0.39	alleging	12	0.08
agreement	48	0.34	denying	11	0.07
states	48	0.34	substantiate	10	0.07
allegations	47	0.33	claims [verb]	9	0.06
confirmed	41	0.29	inform	9	0.06
contended	38	0.27	said [verb]	9	0.06
confirmations [all referred to 'trade']	33	0.23	claim [verb]	8	0.05
assured	28	0.19	communicated	8	0.05
prayed	25	0.17	prays	8	0.05
response	24	0.17	admitted	7	0.04
claiming	23	0.16	substantiated	7	0.04
stating	21	0.14	confirmed [adjectival role]	6	0.04
claims [noun]	20	0.14	admits	5	0.03
argued	19	0.13	answer [noun]	5	0.03
reiterated	18	0.12	communicating	5	0.03
Total hearsay evidential hits			*1,568*	*TTR*	*11.17*

Table 2. Hearsay evidentials.

Such evidentials are the most frequently adopted because the award itself is mainly composed of a consistent part in which there is the reconstruction by the arbitrators of what the applicant and the respondent did and said:

(12) He confirmed that JRG Securities was having a branch office at Korutla headed by Mr G.Sadanand and assisted by 3 other employees. (arb_F&O_H_0002_2012)

(13) The respondent replied that Regulation 3.2.1 of the NSE merely provides […]. (arb_CM_K_0013_2013)

(14) The Applicant has therefore prays [sic] that the Respondent be ordered to pay Rs, 64,612,03. (arb_F&O_M_0047_2013)

(15) However, during the hearing the Applicant clearly stated that she did not make the above-referred two payments of Rs. 20,000. (arb_CM_K_0004_2013)

None of the items above refers to people other than the Applicant or the Respondent involved in the arbitral proceedings.

6.2 *Belief evidentials*

The category of belief evidentials is characterized by those markers that express a mode of knowing with a lack of evidence (Chafe 1986). The evidentials found in my corpus are those indicated in Table 3 below:

Belief evidentials		
		Award word count 140,357
Item	*hits*	*TTR*
duly	64	0.45
regularly	52	0.37
false	50	0.35
true	14	0.09
acceptable	10	0.07
believe	9	0.06
questionable	7	0.04
apparently	6	0.04
TOTAL	*212*	*1.51*

Table 3. Belief evidentials.

The distribution of these evidentials shows a regular pattern. Indeed, *duly* and *regularly* always occur in the second move of awards, that of 'establishing the facts of the case', and refer to documents or papers which have been presented according to procedures established by law, as in example (16), or routinely foreseen as required by business practices, as in (17) below:

(16) […] from 27th March, 2012 to 31st March, 2012 in derivatives segment was duly confirmed and acknowledged by the Director of the Respondent. (arb_CM_M_0052_2012)

(17) The Applicant filed the Arbitration claim on 21.07.2008 and the case is that it signed Member Client Agreement (referred for brevity as 'MCA') in November 2006 and was trading regularly. (arb_F&O_M_0086_2013)

The adjective *false* also occurs in the second move and mainly refers to the Respondent's opinion that the Applicant's reconstruction of the facts are 'fraudulent', as examples (18) and (19) indicate:

(18) Keeping in view above the allegations made by the applicant are false and against the true facts. (arb_F&O_H_0006_2012)

(19) The applicant has filed a false claim to harass and humiliate the respondent and the claim therefore has to be dismissed. (arb_F&O_K_0010_2013)

The adjective *true* (second move, 'establishing the facts of the case'), on the other hand, normally refers to the Applicant:

(20) Assuming that the averment of the applicant is true, there is nothing to show that the applicant either followed up with request to close the account or wrote any mail. (arb_CM_K_0039_2012)

(21) […] the allegation that the Applicant's email dated 2.8.2010 was to camouflage the true facts and wriggle out of its legal obligations, is false. (arb_CM_C_0006_2013)

In (21), it is the allegation made by the respondent that is *false*, rather than what the applicant said. In other words, the arbitral panel never uses the word *false* for the applicant when reporting the respondent's reconstruction of the facts, which are always 'true'. Paradoxically, the word *true* is employed for the applicant even if it does indicate the contrary of 'true' and in doing so seems to reinforce the concept of 'falsehood'. Indeed, this adjective can be found in the expression *against true facts*, commonly used against the applicant:

(22) Keeping in view above the allegations made by the applicant are false and against the true facts. (arb_F&O_H_0006_2012)

In two cases, the evidential *true* collocates with the adjective *acceptable* in the expression *true and acceptable* referring to the applicant's claim. When it occurs, the arbitral panel introduces the reasoning path which leads the arbitrators to the *ratio decidendi* move (third move), i.e. the acceptance or the rebuttal of the applicant's claim:

(23) POINTS: 1. Whether the Claim of the Applicant is barred by Limitation? 2. Whether the Claim of the Applicant is true and acceptable? [...] Hence I conclude that the claim of the Applicant for a sum of Ra. 1,93,100/- is true and acceptable. (arb_F&O_C_0002_2013)

(24) POINT: Whether the claim of the applicant is true and acceptable? [...] I am of the considered view that the claim of the applicant is not acceptable and I answer to the above point against the applicant. (arb_CM_C_0022_2013)

The same can be said whenever the items *questionable* (found in the third move, *ratio decidendi*) and *apparently* (in the second move, establishing the facts of the case) are present: if used, the arbitrators are anticipating a view of the facts which is not completely positive within their reasoning:

(25) Due to ambiguity, the validity of such documents may be questionable. (arb_CM_H_0005_2013)

(26) [...] complaints with the police for investigation in the fraudulent activities leading to the apparently huge losses suffered by the applicant. (arb_CM_K_0043_2012)

The only verb used as a belief evidential is *believe*. It is mainly used in the infinitive form and mainly, but not necessarily, in impersonal constructions: *it is difficult to believe*; *X has every reason to believe*; *X gives room to believe*; *it is impossible to believe*:

(27) It is, therefore, not susceptible to reason to believe that he was unaware of the NEAT trading system. (arb_CM_K_0025_2013);

(28) *I am inclined* to believe this because this is a 'Common Experience' with ordinary investors [...]. Rather, on the other hand, there is no reason at all to believe that the applicant investor would go in for a litigation of sorts. (arb_F&O_K_0030_2013)

(29) […] in favour of The Broker and the stand of the Constituent is impossible to believe […] it is difficult to believe that constituent had placed trade in her account. (arb_F&O_M_0044_2012)

As we can see, in these examples the verb is mainly used in the *ratio decidendi* move, that is, in the part of the award where the arbitral panel has to explain the reasoning on which the award is based. The data suggest that there is a form of depersonalisation whenever the claim has to be dismissed. In other words, there seems to be a form of negative politeness in the Indian arbitral practice by means of which the arbitrators never impose on others. By contrast, as we can see in (28) above, whenever there is no danger of a face-threatening act, the arbitrator is likely to use the first personal form and say *I am inclined to believe.*

6.3 Deduction evidentials

According to Chafe (1986), the category of deduction evidentials includes those evidential markers which indicate a mode of knowing based on predictions grounded on hypotheses. Clearly, the way in which predictions are expressed in terms of 'top-down' maxims may be realized along a cline which indicates different degrees of reliability (cf. §3.2.1), including probability, possibility and certainty. The deduction evidential markers found in my corpus are listed in Table 4:

Deduction evidentials		
Award word count 140,357		
Items	*Hits*	*TTR*
should	76	0.54
could	69	0.49
would	61	0.43
can	61	0.43
may	52	0.37
will	33	0.23
must	14	0.09
ought to	12	0.08

Deduction evidentials		
Award word count 140,357		
Items	*Hits*	*TTR*
cannot	8	0.05
it is clear	10	0.07
logic	6	0.04
TOTAL	*410*	*2.92*

Table 4. Deductive evidentials.

As stated previously, modal expressions convey different degrees of evidential reliability. While *ought to* and *should* express deontic suggestion, *could*, *can*, *may* and *must* account for epistemic possibility, given the premises explained by the author of the text, as excerpts (30)-(35) indicate:

(30) It ought to be borne in mind that the Exchange/SEBI rules, regulation and circulars repeatedly speak of more transparency and discipline [...]. (arb_CM_K_0010_2013)

(31) [...] the counter claim of the Respondent is not only time barred but devoid of any merit and should be dismissed. (arb_F&O_M_0078_2012)

(32) The least that they could have done was to produce to this tribunal the original letters bearing the signatures of the Applicant thereon. (arb_CM_K_0004_2013)

(33) Such blatant disregard of legal and ethical principles can hardly be countenanced. (arb_CM_K_0013_2013)

(34) So the said claim also may be considered while passing an award in the above mailer. (arb_CM_C_0006_2013)

(35) [...] the inference could be, she only must have been trading. (arb_CM_H_0005_2013)

The way in which these evidentials are distributed in the text varies, as does their pragmatic function within the text. A quantitative summary of their distribution is given in Table 5 below:

Evidentials	*Proceeding identification*	*Establishing facts*	*Ratio Decidendi*	*Award Pronouncement*
Could	0	53	16	0
Can	1	12	46	2
Cannot	0	5	3	0
Ought to	0	0	16	0
Should	0	0	61	0
May	0	32	20	0
Might[5]	0	1	16	0
Must	0	1	12	1
Will	0	0	26	7
Total	*1*	*104*	*216*	*12*

Table 5. Distribution of deductive evidentials across awards.

Whenever *could, can, may* or *should* are used in the second move – establishing the facts of the case – they are used by either the respondent or the applicant to indicate what, in their own opinion, the other party could have done or should have done in order not to cause the damage, as examples (36) and (37) suggest:

(36) Had the Respondent really intended to attend the hearing he could have made a telephone call without waiting for the representative of the NSE to contact him over phone. (arb_F&O_D_0093_2012)

(37) Therefore the Applicant's arbitration reference may please be dismissed on merits. (arb_F&O_H_0006_2012)

Excerpt (37), however, seems to be a cliché form used either by the applicant or by the respondent to formally invite the arbitral panel to dismiss the other party's request.

As we can see in Table 5 above, all evidential modals occur mainly in the *ratio decidendi* move. It is here where the arbitral panel offers the juridical reasons on which the award is based. Therefore, in

5 Although *might* has not been found as an evidential in the sample I used to determine the type of evidentials my corpus could characterize, it has been included in this table so as to give a more complete framework of the use of evidential modality in Indian awards.

this move all modals are uttered by the arbitrators. They express either epistemicity (as in the case of *could*, *can*, *cannot*, *may*, *might, must*), or predictivity (as in the case of *would*, and *will*):

(38) Due to ambiguity, the validity of such documents may be questionable. (arb_CM_H_0005_2013)

(39) It is quite unbelievable that the loan would have been given without formalities like Board Resolution etc. (arb_CM_C_0006_2013)

The evidentials *ought to* and *should* are used by the arbitrators in the third move with a slightly different distribution within the move itself: *ought to* is always used at the beginning of the *ratio decidendi* section, while *should* appears at the end. In this case, *should* indicates a more conciliatory tone adopted by the tribunal:

(40) Both should share the losses. (arb_CM_K_0015_2013)

This is also maintained while pronouncing the award:

(41) Alternatively the 90 equity shares should be restored to the applicant by the respondent. No order as to cost. (arb_CM_D_0044_2013)

Apart from epistemic, predictive or tentative modals, Chafe (1986) indicates as deduction modals a set of expressions which are perceived by the reader as commonly-shared knowledge, namely *it is clear* and *logic*. Although *clear* may seem an inference evidential and therefore appear inductive (*clear* metaphorically indicates 'inferred from vision'), in Chafe's opinion it adopts the extensive meaning of 'easy to understand, fully intelligible' (OED). The propositions introduced by the evidential expression *it is clear that* are thus presented as common-sense concepts and perceived by the addressee as perfectly understandable without the need for any debate:

(42) In the present dispute after going through the pleadings and documents it is clear that the Constituent [...]. (arb_F&O_M_0044_2012)

Interestingly, the expression *it is clear that*, which always occurs in the *ratio decidendi* move and is always uttered by the arbitrators, seems to be a linguistic signal in favour of the respondent in the arbitral procedure: when pronounced, nine times out of ten it is in favour of the plaintiff.

Logic, on the contrary, is found in the second move, normally in the respondent's or applicant's reconstruction of the facts and always in such negative expressions as *X baffles logic*, *X has no logic*, *X defies logic*, *X is not supported by logic*, used to emphasize the false logic on which the counterpart's reasoning is based:

(43) […] is false and not supported by proof or logic and deserve to be rejected. (arb _F&O_M_0078_2012)

6.4 Induction evidentials

Induction evidentials are defined by Chafe (1986) as those lexical terms whose source of knowledge is based on evidence. Evidentiality, in this case, is grounded on a 'bottom-up' reasoning process. Hence, as we can see in Table 6 below, the presence of such terms as *proof*, *information*, *knowledge*, *evidences*, etc., or such verbs as *find*, *observed*, *proved*, etc.:

Induction evidentials		
Award word count 140,357		
Items	*Hits*	*TTR*
knowledge	86	0.61
proof	67	0.47
information	44	0.31
evidences	8	0.05
finding [noun]	6	0.05
know	43	0.30
prove	31	0.22
find	27	0.19
proved	17	0.12
found	15	0.10
observed	15	0.10
acknowledged	13	0.09

Induction evidentials		
Award word count 140,357		
Items	*Hits*	*TTR*
perused	8	0.05
conclude	5	0.03
concluded	5	0.03
knew	5	0.03
TOTAL	*407*	*2.89*

Table 6. Induction evidentials.

Nouns – i.e. *knowledge*, *information*, and *evidences* – are found in the 'establishing the facts of the case' move and refer to all the types of evidence deemed necessary to reconstruct the case. The term *proof* is also found mainly in this section (47 hits), but it may also occur in the *ratio decidendi* section of the arbitral award, whenever the arbitral panel refer to the actual proof on which they base their own reasoning:

(44) REASONING AND CONCLUSION: […] There is no proof that the dongle purportedly used by the unknown fraudster for accessing the respondent's system was procured with a forged voter ID card as alleged by the applicant. (arb_CM_K_0043_2012)

Finding, on the contrary, occurs only in the *ratio decidendi* move, and refers to the conclusion the tribunal can reach thanks to it:

(45) we have decided the case on the basis of the materials including documentary evidence on the record and the same is sufficient for us to render finding either in support of the claim or against the claim. (arb_F&O_M_0044_2012)

The verbs found in the category of induction evidentials appear mainly in two moves: either in the 'establishing of the facts' move, or in the *ratio decidendi* move. In the former we can find: *know*, *knew*, *acknowledged* and *concluded*; in the latter: *prove*, *find*, *found*, *observed*, *perused* and *conclude*. The verbs used in the second move – in which facts are reconstructed thanks to the documents, papers, evidence and reports presented to the tribunal by the people involved in the arbitral procedure – are those used by the respondent or the applicant. The texts of the awards indicate that either the respondent or the applicant gets to *know*, *acknowledge*, or *conclude* something based on their reconstruction, as excerpt (46) seems to indicate:

(46) She has contended that she came to know about the unauthorised transactions only in April [...]. (arb_F&O_M_0044_2012)

Interestingly, the term *concluded*, found only in the 'establishing of the facts' move, is attributed to the parties involved in the arbitral procedure, whereas its present form *conclude(s)* occurs exclusively in the *ratio decidendi* move. This verb, as well as the other verbs above mentioned – namely *prove*, *find*, *found*, *observed* and *perused* – are used solely by the arbitrators and indicate the final reasoning process which will lead them to the granting of the award, as the examples below indicate:

(47) Hence so far as the Applicant is concerned they are able to substantially prove their claim and I pass the following award. (arb_F&O_A_0001_2014)

(48) Thus taking into facts involved in the case we find that in the present position Regulation 3.10. (arb_F&O_M_0086_2013)

(49) The Supreme Court also observed that "In the present dispute faced by us, the appellant has made serious allegations [...]". (arb_CM_C_0006_2013)

Together with *prove*, the past form *proved* has been detected as an induction evidential. Yet, unlike *concluded*, it occurs in both the 'establishing of the facts' (9 hits) and the *ratio decidendi* (8 hits) moves.

7. Conclusion

Arbitration has recently developed into a powerful tool used to solve commercial disputes in international settings, particularly in Asian countries, where there has been an increase in global trade. While much of the published literature on arbitration deals with aspects related to the juridical and business perspectives, little attention has been paid to the linguistic and textual analysis of arbitration. My investigation has tried to bridge the gap between normative and linguistic procedures by looking at linguistic evidentiality in Indian arbitration awards.

My analysis has shown that all evidentials are mainly concentrated in the 'establishing the facts of the case' and the *ratio decidendi* moves. These are indeed the most important parts of the arbitral award: the 'establishing of the facts of the case' move corresponds to the *disclosure* or *discovery* part, i.e. where the case is reconstructed according to the parties involved. Instead, the *ratio decidendi* move offers the objective and juridical reasoning path followed by the arbitral panel in order to decide the outcome of the case.

As seen above, hearsay evidentials occur mainly in the *discovery* section of Indian arbitral awards. This does not come as a surprise: things, behaviours and facts are reported by the parties.

Belief evidentials appear mainly in the 'establishing the facts of the case' move: they are used to show the regularity of the reconstruction of the facts; if they are exploited in the *ratio decidendi* move, they are used in depersonalised forms and whenever the claim has to be dismissed. In other words, they are employed in negative politeness cases.

Deduction evidentials include modal verbs. Epistemic modals are mainly used by the parties in the 'establishing the facts of the case' to show what the other party might have done in order not to cause the harm or damage in question. Deontic modality, on the other hand, is used only in the *ratio decidendi* move by the arbitral panel: in this case, the tone is more conciliatory and the arbitrators are suggesting a way to solve the dispute in a satisfactory way for both parties. In this category, lexical expressions such as *it is clear* are exploited in order to indicate deductions. When this occurs, not only are they to be interpreted as commonly-shared knowledge, which does not need to be counterclaimed, but also as linguistic foretelling, anticipating that the respondent will win the case and that the proof presented by the other party will be dismissed.

Induction evidentials are found in 'establishing the facts of the case' in the form of nouns; when they are verbs, they belong to the class of cognitive verbs, such as *know*. In the *ratio decidendi* move only mental verbs are found – like *find* (with the meaning of 'come to the knowledge of' (a fact or state of things) by experience or trial)

– or observational verbs, such as *perused* (in the sense of 'scrutinize). Clearly, cognitive verbs help the parties involved in the arbitral process to reconstruct what they knew and what they did not know, whereas mental verbs indicate how the arbitral panel examined all the documents and how it reached the conclusions which allowed the granting of the award.

Although this preliminary study concerning evidentiality and Indian arbitration still requires further investigation, particularly regarding those aspects related to issues of reliability (Chafe 1986), it has proved to be useful as it has offered a better understanding of the linguistic and textual choices adopted in the expression of evidentiality in the drafting of arbitral awards.

References

Agarwal, Anurag 2008. Resolving Business Disputes in India by Arbitration: Problems due to the Definition of 'Court'. *IIMA Working Papers*. <http://www.iimahd.ernet.in/publications/data/2008-12-03Agarwal.pdf>.

Aikhenvald, Alexandra 2003. Evidentiality in Typological Perspective. In Aikhenvald/Dixon (eds), 1–32.

Aikhenvald, Alexandra 2004. *Evidentiality*. Oxford: Oxford University Press.

Aikhenvald, Alexandra 2007. Information Source and Evidentiality: What can we Conclude? *Rivista di Linguistica* 19/1, 209–227.

Aikhenvald, Alexandra / Dixon, R.M.W. (eds) 2003. *Studies in Evidentiality*. Amsterdam: John Benjamins.

Aksen, Gerald 2007. Reflection on International Arbitration. *Arbitration International* 23/2, 255–259.

Ali, Shahla 2010. Barricades and Checkered Flags: Comparing Views on Roadblocks and Facilitators of Settlement among Arbitration Practitioners in East Asia and the West. *Pacific Rim Law and Policy Journal* 18 <http://blogs.law.nyu.edu/transnational/2012

/12/confidentiality-vs-transparency-in-commercial-arbitration-a-false/>.

Anderson, Lloyd B. 1986. Evidentials, Paths of Change, and Mental Maps: Typologically Regular Asymmetries. In Chafe/Nichols (eds), 273–312.

Bednarek, Monika 2006. Epistemological Positioning and Evidentiality in English News Discourse: A Text-driven Approach. *Text & Talk* 26/6, 635–660.

Bhatia, Vijay / Candlin, Christopher / Gotti, Maurizio (eds) 2010. *The Discourses of Dispute Resolution*. Bern: Peter Lang.

Bhatia, Vijay / Evangelisti Allori, Paola (eds) 2011. *Discourse and Identity in the Professions: Legal, Corporate and Institutional Citizenship*. Bern: Peter Lang.

Bhatia, Vijay / Garzone, Giuliana / Degano, Chiara (eds) 2012. *Arbitration Awards: Generic Features and Textual Realisations*, Newcastle upon Tyne: Cambridge Scholars.

Bhatia, Vijay / Garzone, Giuliana / Salvi, Rita / Tessuto, Girolamo / Williams, Christopher (eds) 2014. *Language and Law in Professional Discourse: Issues and Perspectives*. Newcastle upon Tyne: Cambridge Scholars.

Biber, Douglas / Conrad, Susan 2009. *Register Genre Style*. Cambridge: Cambridge University Press.

Biswas, Tushar Kumar 2012. Right to Appeal in Arbitration under Indian Laws: An Interpretive Critic of Judicial Response. *Commonwealth Law Bulletin* 38/2, 301–320.

Boas, Franz 1911. *Handbook of American Indian Languages*. Washington: Government Printing Office.

Brower, Charles 2008. W(h)ither International Arbitration? The Goff Lecture 2007. *Arbitration International* 24/2, 181–197.

Chafe, Wallace 1986. Evidentiality in English Conversation and Academic Writing. In Chafe/Nichols (eds), 261–272.

Chafe, Wallace / Nichols Johanna (eds) 1986. *Evidentiality: The Linguistic Coding of Epistemology*. Norwood, NJ: Ablex.

Coffey, Amanda / Atkinson, Paul 1996. *Making Sense of Qualitative Data: Complimentary Research Strategies*. Thousand Oaks, CA: Sage.

Debattista, Charles 2005. Drafting Enforceable Arbitration Clauses. *Arbitration International* 21/2, 233–240.
DeLancey, Scott 1997. Mirativity: The Grammatical Marking of Unexpected Information. *Linguistic Typology* 1, 33–52.
Dessemontet, François 2001. Arbitration and Confidentiality. *The American Review of International Arbitration* 7/1, 299.
Hafner, Christoph A. 2011. Professional Reasoning, Legal Cultures, and Arbitral Awards. *World Englishes* 30/1, 117–128.
Jakobson, Roman 1957. *Shifters, Verbal Categories, and the Russian Verb*. Cambridge, Mass.: Harvard University Press.
Kurkela, Matti / Levin, Richard / Liebscher, Christoph / Sommer, Patrick 2007. Certain Procedural Issues in Arbitrating Competition Cases. *Journal of International Arbitration* 24/2, 189–210.
Maci, Stefania M. 2009. Litigation Procedures in Arbitral Practice: A Case of Arbitral Litigation? In Sarcevic, Susan (ed.) *Legal Language in Action: Translation, Terminology, Drafting and Procedural Issues*. Zagreb: Kakladini zadov Globus, 393–410.
Maci, Stefania M. 2010. The *Modus Operandi* of Litigation in Arbitration. In Bhatia/Candlin/Gotti (eds), 69–83.
Maci, Stefania M. 2011. Arbitration in Italy. Litigation Procedures in Arbitral Practice. In Bhatia/Evangelisti Allori (eds), 213–137.
Maci, Stefania M. 2012. Arbitration in Action: the Display of Arbitrators' Neutrality in Witness Hearings. In Bhatia, Vijay / Candlin, Christopher / Gotti, Maurizio (eds) *Discourse and Practice in International Commercial Arbitration: Issues, Challenges and Prospects*. London: Ashgate, 225–238.
Mair, Christian 1991. Quantitative or Qualitative Corpus Analysis? Infinitival Complement Clause in the Survey of English Usage Corpus. In Johansson, Stig / Stenström, Ana-Brita (eds) *English Computer Corpora: Selected Papers and Research Guide*. Berlin: Mouton de Gruyter, 67–80.
Malatesta, Alberto / Sali, Rinaldo (eds) 2013. *The Rise of Transparency in International Arbitration*. New York: JurisNet.
Marriott, Arthur 2004. Less is More: Directing Arbitration Procedures. *Arbitration International* 16/3, 261–278.
McEnery, Tony / Wilson, Andrew 2001. *Corpus Linguistics*. Edinburgh: Edinburgh University Press.

Miles, Matthew / Huberman, A. Michael 1994. *Qualitative Data Analysis: An Expanded Sourcebook.* Thousand Oaks, CA: Sage.

Miles, Wendy 2003. Practical Issues for Appointment of Arbitrators: Lawyer vs. Non-Lawyer and Sole Arbitrator vs. Panel of Three (or More). *Journal of International Arbitration* 20/3, 219–232.

Motiwala, Mustafa / Mukhi, Ashis / Shetti, Ranjit 2014. India. In *The Asia-Pacific Arbitration Review* <http://globalarbitrationreview.com/reviews/55/sections/194/chapters/2171/india/> 22/08/2014.

Mushin Ilana 2001 *Evidentiality and Epistemological Stance: Narrative Retelling.* Amsterdam: John Benjamins.

Nicholas, Geoff / Partasides, Constantine 2007. LCIA Court Decisions on Challenges to Arbitrators: A Proposal to Publish. *Arbitration International* 23/1, 1–41.

Parthasarathy, Suhrith / Visalakshi, AK. 2007 Stretching the Limits of Statutory Interpretation: The Indian Arbitration and Conciliation Act 1996. *Arbitration: the Journal of the Chartered Institute of Arbitrators* 73/4, 394–399.

Rai, Sumit 2012. Proposed Amendments to the Indian Arbitration Act: A Fraction of the Whole? *Journal of International Dispute Settlement* 3/1, 169–204.

Rendeiro, Amelia C. 2011. Indian Arbitration and 'Public Policy'. *Texas Law Review* 89/3, 699–728.

Shah, Namrata / Gandhi, Niyati 2011. Arbitration: One Size Does Not Fit All: Necessity of Developing Institutional Arbitration in Developing Countries. *Journal of International Commercial Law and Technology* 6/4, 232.

Scott, Mike 2012. *WordSmith Tools version 6.* Liverpool: Lexical Analysis Software.

Tognini-Bonelli, Elena 2001. *Corpus Linguistics at Work.* Amsterdam: John Benjamins.

Webster, Thomas H. 2006. Evolving Principles in Enforcing Awards Subject to Annulment Proceedings. *Journal of International Arbitration* 23/3, 201–226.

Willett, Thomas 1988. A Cross-linguistic Survey of the Grammaticalization of Evidentiality. *Studies in Language* 12, 51–97.

Zaiwalla, Sarosh 2003. Challenging Arbitral Awards: Finality is Good but Justice is Better. *Journal of International Arbitration* 20/2, 199–204.

Ziccardi, Fabio E. 2012. Evidence, Oral Testimony and Cross Interrogatory in International Arbitration. In Bhatia/Evangelisti Allori (eds), 63–71.

Patrizia Anesa

Discursive Peculiarities of Indian Arbitral Awards

1. Introduction

Given the enormous economic growth taking place on the Indian subcontinent and the relative increase in the number of national and cross-border agreements involving Indian parties, the number of commercial disputes is also constantly growing. Nowadays, the use of arbitration in India is particularly significant as, notoriously, litigative proceedings are inefficient. As Biswas (2014: xi) states, "the failings of the Indian judiciary, real and perceived, have prompted parties engaged in commercial activity to settle their disputes primarily through the mechanism of arbitration".

In light of the importance that arbitration is acquiring, gaining new insights into arbitration practice seems particularly relevant. This chapter is based on the consideration that investigation should not be limited to legal and procedural viewpoints but should also take into account a linguistic perspective. Thus, the analysis focuses on a corpus of Indian awards in order to observe their general characteristics and their linguistic and discursive peculiarities with the aim to contribute to the identification of areas of concern and potential improvements to be implemented.

The starting assumption of this study is that the professional and educational background of arbitrators may influence their discursive practices. Indeed, it has been argued that in some contexts the arbitrator's writing style, especially when arbitrators belong to the legal profession, is inevitably influenced by the discursive features of a specific legal tradition. More specifically, "arbitrators draw upon legal discourse structures (raising issues, stating and applying legal rules) in order to account for the decisions and orders that they make" (Bhatia/Candlin/

Hafner 2012: 158). In India, arbitrators are often legal experts, and in particular retired judges (Anesa 2014). It is thus possible to assume that awards may display features such as formality, linguistic accuracy and a certain level of wordiness, and the analysis will primarily aim at verifying this hypothesis.

Moreover, it has been stated that arbitration awards, i.e. the final outcome of the proceedings, are becoming "an increasingly conventionalized and codified genre" (Bhatia/Garzone/Degano 2012: 1). The analytical section will also observe in particular if Indian awards present discrepancies in comparison with awards written in other countries, both from a macro and micro perspective.

2. Material and method

The analysis is based on a small corpus consisting of 29 arbitration awards rendered in India. They are available on the National Stock Exchange of India Ltd. (NSE or NSEIL) website (<www.nseindia.com>). For the sake of consistency, all cases refer to initial arbitration awards and no appellate arbitration awards were considered; all cases were settled by a sole arbitrator. The awards date from 2010 to 2014 and were produced in four of the main Indian cities: Delhi, Mumbai, Kolkata and Ahmedabad. The total number of arbitrators involved is 13. In Table 1 a code has been assigned to each arbitrator and their professional background is indicated. This is functional to allow testing our preliminary hypothesis that these texts should comply with specific linguistic expectations, given the writers' expertise. Obviously the professional experience that arbitrators have acquired is often heterogeneous, but for the sake of conciseness only their current position or their principal activities are shown:

No.	*Arbitrator Code*	*Arbitrator's professional background*	*City*	*Year*
1	A	Retired from the Indian Administrative Service (IAS)	New Delhi	2014
2	B	Fellow member of the Institute of Chartered Accountants of India	New Delhi	2014
3	C	Retired judge	Mumbai	2014
4	D	Consultant to Institute of Public Enterprises, Osmania University, Hyderabad and ICRIER, India Habitat Centre	New Delhi	2014
5	E	President of the Institute of Company Secretaries of India (ICSI)	New Delhi	2014
6	E	President of the Institute of Company Secretaries of India (ICSI)	New Delhi	2014
7	F	Chairman	Kolkata	2014
8	G	Lawyer	New Delhi	2014
9	H	Former Add. Secretary to the Govt. of India, Former Member Central Administrative Tribunal Principal Bench	New Delhi	2014
10	C	Retired judge	Mumbai	2014
11	I	Chartered accountant	Ahmedabad	2014
12	C	Retired judge	Mumbai	2014
13	J	Advocate	New Delhi	2014
14	B	Fellow member of the Institute of Chartered Accountants of India	New Delhi	2010
15	B	Fellow member of the Institute of Chartered Accountants of India	New Delhi	2010
16	G	Lawyer	New Delhi	2011
17	G	Lawyer	New Delhi	2011
18	G	Lawyer	New Delhi	2010
19	G	Lawyer	New Delhi	2014
20	K	Retired judge	New Delhi	2014
21	L	Advocate	Mumbai	2013
22	K	Retired judge	Mumbai	2011
23	K	Retired judge	Mumbai	2011
24	C	Retired judge	Mumbai	2013

No.	*Arbitrator Code*	*Arbitrator's professional background*	*City*	*Year*
25	K	Retired judge	Mumbai	2011
26	G	Lawyer	New Delhi	2010
27	G	Lawyer	New Delhi	2011
28	M	Retired judge	Mumbai	2010
29	K	Retired judge	Mumbai	2011

Table 1. Corpus.

Data analysis includes a preliminary genre analysis (Bhatia 1993, 2004) with identification of the different moves and steps and their pragmatic functions. A comparison with the generic features of awards rendered in other studies is also offered (following Bhatia/Lung 2012, Bhatia/Han 2012, Han/Li 2012, Tessuto 2012). Subsequently, the second part of the analysis focuses on the discursive strategies used within the different sections of the awards. The final phase depicts the micro-textual features present in the awards and identifies their peculiarities in order to observe if any clear discrepancies emerge in relation to the standard linguistic features of awards written in the English language.

3. Awards as a genre

3.1 Discursive hierarchical pattern

Some recent studies have been conducted on the discursive hierarchical pattern of awards. For instance, Bhatia and Lung (2012) focus on the structure of awards across different countries, Han and Li (2012) investigate Chinese arbitration awards, Bhatia and Han (2012) offer a comparative analysis of awards and litigation judgments in China, and Tessuto (2012) provides insights into reasoned awards rendered in Canada. The Indian awards analyzed typically take the following pattern:

Move 0:	Heading	
Move 1:	Introduction	
	Step 1:	Identification of type of arbitration
	Step 2:	Identification of parties
	Step 3:	Status of the parties
Move 2:	Background	
	Step 1:	Basic Facts
	Step 2:	Parties' Arguments
Move 3:	Cases	
	Step 1:	Claimant's case
	Step 2:	Defendant's case
Move 4:	Hearings	
Move 5:	Analysis of claims	
Move 6:	Reasoning	
Move 7:	Order	
	Step 1:	Decisions
	Step 2:	Notification of Arbitration Authority
Move 8:	Closing	

Table 2. Discursive hierarchical pattern in NSE Indian awards.

Although the order in which the moves are introduced is quite standardized, it may be subject to minor variations. For example, the corpus shows instances of the following pattern:

- Heading
- Introduction
- Background
- Hearings
- Claims
    - Step 1: Claim of the applicant
    - Step 2: Respondent's defense
- Analysis of Claims
- Award

Occasionally, the award may also be further simplified, thus including:

- Heading
- Introduction
- Applicant's claims
- Award *(award no. 17)*

This pattern is however quite rare, in that it seems to ignore the case of the respondent. Indeed, all the facts are described within the section named 'Applicant's claims' and no description of the respondent's arguments is offered. Moreover, no reasoning is presented. This structure may be used in disputes where resolution is deemed obvious and uncomplicated and when the respondent does not offer any arguments in his/her defence. As a tendency it is however preferable to provide a specific step for the claims made by the respondent in that such an approach offers a clear idea of impartiality and neutrality and follows a standardized practice.

Awards may present different levels of structural complexity and some of the moves or steps may be merged into heterogeneous paragraphs, but the principal elements tend to be present. The typographical layout may also change. In some cases the different parts are clearly identified by headings. In others, only one long section preceded by the term 'award' is presented. However, this part still tends to incorporate all the typical moves in the standard order.

The macro-structural analysis shows that the discursive hierarchical pattern of the Indian arbitration awards is largely in line with the patterns of awards produced in other countries. For instance, in their analysis of arbitration awards as a genre Bhatia and Lung (2012: 25–26) illustrate the typical moves and steps which characterize this genre across different countries:

– Heading
– Recitals, which include four steps:
    a. Introducing the parties
    b. Competence of the tribunal
    c. Pre-hearing proceedings and applicable law
    d. General statements of a dispute
– Details of the disputes, which include:
    a. Summary of agreed facts
    b. Submissions and Claims / Counterclaims by the parties
    c. Relief sought by the parties
– Reviews of contentions and claims, including
    a. Analyses
    b. Conclusions of factual analysis and conclusions of legal analysis
– Closure

Table 3. Discursive hierarchical pattern of awards (adapted from Bhatia/Lung 2012: 25–26).

The principal moves illustrated by Bhatia and Lung (2012) are also present in the Indian awards analyzed, although some terminological differences may be present. For instance, the word 'Recitals' is not present in the Indian texts, but the move called 'Introduction' (Move 1, see Table 2) commonly fulfils a similar function. The general move 'Details of the dispute' broadly covers the moves 'Background', 'Cases' and 'Hearings' (Moves 2, 3 and 4 in the typical structure of the Indian texts). Section 3.2 will describe the function and the structure of the moves and steps identified in Indian awards in more detail.

3.2 Moves and steps

A closer analysis of the different moves and steps has to take into account their rhetorical functions. All awards analyzed are introduced by a clear heading (Move 0, see Table 2), the aim of which is merely to define the case number and to indicate the name of the arbitrator(s):

(1) BEFORE ***[1], SOLE ARBITRATOR
ARBITRATION MATTER NO. F&O/D-024/2010 (*Award no. 26*)

The heading is generally followed by an introductory section (Move 1, Introduction), which may include the type of arbitration and the names of the parties involved. The parties are generally defined 'applicant' (or 'claimant') and 'respondent'.

(2) In the matter of Arbitration as per the Bye Laws and Regulations of National Stock Exchange of India Ltd
And in the matter of
*** Applicant
(Constituent)
****
Vs
***
(Trading Member)
**** Respondent (*Award no. 26*)

1 Although the awards analyzed are publicly available, the excerpts illustrated have been anonymized.

The definition of the parties may be followed by the step defined as 'Status of the parties'.

(3) Status of the Parties
As per the application dated 28.01.2013 the applicant is the member of the BSE and respondent is a constituent of the applicant. (*Award no. 14*)

This section is however only occasionally present and may also be found within other moves. While the introduction is usually visually separated from the rest of the document, the following sections are sometimes not clearly identified by a heading. The introductory phase is generally followed by a 'Background' or 'History' (Move 2), which serves as an informative summary of the events. It should be pointed out that in some awards this move is referred to as 'Introduction', but this term in this analysis refers specifically to Move 1 as previously described.

(4) Background:
The applicant had filed a reference with the NSEIL being reference CM/A-0026/2013 on 25/10/2013. The reference in this dispute being Reference No.: NSE/ARBN/CM/A-0026/2013 was entrusted to me by the National Stock Exchange of India Limited (herein referred to as 'NSEIL') to consider and adjudication [sic] the dispute and difference between the applicant and the Respondent mentioned herein above and to deliver the arbitration award. *(Award no. 11)*

Step 1 usually presents the basic facts of the disputes and Step 2 briefly introduces the parties' arguments. Step 2 may also be avoided and parties' arguments may be presented within the third move. Move 3, 'Claims', includes claims and counterclaims by the parties. First, the 'applicant's claims' (also called 'Case of the applicant' or 'Claims of the applicant') are presented:

(5) The applicant * has filed the present reference claiming a sum of Rs. 1,17,097.79 (Rupees One Lc, Seventeen Thousand, Ninety Seven and Paisa Senty Nine Only) together with interest @ 24% p.a. till payment or realization. *(Award no. 14)*

These claims are typically followed by a detailed description of the events in support of the applicant's case and may also include references to the applicable law to be considered. In one case, a specific subsection called 'Prayer of the applicant' is present and its function is to briefly summarize the claims:

(6) Prayer of the applicant
In the view of the above facts and circumstances it is most respect fully [sic] prayed that the Hon'ble Arbitrator may kindly pass an order(s):
a) Directing the respondent to pay the sum of Rs. 1,17,097.79 (Rupees One Las, Seventeen Thousand, Ninety and Paisa Seventy Nine Only) along with interest @ 24% per annum till the date of payment and/or realization.
b) Directing the respondent to pay the arbitration costs.
c) Pass any other/further order(s) in favour of the applicant and against the respondent as may deem fit and proper. *(Award no. 14)*

The Applicant's case (Step 1) is generally followed by the Respondent's case (or 'Case of the respondent' or 'Respondent's claims', or 'Defence') (Step 2):

(7) CASE OF THE RESPONDENT:
19. The respondent denied all claims of (made by) the Applicant and submitted that while applying for opening of trading account, the Applicant had carefully read and understood the contents of the agreement and proceeded to invest knowing fully well that the said investment is based on market fluctuations and risk is involved. Therefore, the Applicant cannot be allowed to raise plea that he was not aware of the risks and technicalities involved. *(Award no. 5)*

If the respondent is absent and no arguments are offered to support his/her case, this is clearly illustrated in the Respondent's claims.

(8) No one appeared for the respondent despite proper service of notices and communications. *(Award no. 14)*

The main parties' arguments may be summarized into lists which facilitate readability:

(9) The respondent in his reply has stated that:
1. The Applicant has voluntary [sic] opted for VAS Plan [...]
2. All the trading confirmations were sent to the Applicant by the Respondent on a regular basis [...]. *(Award no. 15)*

Move 4, labelled 'Proceedings' or 'Hearings', tends to be quite concise and includes a summary of the proceedings and/or hearings conducted.

(10) HEARINGS:
31. The matter for the first time came for hearing on 5th August 2013 before the Sole Arbitrator in which the parties to the arbitration were asked to submit their respective submissions. The hearings in the matter were held on 30th August 2013, 25th September2013 [sic], 31st October 2013, 6th November, 2013 and 21st November 2013. On the last date of hearing, 21st November 2013, the case was concluded and Order was reserved. *(Award no. 5)*

Some awards then present the move 'Analysis of claims', which is generally a detailed section in which the applicant's and respondent's claims are analyzed in the light of the relevant documentation. For example, award 27 cites the bye-laws of the Indian Stock Exchange:

(11) I have carefully considered the preliminary objection. In accordance with Regulation 5.9 (c) of the Exchange, if any deficiency/defect in the arbitration application filed by any party is found, the Exchange shall call upon the party to rectify the deficiency/defect and the party concerned shall rectify the deficiency/defect within 15 days of receipt of intimation from the Exchange. *(Award no. 27)*

The next move, 'Reasoning', may be replaced by other sections which have similar functions, such as 'Opinion', 'Discussion', 'Discussion and conclusion' or 'Reasoning and findings'. This section is optional in that it is intrinsic in the nature of arbitration that the arbitrators have the power to make an award without having to write a specific reasoning section. Indeed, parties may tend to be more concerned by the outcome rather than by the process which has led to a particular decision, and lengthy opinions may contribute to increasing costs and time. In this regard, Hafner (2011: 121) points out that reasoning in awards has an important function and has to be used within certain limitations:

> The presence of reasoning may serve to secure the parties' compliance with the award: either voluntarily or by enforcement through the courts. However, there is a desire to keep such reasoning to a minimum, both in order to discourage future litigation and to streamline the arbitration process.

Reasoning may be introduced by a brief introductory statement which highlights that all documents and elements have been considered, thus enhancing the professionalism, the competence and the impartiality of the arbitrator:

(12) I have carefully considered the records, documents and statement filed by the Applicant and Respondent and hearing [sic] the arguments of both the parties. *(Award no. 15)*

This move may also include inter-textual references to the documentation provided by the parties:

(13) Taking into account the documents on record and oral and written submissions made by both the parties, I am convinced that the claim of the Applicant as reflected in para 6.12 is justified and accordingly admitted. *(Award no. 21)*

It should be noted that the pragmatic function of moves such as 'Analysis of claims' and 'Reasoning' often overlap, in that they both frequently provide an explanation for the subsequent order. Moreover, both of them may include the arbitrator's opinion regarding a certain issue. Very often such an opinion is not impersonally suggested, but is clearly expressed through the use of first-person pronouns and glosses that plainly emphasize the arbitrator's personal perspective. It has been observed that the arbitrator's personal tenor may follow different identity-marking schemes (Tessuto 2012: 119). In particular 'self-referential items' (Tessuto 2012: 119, following Hyland 2005) can be observed in awards. More specifically, the moves 'Analysis of claims' and 'Reasoning' offer a series of elements which are an indication of the writer's orientation and of the explicitness of the authorial presence in the text:

(14) I am of the considered view that *(Award no. 16; Award no. 6)*
I am of the opinion that *(Award no. 14)*
I consider justified to allow *(Award no. 18)*
I am convinced that *(Award no. 21)*
I am of the view that *(Award no. 14)*

As Tessuto observes (2012: 120), the 'I-orientation' is not the only one present in awards. Other expressions such as 'the arbitrator' may be found and they contribute to encoding the authority stance. However, the noun phrase 'the arbitrator' is present in only three of the texts analyzed. In these texts, the arbitrators tend to use first person pronouns both when expressing their role as evaluators and as adjudicators. The I-orientation is clearly present also in the subsequent move, 'Award' or 'Order', which is generally preceded by a preamble, such as:

(15) Hence, I pass the following Award *(Award no. 20)*
In the result, I pass the following Award *(Award no. 29)*
For all these reasons the claim is required to be allowed and I pass the following award *(Award no. 28)*

The award itself tends to be very short and concise and is always introduced by a heading ('Award', 'Final award') even in texts which are not divided into headed sections:

(16) Final Award
The claim of the Applicant for Rs. 5000.00, is allowed plus Rs. 1091.99 with costs.
Respondent to bear his own cost. The Awarded amount to carry interest @ 12% p.a. from the date of this arbitration proceedings till actual payment. *(Award no. 28)*

The award may be presented making use of ordered or numbered lists with the aim to improve clarity:

(17) AWARD
(a) The Claim Application filed by the Applicant is dismissed for want of evidence in support of the Applicant's case.
(b) There will be no order as to costs.
(c) The Award is signed and issued in three originals, one for the record of The National Stock Exchange and the NSC will forward one signed original to each of the parties. *(Award no. 29)*

Point *c* in the previous example also represents a closing formula which may be included in Move 6 or may be intended as a separate move (identifiable as Move 7).

(18) Made and signed at New Delhi on this 14th day of January in three counterparts. *(Award no. 8)*

The closing move always includes place, date and the arbitrator's name in print and his/her signature.

4. Discursive features

4.1 The use of the English Language

English is generally used in Indian arbitration, and awards are commonly drafted in English. The variety of English used depends to a large extent on the arbitrator's background, and, given the multifaceted linguistic situation of India, a wide range of levels of proficiency may be present. The majority of NSE related awards are produced in English. However, some of the awards may refer to documentation produced in other languages, such as Hindi, which may occasionally be used:

(19) The Respondent by his letter dated 31/01/2013 in Hindi which is handwritten admitted the amount claimed by the Applicants. *(Award no. 24)*

(20) The Respondent's reply / letter dated 31/01/2013 was handwritten and was absolutely unreadable because of a very bad handwriting. He was, therefore, directed to file English translation of the same in triplicate within a week's time. *(Award no. 24)*

The preliminary hypothesis of this study was that awards should display a high level of accuracy from a linguistic perspective and comply with standard discursive features. However, some peculiarities clearly emerge in Indian awards rendered in English, as will be illustrated in Section 4.2.

4.2 Non-standard features

With rcfcrcncc to othcr countries, it has been shown that, although arbitrators' writing styles may change according to their professional background, linguistic accuracy is generally present across different professions (see Gotti/Anesa 2011 on the Italian situation). Indeed, linguistic correctness and a certain level of formality are commonly expected, given that an award is an enforceable legal decision. It has also been shown that awards and litigation judgments display considerable textual similarities (Antelmi/Santulli 2012, Bhatia/Han 2012, Gotti 2012, Preite 2012, Vázquez/Giner 2012).

As shown in Table 1, the majority of the awards analyzed have been written by arbitrators with considerable legal expertise. More precisely, ten of the awards have been written by retired judges and nine by lawyers/advocates. Consequently, it would be plausible to predict that the writing style adopted by arbitrators should be in line with many of the typical aspects of legal style which is often adopted by professionals in other legal contexts.

However, the Indian awards analyzed tend to display a certain level of informality, especially in the analysis of moves such as 'Claims' and 'Reasoning'. For example, arbitrators may include colloquialisms and idioms (*the Applicant is heard to sing only one song)* in order to clarify certain points. Moreover figurative language is employed to support the arbitrator's perspective, and in particular the use of metaphors is often present (*This weapon of alleged ignorance is sought to be used by him as a shield as well as a sword).*

In some cases syntactic and grammatical accuracy does not seem to represent the final goal of the arbitrator's approach in writing awards, at least in NSE issues. As long as clarity in the definition of the final decision is guaranteed, verbal correctness is not perceived as a fundamental aspect. Indeed, unexpectedly, several inaccuracies and typos are found in the corpus. Firstly, the use of punctuation often disregards the standard practice. For instance, punctuation marks are sometimes introduced where unnecessary:

(21) in case, the security amount lying with the NSE is not adequate to comply with this direction, the respondent shall ensure that the shortfall, if any, is made good by them. *(Award no. 24)*

(22) The satisfaction letter obtained by Amit Karle on 01.09.2009 from the Claimant is important, that letter dated 01.09.2009, is annexed by the Claimant along with their complaint it is exhibit C of the WS it is addressed to the Manager of the Respondent and it contains the following *(Award no. 28)*

The following excerpt includes a series of long sentences where punctuation is not used in the most effective way, which is quite unexpected for a formal document, as will be shown later:

(23) It is submitted that in trading there is always loss or gain and once an agreement is arrived at after having understood the same, the claimant cannot be allowed to raise such contentions before this Hon'ble Tribunal which are infact (*sic*) after thought as due to market fluctuations the claimant has lost certain amount of money which is not the fault of the Respondent and therefore the claim is not maintainable and is liable to be rejected. *(Award no. 11)*

Quotation (24) also shows inconsistencies in the date format, a feature that occurs across different texts:

(24) Notice of hearing [...] which has been delivered to him on 8th March 2013
Minutes of arbitral hearing [...] vide consignment note no. V12650244 dated 12 April 2013. *(Award no. 14)*

Numerous texts also include inconsistent capitalization. For instance in award 15 the definite article *the* is sometimes capitalized without clear reason and without any consistency.

(25) Further, *The Applicant* contention that unauthorized trade has been carried out in his account by the Respondent without taking the consent and permission of *the applicant. (Award no. 15).*

Quotation (25) is also atypical in terms of syntax in that no verb is expressed in the sentence.

As far as spelling is concerned, some inaccuracies are present, especially as regards foreign words:

(26) The intimation by the Respondents about the Applicant's Ledger balance showing debit of Rs.38,461.76 might be the reason for the Applicant to come with such a demand by way of *fate accompli. (Award no. 10)*

In this case the French expression *fait accompli* (denoting an accomplished deed or fact which is presumably irreversible) is here indicated as *fate accompli*. Although the original form is easily identifiable, thus not causing a communicative breakdown, the standard spelling is not maintained. Other linguistic peculiarities which do not follow standard syntactic and lexical conventions as well other typos found in the corpus are listed in Table 4.

Excerpt (27) also presents other non-standard characteristics, namely:

- Acronym explained after it has already been used (*NSEIL*)
- Use of noun forms instead of verb forms (*To consider and adjudication the dispute*)
- Use of infinite forms instead of past participles (*was schedule*)

Award no.	*Excerpt*
2	– The respondent has deny
4	– in both the hearing – the applicant has subsequently on 16 September 2013 filed a second document – had the respondent being doing unauthorized trades – without investing a singly penny
9	– They better made a complaint
11	– There would have not been so much losses– They did not fulfilled their promise – Infact
14	– Notice of hearing [...] which has been delivered to him on 8th March 2013 – New Dated, dated 20th day of January, 2014.
15	– Both parties was intimated – The Applicant has voluntary opted for VAS Plan
21	– The Applicant has in her arbitration application has claimed

Table 4. Examples of linguistic peculiarities.

(27) The applicant had filed a reference with the *NSEIL* being reference CM/A-0026/2013 on 25/10/2013. The reference in this dispute being Reference No.: NSE/ARBN/CM/A-0026/2013 was entrusted to me by the *National Stock Exchange of India Limited (herein referred to as 'NSEIL')* to *consider and adjudication* the dispute and difference between the applicant and the Respondent mentioned herein above and to deliver the arbitration award.
The hearing in the said reference *was schedule* on 22/11/2013 *(award no. 11)*

Non-standard features are present across several awards written by different arbitrators, most of whom have a legal background. These peculiarities denote an interest in the final result rather than in the linguistic accuracy in the formulation of the award in English. In this regard ethnographic data also demonstrates that minor linguistic inaccuracies do not represent a major issue for arbitrators in India. In particular, experienced Indian arbitrators have stressed that no award is generally challenged for linguistic reasons (Anesa 2014). Indeed, awards may be set aside only under specific circumstances illustrated in Chapter VII of the Arbitration and Conciliation Act, 1996 (see Appendix), and language inaccuracies do not constitute cases under which an application for setting aside may be made.

5. Conclusions

In India, English is the most common language in both international and domestic arbitration and awards are generally drafted in English. From a macro-structural perspective the awards analyzed are in line with the move pattern which characterizes international and domestic awards in other countries. However, the micro-linguistic analysis shows some significant peculiarities.

Starting from the consideration that in several countries awards tend to display a relatively high level of formality and linguistic accuracy, this study aimed to observe whether Indian domestic awards also exhibit similar characteristics and which unique and distinctive traits tend to emerge. Given that the majority of arbitrators involved in the writing of the awards analyzed have a legal background (with many of them being retired judges), it would be plausible to postulate that the linguistic accuracy and the high level of formality which are typical of the legal style are likely to be present in Indian awards. Nonetheless, this does not always hold true in the awards analyzed. An inevitable trade-off exists between time and cost efficiency on the one hand and linguistic precision on the other and the former aspect is generally favored. Thus, contrary to plausible expectations, linguistic correctness is not deemed fundamental in the process of writing Indian awards.

Indeed, some peculiar features are present across many of the awards under investigation, which tend to exhibit instances of informalities and inaccuracies, especially in moves such as 'claims' and 'reasoning'. Award drafters occasionally include colloquialisms, idioms and figurative language (such as metaphors) for clarifying purposes.

Moreover, spelling is at times inaccurate, the use of punctuation is not always in line with standard practices, and redundancies, repetitions and typing errors are present in several texts. The syntax is generally quite simple and in some cases it is possible to identify some grammatical features which are unique and differ considerably from canonical ones present in mainstream varieties.

To conclude, it can be argued that in this corpus of Indian domestic awards, linguistic accuracy does not assume a fundamental role. This derives from the fact that awards are not generally challengeable on the basis of lexical or grammatical incorrectness.

References

Anesa, Patrizia 2014. Arbitration Practice in India: A Discursive Perspective. Paper presented at the International Round Table *Asian Arbitration Law*, 18–19 September 2014, University of Bergamo, Italy.

Antelmi, Donatella / Santulli, Francesca 2012. Arbitration Awards in Italy: Some Argumentative Features in the Discourse Analytical Perspective. In Bhatia/Garzone/Degano (eds), 91–108.

Bhatia, Vijay K. 1993. *Analysing Genre – Language Use in Professional Settings*. London: Longman.

Bhatia, Vijay K. 2004. *Worlds of Written Discourse: A Genre-based View*. London: Continuum.

Bhatia, Vijay K. / Candlin, Christopher / Hafner, Christoph 2012. Arbitration Awards as Accounts. In Bhatia/Candlin/Gotti (eds), 147–161.

Bhatia, Vijay K. / Garzone, Giuliana / Degano, Chiara 2012. Arbitration Awards: Generic Features and Textual Realisations: An Introduction. In Bhatia/Garzone/Degano (eds), 1–13.

Bhatia, Vijay K. / Han, Zhengrui 2012. Comparative Genre Analysis of Chinese Legal Judgments and Arbitration. In Bhatia/Garzone/Degano (eds), 192–217.

Bhatia, Vijay K. / Lung, Jane 2012. Analysing International Commercial Arbitration Awards as Genre. In Bhatia/Garzone/Degano (eds), 23–46.

Bhatia, Vijay K. / Candlin, Christopher / Gotti, Maurizio (eds) 2012. *Discourse and Practice in International Commercial Arbitration: Issues, Challenges and Prospects*. Farnham: Ashgate.

Bhatia, Vijay K. / Garzone, Giuliana / Degano, Chiara (eds) 2012. *Arbitration Awards: Generic Features and Textual Realisations*. Newcastle upon Tyne: Cambridge Scholars.

Biswas, Tushar Kumar 2014. *Introduction to Arbitration in India*. Alphen aan den Rijn, The Netherlands: Kluwer Law International.

Gotti, Maurizio 2012. The Judicialization of Arbitration Discourse in the Italian Context. In Bhatia/Candlin/Gotti (eds), 129–146.

Gotti, Maurizio / Anesa, Patrizia 2011. Professional Identities in Italian Arbitral Awards: the Spread of Lawyers' Language. In Bhatia, Vijay K. / Evangelisti Allori, Paola (eds) *Discourse and Identity in the Professions*. Bern: Peter Lang, 189–212.

Hafner, Christoph 2011. Professional Reasoning, Legal Cultures, and Arbitral Awards. *World Englishes* 30/1, 117–128.

Han, Zhengrui / Li, Xiaoyu 2012. Discourse of International Commercial Arbitration: The Case of Mainland China. *Journal of Pragmatics* 43, 1380–1391.

Hyland, Ken 2005. *Metadiscourse*. London: Continuum.

Preite, Chiara 2012. Performativity and Deontic Strategies in French Arbitration Awards. In Bhatia/Garzone/Degano (eds), 47–66.

Tessuto, Girolamo 2012. Canadian Arbitration Awards: A Genre-Oriented Linguistic Description of Professional Discursive Practices. In Bhatia/Garzone/Degano (eds), 109–136.

Vázquez, Ignacio / Giner, Diana 2012. Contrastive Study of International Commercial Arbitration Awards and Court Judgments: Intertextuality through Metadiscourse in Action. In Bhatia/Garzone/Degano (eds), 171–191.

Appendix

Arbitration and Conciliation Act 1996

Chapter VII Recourse against arbitral award

34. Application for setting aside arbitral award.

(1) Recourse to a court against an arbitral award may be made only by an application for setting aside such award in accordance with sub-section (2) and subsection (3).

(2) An arbitral award may be set aside by the court only if

(a) The party making the application furnishes proof that

(i) A party was under some incapacity, or

(ii) The arbitration agreement is not valid under the law to which the parties have subjected it or, failing any indication thereon, under the law for the time being in force; or

(iii) The party making the application was not given proper notice of the appointment of an arbitrator or of the arbitral proceedings or was otherwise unable to present his case; or

(iv) The arbitral award deals with a dispute not contemplated by or not falling within the terms of the submission to arbitration, or it contains decisions on matters beyond the scope of the submission to arbitration:

Provided that, if the decisions on matters submitted to arbitration can be separated from those not so submitted, only that part of the arbitral award which contains decisions on matters not submitted to arbitration may be set aside; or

(v) The composition of the arbitral tribunal or the arbitral procedure was not in accordance with the agreement of the parties, unless such agreement was in conflict with a provision of this Part from which the parties cannot derogate, or, failing such agreement, was not in accordance with this Part; or

(b) The court finds that

(i) The subject-matter of the dispute is not capable of settlement by arbitration under the law for the time being in force, or

(ii) The arbitral award is in conflict with the public policy of India.

Explanation. –Without prejudice to the generality of sub-clause (ii), it is hereby declared, for the avoidance of any doubt, that an award is in conflict with the public policy of India if the making of the award was induced or affected by fraud or corruption or was in violation of section 75 or section 81.

(3) An application for setting aside may not be made after three months have elapsed from the date on which the party making that application had received the arbitral award or, if a request had been made under section 33, from the date on which that request had been disposed of by the arbitral tribunal:
Provided that if the court is satisfied that the applicant was prevented by sufficient cause from making the application within the said period of three months it may entertain the application within a further period of thirty days, but not thereafter.

(4) On receipt of an application under sub-section (1), the court may, where it is appropriate and it is so requested by a party, adjourn the proceedings for a period of time determined by it in order to give the arbitral tribunal an opportunity to resume the arbitral proceedings or to take such other action as in the opinion of arbitral tribunal will eliminate the grounds for setting aside the arbitral award.

Notes on Contributors

PATRIZIA ANESA holds a Ph.D. in English Studies, with a specialization in professional and legal communication. She is a member of the Research Centre on Specialized Languages (CERLIS) at the University of Bergamo and teaches courses in the field of English Language and Translation at the same university. Her research interests lie mostly in the area of specialised discourse, with particular reference to legal language and courtroom communication. She is currently interested in the analysis of arbitration practices, the applications of Conversation Analysis in LSP and the investigation of knowledge asymmetries in expert-lay communication.

ULISSE BELOTTI is a tenured researcher in English Language and Translation at the University of Bergamo (Italy) where he teaches English for Business and Law studies at both undergraduate and postgraduate level. His research interests concern word-formation in IT language, genre analysis, business and legal discourse. His recent work centres on the genre characteristics of business related documents through the analysis of specialized corpora. His publications are mostly in the areas of specialised discourse, particularly legal (arbitration) and business communication He is currently researching genre and narrative analysis in the domains of arbitration and business.

VIJAY K. BHATIA retired as Professor from the Department of English, City University of Hong Kong. His research interests include Critical Genre Analysis, academic and professional discourses in legal, business, newspaper, and promotional contexts, ESP and Professional Communication; simplification of legal and other public documents; and intercultural and cross-disciplinary variations in professional genres. Two of his books, *Analysing Genre: Language Use in Professional Settings* and *Worlds of Written Discourse: A Genre-based View*, are widely used in genre theory and practice. He is working on his next book on genre theory *Critical Genre Theory* to be published by Routledge.

GIULIANA GARZONE is Full Professor of English, Linguistics and Translation at Università degli Studi di Milano, Italy. Her research interests are mainly in English for Specific Purposes, which she has explored in a discourse analytical perspective, integrating it with corpus linguistics. She has co-ordinated several research projects and published extensively on legal, scientific and business discourse as well as on translation and interpreting. Her latest publications include 'Variation in the use of modality in legislative texts: focus on *shall*' (2013), 'Evolutions in Societal Values and Discursive Practices: Their Impact on Genre Change' (2014), 'Investigating Blawgs through Corpus Linguistics: Issues of Generic Integrity' (2014), and the volume *Le traduzioni come 'fuzzy set': percorsi teorici e applicativi* [*Translations as a fuzzy set: theoretical perspectives and applications*] (2015). She is Editor-in-Chief of the journal *Lingue Culture Mediazioni / Languages Cultures Mediation* and is co-editor of the series *Lingua, traduzione, didattica* for the publisher FrancoAngeli. She sits on the advisory board of the international journals *Text & Talk* and *Journal of Multicultural Discourses*.

MAURIZIO GOTTI is Professor of English Language and Translation, Head of the Department of Foreign Languages, Literatures and Communication, and Director of the Research Centre for LSP Research (CERLIS) at the University of Bergamo. His main research areas are the features and origins of specialized discourse (*Robert Boyle and the Language of Science,* 1996; *Specialized Discourse: Linguistic Features and Changing Conventions*, 2003; *Investigating Specialized Discourse*, ^{3}2011). He is also interested in English syntax and English lexicology and lexicography, with particular regard to specialized terminology and canting. He is a member of the Editorial Board of national and international journals, and edits the *Linguistic Insights* series for Peter Lang.

MARIACARLA GIORGETTI graduated summa cum laude in 1992. Presently she holds the professorship of Civil Procedural Law at the University of Bergamo and she also holds the university chairs of Arbitration Law and of Bankruptcy Law within the same university. She is the author of more than 125 publications (monographs, articles and case notes) about Civil Procedural Law, Arbitration Law and Bankruptcy Law. She is a lawyer in Milan, Bergamo and Ancona (Italy). She presided over hundreds of arbitration panels, also international and abroad. She is lawyer of various bankruptcies and arrangements with creditors.

JOANNA JEMIELNIAK, Ph.D., is an associate professor at the Faculty of Law, University of Copenhagen. She specializes in international business law and arbitration, as well as in theory of legal interpretation. She graduated from Harvard Law School and University of Warsaw (*summa cum laude*). She held visiting appointments at Harvard University (2004/05 and 2007), UNIDROIT (2006), University of California, Berkeley (2008) and Renmin University, Beijing (2013). Her most recent publications include the book *Legal Interpretation in International Commercial Arbitration* (Ashgate 2014) and the forthcoming volume *Judicial Authority in International Economic Law* (Cambridge University Press; co-edited with Laura Nielsen and Henrik Palmer Olsen).

FRANCESCA LOCATELLI is a Researcher in Civil Procedural Law and Assistant Professor of Institutions of Civil Procedure at the University of Bergamo, Department of Law. Since 2005 she has lectured extensively in the areas of Civil Procedure, Arbitration and other ADR systems. She also teaches at the School of Specialization for arbitrators at the Foundation of Chartered Accountants of Milan and at School 'Luigi Martino' of the same Foundation. She has been a qualified lawyer since 2004.

STEFANIA M. MACI is Associate Professor of English Language and Translation at the University of Bergamo, where she teaches English linguistic courses at graduate and undergraduate level. Her research is focussed on the study of the English language in academic and professional contexts, with particular regard to the analysis of medical, legal and tourism discourse. Her most recent publications include: the volume *Tourism Discourse: Professional, Promotional, Digital Voices* (2013); and the papers 'What Does he Think this Is? The Court of Human Rights or the United Nations?' (2014). '(Plain) Language in the Written Memories of Arbitral Proceedings: A Cross-Cultural Case Study' (2014); 'Investigating Variation in Medical Poster Abstracts' (2014); 'Institutional Popularization of Medical Knowledge: the Case of Pandemic Influenza A (H1N1)' (2014); 'Popularizing Scientific Discourse for an Academic Audience: the Case of Nobel Lectures' (2013).

Piera Pellegrinelli received her doctorate in Civil Procedural Law at the University of Milan. Currently she has a fellowship to undertake research activities at the Department of Law, University of Bergamo, where she is also adjunct professor of Law of Arbitration. She is the author of several publications on arbitration, such as 'The Management of a Mediation Organization According to the Italian Law' (*Beijing Law Review*, 2012), 'Il termine per la pronuncia del lodo' and 'Profili critici in tema di responsabilità degli arbitri' (both in *La giustizia sostenibile. Scritti vari*, Roma 2014), 'Commento all'art. 817 c.p.c. (in A. Briguglio / B. Capponi (eds) *Commentario alle riforme del processo civile*, Padova 2009). She is a lawyer.

Michele Sala, PhD (University of Bergamo), MA (Youngstown State University, Ohio), is a researcher in English Language and Translation at the University of Bergamo, where he teaches English linguistic courses at graduate and undergraduate level. He a member of CERLIS (Centro di Ricerca sui Linguaggi Specialistici) and a member of the scientific and editorial board of the CERLIS Series (international peer-reviewed volumes on specialized languages). His research activity and major publications deal with language for specific purposes and, more specifically, the application of genre and discourse analytical methods to a corpus-based study of legal-academic discourse and to the analysis of the linguistic, textual and pragmatic aspects of legal translation. He has also published in the field of academic discourse (*Persuasion and Politeness in Academic Discourse*, 2008, *Genre Variation in Academic Communication. Emerging Disciplinary Trends*, 2012 [co-edited with S. Maci]; *Corpora in specialized communication*, 2013 [co-edited with C. Desoutter and D. Heller]) and in the domain of pragmatics and cognitive linguistics (*Differently Amusing* 2012).

Elena Signorini is a Research Fellow and Adjunct Professor of Labour Law and of Welfare Law at the University of Bergamo. She has written on unquestionable rights of the worker, health protection in the workplace, employment promotion and fair work, informal economy and undeclared work, youth employment, labour market discrimination, labour law. She is the author of several publications, such as 'Diritto al lavoro. Crisi. Lavoro dei Giovani' 2013; 'Le politiche di contrasto al lavoro sommerso nei Paesi dell'Unione Europea' (co-autor with M. Sala Chiri) 2014; 'Invecchiamento attivo: il senso delle stagioni della vita. Evoluzione o sfida ai sistemi?' 2014; 'La salute mentale, ritmi, assenze e presenze: nuovi rischi sul fronte del lavoro?' 2014; 'Apprendistato: modulabilità della formazione' 2012; 'Il lavoro decente' 2012. She is a lawyer, and arbitrator and mediator at the Chambers of Commerce of Bergamo and Modena.

TARJA SALMI-TOLONEN, LL.D., Phil.Lic., is currently a Research Fellow at the Faculty of Law, University of Turku, Finland. She has held a chair of legal linguistics and lectured and on law and language at several universities in Finland, the US and Europe and worked as a visiting scholar at Cambridge University, UK. She is an expert member of the language department of the Finnish Prime Minister's Office. She is a referee for publications on language and law. Selected publications: Persuasion in Judicial Argumentation (In Halmari *et al.* 2003), *Language and the Functions of Law* (2008), Contracts and Language (2014) (In Finnish in Haapio *et al.*), A Respected Neutral Expert: Arbitrator Profile in Focus (2014) (In Bhatia *et al.*).

GIROLAMO TESSUTO is Associate Professor of English, Linguistics and Translation at the University of Naples 2, Italy. He also teaches at the Law Department of University of Federico II and the Medicine Department of University of Naples 2. His research interests are in applied linguistics, genre analysis of academic, institutional and professional discourses in legal contexts. Several of his publications have appeared as research papers, book chapters and co-edited volumes. His most recent publications include 'Generic structure and rhetorical moves in English-language empirical law research articles: sites of interdisciplinary and interdiscursive cross-over' (*Journal of English for Specific Purposes*) and *Investigating English Legal Genres in Academic and Professional Settings* (Cambridge Scholars). He is Chief Editor of the *Legal Discourse and Communication* series (formerly *Explorations in Language and Law*), and Editorial Board member of international linguistic journals.

Linguistic Insights

Studies in Language and Communication

This series aims to promote specialist language studies in the fields of linguistic theory and applied linguistics, by publishing volumes that focus on specific aspects of language use in one or several languages and provide valuable insights into language and communication research. A cross-disciplinary approach is favoured and most European languages are accepted.

The series includes two types of books:

- **Monographs** – featuring in-depth studies on special aspects of language theory, language analysis or language teaching.
- **Collected papers** – assembling papers from workshops, conferences or symposia.

Each volume of the series is subjected to a double peer-reviewing process.

Vol. 1 Maurizio Gotti & Marina Dossena (eds)
Modality in Specialized Texts. Selected Papers of the 1st CERLIS Conference.
421 pages. 2001. ISBN 3-906767-10-8 · US-ISBN 0-8204-5340-4

Vol. 2 Giuseppina Cortese & Philip Riley (eds)
Domain-specific English. Textual Practices across Communities and Classrooms.
420 pages. 2002. ISBN 3-906768-98-8 · US-ISBN 0-8204-5884-8

Vol. 3 Maurizio Gotti, Dorothee Heller & Marina Dossena (eds)
Conflict and Negotiation in Specialized Texts. Selected Papers of the 2nd CERLIS Conference.
470 pages. 2002. ISBN 3-906769-12-7 · US-ISBN 0-8204-5887-2

Vol. 4 Maurizio Gotti, Marina Dossena, Richard Dury, Roberta Facchinetti & Maria Lima
Variation in Central Modals. A Repertoire of Forms and Types of Usage in Middle English and Early Modern English.
364 pages. 2002. ISBN 3-906769-84-4 · US-ISBN 0-8204-5898-8

Editorial address:

Prof. Maurizio Gotti Università di Bergamo, Dipartimento di Lingue, Letterature Straniere e Comunicazione, Piazza Rosate 2, 24129 Bergamo, Italy
Fax: +39 035 2052789, E-Mail: m.gotti@unibg.it

Vol. 5 Stefania Nuccorini (ed.)
Phrases and Phraseology. Data and Descriptions.
187 pages. 2002. ISBN 3-906770-08-7 · US-ISBN 0-8204-5933-X

Vol. 6 Vijay Bhatia, Christopher N. Candlin & Maurizio Gotti (eds)
Legal Discourse in Multilingual and Multicultural Contexts.
Arbitration Texts in Europe.
385 pages. 2003. ISBN 3-906770-85-0 · US-ISBN 0-8204-6254-3

Vol. 7 Marina Dossena & Charles Jones (eds)
Insights into Late Modern English. 2nd edition.
378 pages. 2003, 2007.
ISBN 978-3-03911-257-9 · US-ISBN 978-0-8204-8927-8

Vol. 8 Maurizio Gotti
Specialized Discourse. Linguistic Features and Changing Conventions.
351 pages. 2003, 2005.
ISBN 3-03910-606-6 · US-ISBN 0-8204-7000-7

Vol. 9 Alan Partington, John Morley & Louann Haarman (eds)
Corpora and Discourse.
420 pages. 2004. ISBN 3-03910-026-2 · US-ISBN 0-8204-6262-4

Vol. 10 Martina Möllering
The Acquisition of German Modal Particles. A Corpus-Based Approach.
290 pages. 2004. ISBN 3-03910-043-2 · US-ISBN 0-8204-6273-X

Vol. 11 David Hart (ed.)
English Modality in Context. Diachronic Perspectives.
261 pages. 2003. ISBN 3-03910-046-7 · US-ISBN 0-8204-6852-5

Vol. 12 Wendy Swanson
Modes of Co-reference as an Indicator of Genre.
430 pages. 2003. ISBN 3-03910-052-1 · US-ISBN 0-8204-6855-X

Vol. 13 Gina Poncini
Discursive Strategies in Multicultural Business Meetings.
2nd edition. 338 pages. 2004, 2007.
ISBN 978-3-03911-296-8 · US-ISBN 978-0-8204-8937-7

Vol. 14 Christopher N. Candlin & Maurizio Gotti (eds)
Intercultural Aspects of Specialized Communication.
2nd edition. 369 pages. 2004, 2007.
ISBN 978-3-03911-258-6 · US-ISBN 978-0-8204-8926-1

Vol. 15 Gabriella Del Lungo Camiciotti & Elena Tognini Bonelli (eds)
Academic Discourse. New Insights into Evaluation.
234 pages. 2004. ISBN 3-03910-353-9 · US-ISBN 0-8204-7016-3

Vol. 16 Marina Dossena & Roger Lass (eds)
Methods and Data in English Historical Dialectology.
405 pages. 2004. ISBN 3-03910-362-8 · US-ISBN 0-8204-7018-X

Vol. 17 Judy Noguchi
The Science Review Article. An Opportune Genre in
the Construction of Science.
274 pages. 2006. ISBN 3-03910-426-8 · US-ISBN 0-8204-7034-1

Vol. 18 Giuseppina Cortese & Anna Duszak (eds)
Identity, Community, Discourse. English in Intercultural Settings.
495 pages. 2005. ISBN 3-03910-632-5 · US-ISBN 0-8204-7163-1

Vol. 19 Anna Trosborg & Poul Erik Flyvholm Jørgensen (eds)
Business Discourse. Texts and Contexts.
250 pages. 2005. ISBN 3-03910-606-6 · US-ISBN 0-8204-7000-7

Vol. 20 Christopher Williams
Tradition and Change in Legal English. Verbal Constructions in Prescriptive Texts.
2nd revised edition. 216 pages. 2005, 2007. ISBN 978-3-03911-444-3.

Vol. 21 Katarzyna Dziubalska-Kolaczyk & Joanna Przedlacka (eds)
English Pronunciation Models: A Changing Scene.
2nd edition. 476 pages. 2005, 2008. ISBN 978-3-03911-682-9.

Vol. 22 Christián Abello-Contesse, Rubén Chacón-Beltrán, M. Dolores López-Jiménez & M. Mar Torreblanca-López (eds)
Age in L2 Acquisition and Teaching.
214 pages. 2006. ISBN 3-03910-668-6 · US-ISBN 0-8204-7174-7

Vol. 23 Vijay K. Bhatia, Maurizio Gotti, Jan Engberg & Dorothee Heller (eds)
Vagueness in Normative Texts.
474 pages. 2005. ISBN 3-03910-653-8 · US-ISBN 0-8204-7169-0

Vol. 24 Paul Gillaerts & Maurizio Gotti (eds)
Genre Variation in Business Letters. 2nd printing.
407 pages. 2008. ISBN 978-3-03911-681-2.

Vol. 25 Ana María Hornero, María José Luzón & Silvia Murillo (eds)
Corpus Linguistics. Applications for the Study of English.
2nd printing. 526 pages. 2006, 2008. ISBN 978-3-03911-726-0

Vol. 26 J. Lachlan Mackenzie & María de los Ángeles Gómez-González (eds)
Studies in Functional Discourse Grammar.
259 pages. 2005. ISBN 3-03910-696-1 · US-ISBN 0-8204-7558-0

Vol. 27 Debbie G. E. Ho
Classroom Talk. Exploring the Sociocultural Structure of Formal ESL Learning.
2nd edition. 254 pages. 2006, 2007. ISBN 978-3-03911-434-4

Vol. 28 Javier Pérez-Guerra, Dolores González Álvarez, Jorge L. Bueno-Alonso & Esperanza Rama-Martínez (eds)
'Of Varying Language and Opposing Creed'. New Insights into Late Modern English.
455 pages. 2007. ISBN 978-3-03910-788-9

Vol. 29 Francesca Bargiela-Chiappini & Maurizio Gotti (eds)
Asian Business Discourse(s).
350 pages. 2005. ISBN 3-03910-804-2 · US-ISBN 0-8204-7574-2

Vol. 30 Nicholas Brownlees (ed.)
News Discourse in Early Modern Britain. Selected Papers of CHINED 2004.
300 pages. 2006. ISBN 3-03910-805-0 · US-ISBN 0-8204-8025-8

Vol. 31 Roberta Facchinetti & Matti Rissanen (eds)
Corpus-based Studies of Diachronic English.
300 pages. 2006. ISBN 3-03910-851-4 · US-ISBN 0-8204-8040-1

Vol. 32 Marina Dossena & Susan M. Fitzmaurice (eds)
Business and Official Correspondence. Historical Investigations.
209 pages. 2006. ISBN 3-03910-880-8 · US-ISBN 0-8204-8352-4

Vol. 33 Giuliana Garzone & Srikant Sarangi (eds)
Discourse, Ideology and Specialized Communication.
494 pages. 2007. ISBN 978-3-03910-888-6

Vol. 34 Giuliana Garzone & Cornelia Ilie (eds)
The Use of English in Institutional and Business Settings.
An Intercultural Perspective.
372 pages. 2007. ISBN 978-3-03910-889-3

Vol. 35 Vijay K. Bhatia & Maurizio Gotti (eds)
Explorations in Specialized Genres.
316 pages. 2006. ISBN 3-03910-995-2 · US-ISBN 0-8204-8372-9

Vol. 36 Heribert Picht (ed.)
Modern Approaches to Terminological Theories and Applications.
432 pages. 2006. ISBN 3-03911-156-6 · US-ISBN 0-8204-8380-X

Vol. 37 Anne Wagner & Sophie Cacciaguidi-Fahy (eds)
Legal Language and the Search for Clarity / Le langage juridique et la quête de clarté.
Practice and Tools / Pratiques et instruments.
487 pages. 2006. ISBN 3-03911-169-8 · US-ISBN 0-8204-8388-5

Vol. 38 Juan Carlos Palmer-Silveira, Miguel F. Ruiz-Garrido &
Inmaculada Fortanet-Gómez (eds)
Intercultural and International Business Communication.
Theory, Research and Teaching.
2nd edition. 343 pages. 2006, 2008. ISBN 978-3-03911-680-5

Vol. 39 Christiane Dalton-Puffer, Dieter Kastovsky, Nikolaus Ritt &
Herbert Schendl (eds)
Syntax, Style and Grammatical Norms. English from 1500–2000.
250 pages. 2006. ISBN 3-03911-181-7 · US-ISBN 0-8204-8394-X

Vol. 40 Marina Dossena & Irma Taavitsainen (eds)
Diachronic Perspectives on Domain-Specific English.
280 pages. 2006. ISBN 3-03910-176-0 · US-ISBN 0-8204-8391-5

Vol. 41 John Flowerdew & Maurizio Gotti (eds)
Studies in Specialized Discourse.
293 pages. 2006. ISBN 3-03911-178-7

Vol. 42 Ken Hyland & Marina Bondi (eds)
Academic Discourse Across Disciplines.
320 pages. 2006. ISBN 3-03911-183-3 · US-ISBN 0-8204-8396-6

Vol. 43 Paul Gillaerts & Philip Shaw (eds)
The Map and the Landscape. Norms and Practices in Genre.
256 pages. 2006. ISBN 3-03911-182-5 · US-ISBN 0-8204-8395-4

Vol. 44 Maurizio Gotti & Davide Giannoni (eds)
New Trends in Specialized Discourse Analysis.
301 pages. 2006. ISBN 3-03911-184-1 · US-ISBN 0-8204-8381-8

Vol. 45 Maurizio Gotti & Françoise Salager-Meyer (eds)
Advances in Medical Discourse Analysis. Oral and Written Contexts.
492 pages. 2006. ISBN 3-03911-185-X · US-ISBN 0-8204-8382-6

Vol. 46 Maurizio Gotti & Susan Šarcević (eds)
Insights into Specialized Translation.
396 pages. 2006. ISBN 3-03911-186-8 · US-ISBN 0-8204-8383-4

Vol. 47 Khurshid Ahmad & Margaret Rogers (eds)
Evidence-based LSP. Translation, Text and Terminology.
584 pages. 2007. ISBN 978-3-03911-187-9

Vol. 48 Hao Sun & Dániel Z. Kádár (eds)
It's the Dragon's Turn. Chinese Institutional Discourses.
262 pages. 2008. ISBN 978-3-03911-175-6

Vol. 49 Cristina Suárez-Gómez
Relativization in Early English (950-1250). the Position of Relative Clauses.
149 pages. 2006. ISBN 3-03911-203-1 · US-ISBN 0-8204-8904-2

Vol. 50 Maria Vittoria Calvi & Luisa Chierichetti (eds)
Nuevas tendencias en el discurso de especialidad.
319 pages. 2006. ISBN 978-3-03911-261-6

Vol. 51 Mari Carmen Campoy & María José Luzón (eds)
Spoken Corpora in Applied Linguistics.
274 pages. 2008. ISBN 978-3-03911-275-3

Vol. 52 Konrad Ehlich & Dorothee Heller (Hrsg.)
Die Wissenschaft und ihre Sprachen.
323 pages. 2006. ISBN 978-3-03911-272-2

Vol. 53 Jingyu Zhang
The Semantic Salience Hierarchy Model. The L2 Acquisition of Psych Predicates
273 pages. 2007. ISBN 978-3-03911-300-2

Vol. 54 Norman Fairclough, Giuseppina Cortese & Patrizia Ardizzone (eds)
Discourse and Contemporary Social Change.
555 pages. 2007. ISBN 978-3-03911-276-0

Vol. 55 Jan Engberg, Marianne Grove Ditlevsen, Peter Kastberg & Martin Stegu (eds)
New Directions in LSP Teaching.
331 pages. 2007. ISBN 978-3-03911-433-7

Vol. 56 Dorothee Heller & Konrad Ehlich (Hrsg.)
Studien zur Rechtskommunikation.
322 pages. 2007. ISBN 978 3 03911 436-8

Vol. 57 Teruhiro Ishiguro & Kang-kwong Luke (eds)
Grammar in Cross-Linguistic Perspective.
The Syntax, Semantics, and Pragmatics of Japanese and Chinese.
304 pages. 2012. ISBN 978-3-03911-445-0

Vol. 58 Carmen Frehner
Email – SMS – MMS
294 pages. 2008. ISBN 978-3-03911-451-1

Vol. 59 Isabel Balteiro
The Directionality of Conversion in English. A Dia-Synchronic Study.
276 pages. 2007. ISBN 978-3-03911-241-8

Vol. 60 Maria Milagros Del Saz Rubio
English Discourse Markers of Reformulation.
237 pages. 2007. ISBN 978-3-03911-196-1

Vol. 61 Sally Burgess & Pedro Martín-Martín (eds)
English as an Additional Language in Research Publication and Communication.
259 pages. 2008. ISBN 978-3-03911-462-7

Vol. 62 Sandrine Onillon
Pratiques et représentations de l'écrit.
458 pages. 2008. ISBN 978-3-03911-464-1

Vol. 63 Hugo Bowles & Paul Seedhouse (eds)
Conversation Analysis and Language for Specific Purposes.
2nd edition. 337 pages. 2007, 2009. ISBN 978-3-0343-0045-2

Vol. 64 Vijay K. Bhatia, Christopher N. Candlin & Paola Evangelisti Allori (eds)
Language, Culture and the Law.
The Formulation of Legal Concepts across Systems and Cultures.
342 pages. 2008. ISBN 978-3-03911-470-2

Vol. 65 Jonathan Culpeper & Dániel Z. Kádár (eds)
Historical (Im)politeness.
300 pages. 2010. ISBN 978-3-03911-496-2

Vol. 66 Linda Lombardo (ed.)
Using Corpora to Learn about Language and Discourse.
237 pages. 2009. ISBN 978-3-03911-522-8

Vol. 67 Natsumi Wakamoto
Extroversion/Introversion in Foreign Language Learning.
Interactions with Learner Strategy Use.
159 pages. 2009. ISBN 978-3-03911-596-9

Vol. 68 Eva Alcón-Soler (ed.)
Learning How to Request in an Instructed Language Learning Context.
260 pages. 2008. ISBN 978-3-03911-601-0

Vol. 69 Domenico Pezzini
The Translation of Religious Texts in the Middle Ages.
428 pages. 2008. ISBN 978-3-03911-600-3

Vol. 70 Tomoko Tode
Effects of Frequency in Classroom Second Language Learning.
Quasi-experiment and stimulated-recall analysis.
195 pages. 2008. ISBN 978-3-03911-602-7

Vol. 71 Egor Tsedryk
Fusion symétrique et alternances ditransitives.
211 pages. 2009. ISBN 978-3-03911-609-6

Vol. 72 Cynthia J. Kellett Bidoli & Elana Ochse (eds)
English in International Deaf Communication.
444 pages. 2008. ISBN 978-3-03911-610-2

Vol. 73 Joan C. Beal, Carmela Nocera & Massimo Sturiale (eds)
Perspectives on Prescriptivism.
269 pages. 2008. ISBN 978-3-03911-632-4

Vol. 74 Carol Taylor Torsello, Katherine Ackerley & Erik Castello (eds)
Corpora for University Language Teachers.
308 pages. 2008. ISBN 978-3-03911-639-3

Vol. 75 María Luisa Pérez Cañado (ed.)
English Language Teaching in the European Credit Transfer System. Facing the Challenge.
251 pages. 2009. ISBN 978-3-03911-654-6

Vol. 76 Marina Dossena & Ingrid Tieken-Boon van Ostade (eds)
Studies in Late Modern English Correspondence. Methodology and Data.
291 pages. 2008. ISBN 978-3-03911-658-4

Vol. 77 Ingrid Tieken-Boon van Ostade & Wim van der Wurff (eds)
Current Issues in Late Modern English.
436 pages. 2009. ISBN 978-3-03911-660-7

Vol. 78 Marta Navarro Coy (ed.)
Practical Approaches to Foreign Language Teaching and Learning.
297 pages. 2009. ISBN 978-3-03911-661-4

Vol. 79 Qing Ma
Second Language Vocabulary Acquisition.
333 pages. 2009. ISBN 978-3-03911-666-9

Vol. 80 Martin Solly, Michelangelo Conoscenti & Sandra Campagna (eds)
Verbal/Visual Narrative Texts in Higher Education.
384 pages. 2008. ISBN 978-3-03911-672-0

Vol. 81 Meiko Matsumoto
From Simple Verbs to Periphrastic Expressions: The Historical Development of Composite Predicates, Phrasal Verbs, and Related Constructions in English.
235 pages. 2008. ISBN 978-3-03911-675-1

Vol. 82 Melinda Dooly
Doing Diversity. Teachers' Construction of Their Classroom Reality.
180 pages. 2009. ISBN 978-3-03911-687-4

Vol. 83 Victoria Guillén-Nieto, Carmen Marimón-Llorca & Chelo Vargas-Sierra (eds)
Intercultural Business Communication and Simulation and Gaming Methodology.
392 pages. 2009. ISBN 978-3-03911-688-1

Vol. 84 Maria Grazia Guido
English as a Lingua Franca in Cross-cultural Immigration Domains.
285 pages. 2008. ISBN 978-3-03911-689-8

Vol. 85 Erik Castello
Text Complexity and Reading Comprehension Tests.
352 pages. 2008. ISBN 978-3-03911-717-8

Vol. 86 Maria-Lluisa Gea-Valor, Isabel García-Izquierdo & Maria-José Esteve (eds)
Linguistic and Translation Studies in Scientific Communication.
317 pages. 2010. ISBN 978-3-0343-0069-8

Vol. 87 Carmen Navarro, Rosa Mª Rodríguez Abella, Francesca Dalle Pezze & Renzo Miotti (eds)
La comunicación especializada.
355 pages. 2008. ISBN 978-3-03911-733-8

Vol. 102 Nuria Edo Marzá
The Specialised Lexicographical Approach. A Step further in Dictionary-making.
316 pages. 2009. ISBN 978-3-0343-0043-8

Vol. 103 Carlos Prado-Alonso, Lidia Gómez-García, Iria Pastor-Gómez & David Tizón-Couto (eds)
New Trends and Methodologies in Applied English Language Research. Diachronic, Diatopic and Contrastive Studies.
348 pages. 2009. ISBN 978-3-0343-0046-9

Vol. 104 Françoise Salager-Meyer & Beverly A. Lewin
Crossed Words. Criticism in Scholarly Writing?
371 pages. 2011. ISBN 978-3-0343-0049-0.

Vol. 105 Javier Ruano-García
Early Modern Northern English Lexis. A Literary Corpus-Based Study.
611 pages. 2010. ISBN 978-3-0343-0058-2

Vol. 106 Rafael Monroy-Casas
Systems for the Phonetic Transcription of English. Theory and Texts.
280 pages. 2011. ISBN 978-3-0343-0059-9

Vol. 107 Nicola T. Owtram
The Pragmatics of Academic Writing.
A Relevance Approach to the Analysis of Research Article Introductions.
311 pages. 2009. ISBN 978-3-0343-0060-5

Vol. 108 Yolanda Ruiz de Zarobe, Juan Manuel Sierra & Francisco Gallardo del Puerto (eds)
Content and Foreign Language Integrated Learning.
Contributions to Multilingualism in European Contexts
343 pages. 2011. ISBN 978-3-0343-0074-2

Vol. 109 Ángeles Linde López & Rosalía Crespo Jiménez (eds)
Professional English in the European context. The EHEA challenge.
374 pages. 2010. ISBN 978-3-0343-0088-9

Vol. 110 Rosalía Rodríguez-Vázquez
The Rhythm of Speech, Verse and Vocal Music. A New Theory.
394 pages. 2010. ISBN 978-3-0343-0309-5

Vol. 111 Anastasios Tsangalidis & Roberta Facchinetti (eds)
Studies on English Modality. In Honour of Frank Palmer.
392 pages. 2009. ISBN 978-3-0343-0310-1

Vol. 112 Jing Huang
Autonomy, Agency and Identity in Foreign Language Learning and Teaching.
400 pages. 2013. ISBN 978-3-0343-0370-5

Vol. 113 Mihhail Lotman & Maria-Kristiina Lotman (eds)
Frontiers in Comparative Prosody. In memoriam: Mikhail Gasparov.
426 pages. 2011. ISBN 978-3-0343-0373-6

Vol. 114 Merja Kytö, John Scahill & Harumi Tanabe (eds)
Language Change and Variation from Old English to Late Modern English.
A Festschrift for Minoji Akimoto
422 pages. 2010. ISBN 978-3-0343-0372-9

Vol. 115 Giuliana Garzone & Paola Catenaccio (eds)
Identities across Media and Modes. Discursive Perspectives.
379 pages. 2009. ISBN 978-3-0343-0386-6

Vol. 116 Elena Landone
Los marcadores del discurso y cortesía verbal en español.
390 pages. 2010. ISBN 978-3-0343-0413-9

Vol. 117 Maurizio Gotti & Christopher Williams (eds)
Legal Discourse across Languages and Cultures.
339 pages. 2010. ISBN 978-3-0343-0425-2

Vol. 118 David Hirsh
Academic Vocabulary in Context.
217 pages. 2010. ISBN 978-3-0343-0426-9

Vol. 119 Yvonne Dröschel
Lingua Franca English. The Role of Simplification and Transfer.
358 pages. 2011. ISBN 978-3-0343-0432-0

Vol. 120 Tengku Sepora Tengku Mahadi, Helia Vaezian & Mahmoud Akbari
Corpora in Translation. A Practical Guide.
135 pages. 2010. ISBN 978-3-0343-0434-4

Vol. 121 Davide Simone Giannoni & Celina Frade (eds)
Researching Language and the Law. Textual Features and Translation Issues.
278 pages. 2010. ISBN 978-3-0343-0443-6

Vol. 122 Daniel Madrid & Stephen Hughes (eds)
Studies in Bilingual Education.
472 pages. 2011. ISBN 978-3-0343-0474-0

Vol. 123 Vijay K. Bhatia, Christopher N. Candlin & Maurizio Gotti (eds)
The Discourses of Dispute Resolution.
290 pages. 2010. ISBN 978-3-0343-0476-4

Vol. 124 Davide Simone Giannoni
Mapping Academic Values in the Disciplines. A Corpus-Based Approach.
288 pages. 2010. ISBN 978-3-0343-0488-7

Vol. 125 Giuliana Garzone & James Archibald (eds)
Discourse, Identities and Roles in Specialized Communication.
419 pages. 2010. ISBN 978-3-0343-0494-8

Vol. 126 Iria Pastor-Gómez
The Status and Development of N+N Sequences in
Contemporary English Noun Phrases.
216 pages. 2011. ISBN 978-3-0343-0534-1

Vol. 127 Carlos Prado-Alonso
Full-verb Inversion in Written and Spoken English.
261 pages. 2011. ISBN 978-3-0343-0535-8

Vol. 128 Tony Harris & María Moreno Jaén (eds)
Corpus Linguistics in Language Teaching.
214 pages. 2010. ISBN 978-3-0343-0524-2

Vol. 129 Tetsuji Oda & Hiroyuki Eto (eds)
Multiple Perspectives on English Philology and History of Linguistics.
A Festschrift for Shoichi Watanabe on his 80th Birthday.
378 pages. 2010. ISBN 978-3-0343-0480-1

Vol. 130 Luisa Chierichetti & Giovanni Garofalo (eds)
Lengua y Derecho. líneas de investigación interdisciplinaria.
283 pages. 2010. 978-3-0343-0463-4

Vol. 131 Paola Evangelisti Allori & Giuliana Garzone (eds)
Discourse, Identities and Genres in Corporate Communication.
Sponsorship, Advertising and Organizational Communication.
324 pages. 2011. 978-3-0343-0591-4

Vol. 132 Leyre Ruiz de Zarobe & Yolanda Ruiz de Zarobe (eds)
Speech Acts and Politeness across Languages and Cultures.
402 pages. 2012. 978-3-0343-0611-9

Vol. 133 Thomas Christiansen
Cohesion. A Discourse Perspective.
387 pages. 2011. 978-3-0343-0619-5

Vol. 134 Giuliana Garzone & Maurizio Gotti
Discourse, Communication and the Enterprise. Genres and Trends.
451 pages. 2011. ISBN 978-3-0343-0620-1

Vol. 135 Zsuzsa Hoffmann
Ways of the World's Words.
Language Contact in the Age of Globalization.
334 pages 2011. ISBN 978-3-0343-0673-7

Vol. 136 Cecilia Varcasia (ed.)
Becoming Multilingual.
Language Learning and Language Policy between Attitudes and Identities.
213 pages. 2011. ISBN 978-3-0343-0687-5

Vol. 137 Susy Macqueen
The Emergence of Patterns in Second Language Writing.
A Sociocognitive Exploration of Lexical Trails.
325 pages. 2012. ISBN 978-3-0343-1010-9

Vol. 138 Maria Vittoria Calvi & Giovanna Mapelli (eds)
La lengua del turismo. Géneros discursivos y terminología.
365 pages. 2011. ISBN 978-3-0343-1011-6

Vol. 139 Ken Lau
Learning to Become a Professional in a Textually-Mediated World.
A Text-Oriented Study of Placement Practices.
261 pages. 2012. ISBN 978-3-0343-1016-1

Vol. 140 Sandra Campagna, Giuliana Garzone, Cornelia Ilie & Elizabeth Rowley-Jolivet (eds)
Evolving Genres in Web-mediated Communication.
337 pages. 2012. ISBN 978-3-0343-1013-0

Vol. 141 Edith Esch & Martin Solly (eds)
The Sociolinguistics of Language Education in International Contexts.
263 pages. 2012. ISBN 978-3-0343-1009-3

Vol. 142 Forthcoming.

Vol. 143 David Tizón-Couto
Left Dislocation in English. A Functional-Discoursal Approach.
416 pages. 2012. ISBN 978-3-0343-1037-6

Vol. 144 Margrethe Petersen & Jan Engberg (eds)
Current Trends in LSP Research. Aims and Methods.
323 pages. 2011. ISBN 978-3-0343-1054-3

Vol. 145 David Tizón-Couto, Beatriz Tizón-Couto, Iria Pastor-Gómez & Paula Rodríguez-Puente (eds)
New Trends and Methodologies in Applied English Language Research II.
Studies in Language Variation, Meaning and Learning.
283 pages. 2012. ISBN 978-3-0343-1061-1

Vol. 146 Rita Salvi & Hiromasa Tanaka (eds)
Intercultural Interactions in Business and Management.
306 pages. 2011. ISBN 978-3-0343-1039-0

Vol. 147 Francesco Straniero Sergio & Caterina Falbo (eds)
Breaking Ground in Corpus-based Interpreting Studies.
254 pages. 2012. ISBN 978-3-0343-1071-0

Vol. 148 Forthcoming.

Vol. 149 Vijay K. Bhatia & Paola Evangelisti Allori (eds)
Discourse and Identity in the Professions. Legal, Corporate and Institutional Citizenship.
352 pages. 2011. ISBN 978-3-0343-1079-6

Vol. 150 Maurizio Gotti (ed.)
Academic Identity Traits. A Corpus-Based Investigation.
363 pages. 2012. ISBN 978-3-0343-1141-0

Vol. 151 Priscilla Heynderickx, Sylvain Dieltjens, Geert Jacobs, Paul Gillaerts &
Elizabeth de Groot (eds)
The Language Factor in International Business.
New Perspectives on Research, Teaching and Practice.
320 pages. 2012. ISBN 978-3-0343-1090-1

Vol. 152 Paul Gillaerts, Elizabeth de Groot, Sylvain Dieltjens, Priscilla Heynderickx &
Geert Jacobs (eds)
Researching Discourse in Business Genres. Cases and Corpora.
215 pages. 2012. ISBN 978-3-0343-1092-5

Vol. 153 Yongyan Zheng
Dynamic Vocabulary Development in a Foreign Language.
262 pages. 2012. ISBN 978-3-0343-1106-9

Vol. 154 Carmen Argondizzo (ed.)
Creativity and Innovation in Language Education.
357 pages. 2012. ISBN 978-3-0343-1080-2

Vol. 155 David Hirsh (ed.)
Current Perspectives in Second Language Vocabulary Research.
180 pages. 2012. ISBN 978-3-0343-1108-3

Vol. 156 Seiji Shinkawa
Unhistorical Gender Assignment in Laȝamon's *Brut*. A Case Study of a Late Stage
in the Development of Grammatical Gender toward its Ultimate Loss.
186 pages. 2012. ISBN 978-3-0343-1124-3

Vol. 157 Yeonkwon Jung
Basics of Organizational Writing: A Critical Reading Approach.
151 pages. 2014. ISBN 978-3-0343-1137-3.

Vol. 173 Madalina Chitez
Learner corpus profiles. The case of Romanian Learner English.
244 pages. 2014. ISBN 978-3-0343-1410-7

Vol. 174 Chihiro Inoue
Task Equivalence in Speaking Tests.
251 pages. 2013. ISBN 978-3-0343-1417-6

Vol. 175 Gabriel Quiroz & Pedro Patiño (eds.)
LSP in Colombia: advances and challenges.
339 pages. 2014. ISBN 978-3-0343-1434-3

Vol. 176 Catherine Resche
Economic Terms and Beyond: Capitalising on the Wealth of Notions.
How Researchers in Specialised Varieties of English Can Benefit from Focusing on Terms.
332 pages. 2013. ISBN 978-3-0343-1435-0

Vol. 177 Forthcoming.

Vol. 178 Cécile Desoutter & Caroline Mellet (dir.)
Le discours rapporté: approches linguistiques et perspectives didactiques.
270 pages. 2013. ISBN 978-3-0343-1292-9

Vol. 179 Ana Díaz-Negrillo & Francisco Javier Díaz-Pérez (eds)
Specialisation and Variation in Language Corpora.
341 pages. 2014. ISBN 978-3-0343-1316-2

Vol. 180 Pilar Alonso
A Multi-dimensional Approach to Discourse Coherence. From Standardness to Creativity.
247 pages. 2014. ISBN 978-3-0343-1325-4

Vol. 181 Alejandro Alcaraz-Sintes & Salvador Valera-Hernández (eds)
Diachrony and Synchrony in English Corpus Linguistics.
393 pages. 2014. ISBN 978-3-0343-1326-1

Vol. 182 Runhan Zhang
Investigating Linguistic Knowledge of a Second Language.
207 pages. 2015. ISBN 978-3-0343-1330-8

Vol. 183 Hajar Abdul Rahim & Shakila Abdul Manan (eds.)
English in Malaysia. Postcolonial and Beyond.
267 pages. 2014. ISBN 978-3-0343-1341-4

Vol. 184 Virginie Fasel Lauzon
Comprendre et apprendre dans l'interaction. Les séquences d'explication en classe
de français langue seconde.
292 pages. 2014. ISBN 978-3-0343-1451-0

Vol. 185 Forthcoming.

Vol. 186 Wei Ren
L2 Pragmatic Development in Study Abroad Contexts
256 pages. 2015. ISBN 978-3-0343-1358-2

Vol. 187 Marina Bondi & Rosa Lorés Sanz (eds)
Abstracts in Academic Discourse. Variation and Change.
361 pages. 2014. ISBN 978-3-0343-1483-1

Vol. 188 Forthcoming.

Vol. 189 Paola Evangelisti Allori (ed.)
Identities in and across Cultures.
315 pages. 2014. ISBN 978-3-0343-1458-9

Vol. 190 Forthcoming.

Vol. 191 Ruth Breeze, Maurizio Gotti & Carmen Sancho Guinda (eds)
Interpersonality in Legal Genres.
389 pages. 2014. ISBN 978-3-0343-1524-1

Vol. 192 Paola Evangelisti Allori, John Bateman & Vijay K. Bhatia (eds)
Evolution in Genre. Emergence, Variation, Multimodality.
364 pages. 2014. ISBN 978-3-0343-1533-3

Vol. 193 Jiyeon Kook
Agency in Arzt-Patient-Gesprächen. Zur interaktionistischen Konzeptualisierung von Agency
271 pages. 2015. ISBN 978-3-0343-1666-8

Vol. 194 Susana Nicolás Román & Juan José Torres Núñez (eds)
Drama and CLIL. A new challenge for the teaching approaches in bilingual education.
170 pages. 2015. ISBN 978-3-0343-1629-3

Vol. 195 Alessandra Molino & Serenella Zanotti (eds)
Observing Norm, Observing Usage. Lexis in Dictionaries and in the Media.
430 pages. 2015. ISBN 978-3-0343-1584-5

Vol. 196 Begoña Soneira
A Lexical Description of English for Architecture. A Corpus-based Approach.
267 pages. 2015. ISBN 978-3-0343-1602-6

Vol. 197 M Luisa Roca-Varela
False Friends in Learner Corpora. A corpus-based study of English false friends in the written and spoken production of Spanish learners.
348 pages. 2015. ISBN 978-3-0343-1620-0

Vol. 198 Forthcoming.

Vol. 199 Rita Salvi & Janet Bowker (eds)
The Dissemination of Contemporary Knowledge in English. Genres, discourse strategies and professional practices.
171 pages. 2015. ISBN 978-3-0343-1679-8

Vol. 200 Maurizio Gotti & Davide S. Giannoni (eds)
Corpus Analysis for Descriptive and Pedagogical Purposes. ESP Perspectives.
432 pages. 2014. ISBN 978-3-0343-1516-6

Vol. 201 Ida Ruffolo
The Perception of Nature in Travel Promotion Texts. A Corpus-based Discourse Analysis.
148 pages. 2015. ISBN 978-3-0343-1521-0

Vol. 202 Ives Trevian
English suffixes. Stress-assignment properties, productivity, selection and combinatorial processes.
471 pages. 2015. ISBN 978-3-0343-1576-0

Vol. 203 Maurizio Gotti, Stefania Maci & Michele Sala (eds)
Insights into Medical Communication.
422 pages. 2015. ISBN 978-3-0343-1694-1

Vol. 204-205 Forthcoming.

Vol. 206 Maria Pavesi, Maicol Formentelli & Elisa Ghia (eds)
The Languages of Dubbing. Mainstream Audiovisual Translation in Italy.
275 pages. 2014. ISBN 978-3-0343-1646-0

Vol. 207 Forthcoming.

Vol. 208 Vijay K. Bhatia & Maurizio Gotti (eds)
Arbitration Discourse in Asia.
331 pages. 2015. ISBN 978-3-0343-2032-0

www.ingramcontent.com/pod-product-compliance
Ingram Content Group UK Ltd.
Pitfield, Milton Keynes, MK11 3LW, UK
UKHW021853100926
8556IPUK00020B/1198

9 783034 320320